PARTICIPATION IN COMMUNITY WORK

Participation is a key community work method and this text, written by an international selection of authors, covers innovative approaches in community based education and practice. Including real-life case studies of participatory practice, it offers new definitions of community work, organization and development and will challenge and inspire all those involved in community work practice and research.

Divided into four parts, *Participation in Community Work* begins by exploring theoretical aspects of participation and the co-construction of knowledge, including the ethics of participation. The second part focuses on the potential of participatory learning and action research, with chapters presenting key techniques followed by case studies. The third part looks at power and participation, addressing issues of inclusivity, capacity and democracy building and giving examples from a range of research and field projects. Finally, the fourth part begins the discussion of new and emerging challenges for community work globally.

This unique book is suitable for students, researchers and practitioners interested in participation and community development from a range of disciplines, including community work itself through social work and youth work to health promotion.

Anne Karin Larsen is Associate Professor in the Department of Social Work and Social Education, Bergen University College, Norway.

Vishanthie Sewpaul is Senior Professor in the School of Applied Human Sciences, University KwaZulu Natal, South Africa. She is currently President of the Association of Schools of Social Work in Africa and a Vice-President on the Board of the International Association of Schools of Social Work.

Grete Oline Hole is Associate Professor at the Centre of Evidence Based Practice, Bergen University College, Norway.

PARTICIPATION IN COMMUNITY WORK

International perspectives

Edited by Anne Karin Larsen,
Vishanthie Sewpaul and Grete Oline Hole

Routledge
Taylor & Francis Group

LONDON AND NEW YORK

First Published in 2014
by Routledge
2 Park Square, Milton Park, Abingdon, Oxon OX14 4RN

Simultaneously published in the USA and Canada
by Routledge
711 Third Avenue, New York, NY 10017

Routledge is an imprint of the Taylor & Francis Group, an informa business

British Library Cataloguing in Publication Data
A catalogue record for this book is available from the British Library

Library of Congress Cataloging in Publication Data
Participation in community work : international perspectives / edited by Anne Karin Larsen,
Vishanthie Sewpaul and Grete Oline Hole.
pages cm
1. Community development. 2. Community development--Citizen participation.
3. Social service--Citizen participation. I. Larsen, Anne Karin. II. Sewpaul, Vishanthie.
III. Hole, Grete Oline.
HN49.C6P365 2014
307.1'4--dc23
2013011020

ISBN: 978-0-415-65841-6 (hbk)
ISBN: 978-0-203-07596-8 (ebk)

Typeset in Bembo
by Saxon Graphics Ltd, Derby

Printed and bound in Great Britain by
TJ International Ltd, Padstow, Cornwall

CONTENTS

List of illustrations   *viii*
List of contributors   *x*
Preface   *xiv*
Acknowledgements   *xvi*
List of abbreviations   *xvii*

1 Introduction   1
    Anne Karin Larsen, Vishanthie Sewpaul and Grete Oline Hole

PART 1
**Participation, ethics and co-construction of knowledge
in community work**   **17**

2 The ethics of participation in community work practice   19
    Richard Hugman and Linda Bartolomei

3 Community knowledge and practices after the postmodern   30
    epistemic framework: towards a second modernity
    Andrés Arias Astray, David Alonso and Andoni Alonso

4 The co-construction of knowledge: reflection on experiences   41
    of developing an online international community work course
    Grete Oline Hole, Janet Harris and Anne Karin Larsen

PART 2
Participatory learning and action research 55

5 Participatory learning and action (PLA) techniques for 57
community work
Vivienne Bozalek

6 Mobilizing community strengths and assets: participatory 72
experiences of community members in a garden project
Tanusha Raniga

7 Participatory learning of community work in an 88
e-learning course
Anne Karin Larsen and Grete Oline Hole

PART 3
Power and participation in community work 105

8 Power and participation in community work research 107
and practice
Vishanthie Sewpaul, Ingrid Østhus and Christopher Mhone

9 How do we make room for all? The power of context in 120
shaping action
Bliss Browne and Caroline B. Adelman

10 Community work within the Norwegian welfare state: barriers 133
and possibilities for work with particularly vulnerable groups
Gunn Strand Hutchinson

11 Community work as part of neighbourhood renewal: 145
a case study
Kjell Henriksbø and Anne Line Grimen

12 Partnership and participation: art in community work 159
Rina Visser-Rotgans and Eduardo Marques

PART 4
Addressing new global challenges 173

13 (Re)imagining communities in the context of climate change: 175
a saving grace or the evasion of state responsibilities
during (hu)man-made disasters?
Lena Dominelli

14 Pacific heritage specific conceptual frameworks and family 188
violence preventive training in Aotearoa New Zealand
Vaiolesi Passells

15 Social action for community work in India: grassroots 204
interventions to face global challenges
Sanaya Singh and Prabha Tirmare

16 Community work and the challenges of neoliberalism and new 217
managerialism: resistance, the Occupy Movement and the
Arab Spring
Vishanthie Sewpaul

17 Community development: towards an integrated 230
emancipatory framework
Vishanthie Sewpaul and Anne Karin Larsen

Index 247

ILLUSTRATIONS

Figures

5.1 Community map drawing   62
5.2 Body map of a community member living with HIV/AIDS   63
5.3 River of Life showing the difficult circumstances leading to the
    choice of social work as a profession at UWC   66
5.4 Flow and impact diagram showing the advantages and disadvantages
    of public works programmes in South Africa   67
6.1 A typical informal dwelling built by a resident using mud
    in Bhambayi   77
6.2 A grandmother cooking a meal on fire   82
7.1 Green Park Community Blog, text view   90
7.2 Green Park Community Blog, map view   90
7.3 The Europe Magazine   92
7.4 Community work practice roles   95
8.1 The core group of young street children that actively participated
    in World Social Work day   111
8.2 Children and youth presenting their life situation with a poster at
    the Global Social Work Congress   112
8.3 Drawing reflecting the experience of police round-ups and violence,
    by children and youth living on the streets   113
11.1 A new playground is taking shape among the houses   150
11.2 The community house in the centre of the Neighbours' Day
     festivities   151
12.1 'IkVrouw' theatre group 2009 Delft (The Netherlands)   168

12.2 In one of Coimbra's main squares, the voices of people could be seen.
From the project 'Risen from the Ground' – 'Labyrinth: Checkmate
Poverty', Portugal — 169

17.1 An integrated emancipatory framework for community development — 242

Tables

1.1 Arnstein's and Pretty's typologies of participation — 7
5.1 Things which children gain from preschool — 65
6.1 Outline of the research process — 79
7.1 The action research process with teachers 2009–10 and
students 2010–11 — 93
14.1 Framework for Pacific Islands' theories and models of practice — 199
17.1 Synthesis of Legerton and Castelloe's (1999) organic model — 235
17.2 Illustration of Boehm's and Cnaan's model for community practice
based on binary opposites — 236

CONTRIBUTORS

Caroline B. Adelman (PhD) is a post-doctoral psychology fellow at the Yale University Child Study Center, where she specializes in the treatment of children with anxiety disorders. She co-created the Frameworks for Change workshop with Bliss Browne and has done community development work in the US and abroad.

Andoni Alonso (PhD) is from the University of Navarre (Spain). He was a Research Fellow at Penn State University (1996–1998) and Nevada University (Reno, 2003). He is currently Associate Professor at Universidad Complutense de Madrid.

Andrés Arias Astray (PhD) is a lecturer at the Complutense University of Madrid (Spain), where he also holds the position of Dean at the Faculty of Social Work. The use of ICT in social work practice and education is one of his main research interests. In this sense it is important to underline that he is a member of the Steering Committees of the SW-VirCamp project, where he also collaborates as a teacher and researcher.

Linda Bartolomei is Deputy Director of the Centre for Refugee Research at the University of New South Wales, Australia, where she also co-convenes the Master of Development studies. Her recent writing focuses on refugee policy and practice and in particular on refugee women and gender related violence. She is actively engaged in practice based research community work practice among refugee communities in Australia and internationally.

Vivienne Bozalek (PhD) is Professor of Social Work and the Director of Teaching and Learning at the University of the Western Cape (UWC), South Africa. Her areas of research, publications and expertise include the use of post-structural, social justice and the political ethics of care perspectives, critical family studies, innovative pedagogical approaches in Higher Education, and feminist and participatory research methodologies.

Bliss Browne is founder and president of Imagine Chicago, an Episcopal priest and a community activist. She is a graduate of Yale University (BA, History 1971), Harvard University (M.Div, Theology, 1974) and the Kellogg School of Management of Northwestern (MM, Finance, 1978).

Lena Dominelli is Professor and Co-Director in the Institute of Hazards, Risk and Resilience Research at Durham University. She is an active researcher, holding major projects funded by research councils in the UK and Canada on subjects ranging from earthquakes to tsunamis and from motherhood to fatherhood. She has played a major role in the International Association of Schools of Social Work (IASSW) as President from 1996 to 2004, and is currently chairing the IASSW Committee on Climate Change and Disaster Interventions.

David Alonso Gonzalez has a Bachelor's in Social Work and a Master's in Social and Cultural Anthropology from the Complutense University (Madrid). He is Assistant Professor at the School of Social Work – Complutense University (Madrid).

Anne Line Grimen holds a Master's in Community Work and is a social worker by profession. She is planner and project manager at the Social Housing Company of Bergen Municipality, Norway. Her main field of practice has been related to area based community development and management programs.

Janet Harris (PhD) is Senior Lecturer at the University of Sheffield, UK. She has a Master's degree in Community Organisation, Management and Planning. She is a member of the International Collaboration for Participatory Health Research.

Kjell Henriksbø is Assistant Professor at Bergen University College, Norway. He is a social worker and political scientist, and presently affiliated to the Master's programme in community work at Bergen University College.

Richard Hugman is Professor of Social Work at the University of New South Wales, Australia. He has worked in social work practice, research and teaching. His recent writing has focused mostly on ethics and on international and intercultural practice. He chairs the ethics committee of the International Federation of Social Workers.

Gunn Strand Hutchinson is Associate Professor at the University of Nordland, Norway. Her main research interests are comparative social work and social work in local communities including community work. She has written and contributed to several textbooks mainly in Norwegian including books on community work in social work, models in social work, and social work in local authorities.

Eduardo Marques worked as a lecturer in social work for 20 years at Miguel Torga University College, Portugal, during which time he was involved in several social work international projects about e-learning, community work and youth work. He is currently pursuing a Doctorate in Social Work and is working as executive director of the Social Enterprise Academy and of the NGO Associação Hemisférios Solidários. His area of interest is Community Arts and Human Rights.

Christopher Mhone obtained his Bachelor of Social Work and Master of Social Work degrees Cum Laude at the University of KwaZulu Natal, South Africa.

Ingrid Schärer Østhus obtained the Bachelor and Master of Social Work degrees Summa Cum Laude at the University of KwaZulu Natal, South Africa.

Vaiolesi Passells identifies as a first generation New Zealand born Niue woman of mixed heritage. She has a degree in social work, a MA in Pacific studies and has worked for a Pacific Islands grass roots organization on a voluntary basis. She is a member of the Auckland Women's Refuge Collective. She is a lecturer at the School of Counselling, Human Services and Social Work, University of Auckland.

Tanusha Raniga (PhD) is Senior Lecturer in the School of Applied Human Sciences at the University of KwaZulu-Natal, South Africa. Her teaching areas are community work, social policy and HIV/AIDS at undergraduate and postgraduate levels. Her research interests are integrating radical community work theories in poverty alleviation projects, the psycho-social impact of HIV/AIDS on families and social security policy.

Sanaya Singh is of Indian origin and a graduate from University of Gävle, Sweden with a Bachelors of Science degree in International Social Work. She is currently a teaching assistant at the same university. She has been engaged in community based projects and social activism in India.

Prabha Tirmare is Associate Professor at the College of Social Work, Nirmala Niketan, Mumbai University, India, presently pursuing her PhD with Tata Institute of Social Science, Mumbai, on indigenous knowledge to strengthen social work education. She has been engaged with social activism and numerous community based projects in urban and rural India for the last 25 years.

Rina Visser is a lecturer and Project Manager International Affairs cluster Social Work, Faculty of Health, Sports and Social Work, Inholland University of Applied Sciences, The Netherlands. She studied arts and crafts, art education and art history at University of Leiden. She was involved in the development of the SW-VirCamp module community work from an international perspective and has been teaching in this course.

The editors

Anne Karin Larsen is Associate Professor at Bergen University College, Norway. She is a social worker by profession with a Master's degree in health promotion and health psychology. She has been project leader for several local and international projects; latest the EU funded project SW-VirCamp (Social Work-Virtual Campus). Her research and writings focuses on professional development and learning, and participatory learning in e-learning.

Vishanthie Sewpaul (PhD) is senior Professor in the School of Applied Human Sciences, University KwaZulu Natal, South Africa. She served on several national structures in SA. She is currently President of the Association of Schools of Social Work in Africa and a Vice-President on the Board of the International Association of Schools of Social Work.

Grete Oline Hole is educated as a nurse with a Master's degree in Sociology, as well as degrees in Economics and Pedagogy. She is currently working as Associate Professor at the Centre of Evidence Based Practice, Bergen University College. Her main research interests are within the development of professional practice. Since the early 1990s she has been interested in the best use of computers to support knowledge construction.

PREFACE

This book had its genesis during a research seminar held in Mont Fleur, Cape Town, South Africa in November 2008. The initiative was taken by the VIRCLASS consortium (The Virtual Classroom for Social Work in Europe) research group which under the heading 'VIRCLASS goes worldwide' wanted to expand the network and invited academics and researchers from South Africa and Europe to participate in the seminar. At that time the VIRCLASS consortium had just started a new project, SW-VirCamp (The Social Work-Virtual Campus) funded by the EU-Lifelong Learning programme. One of the expected outcomes of this project was an online course in community work from an international perspective. By using the international network among the VirCamp partners we managed to connect persons with high competence in community work from South Africa, Spain, Denmark, Norway, Sweden and the Netherlands for a weeklong meeting in Mont Fleur. The deliberations of this research seminar stimulated the idea to produce such a book, and it is interesting to observe what started off as merely an idea evolve into a tangible product.

Thanks to Andres Astray, Vivienne Bozalek, Helen Lahti Edmark, Gunn Strand Hutchinson, Anne-Mette Magnussen, Klas-Göran Olsson, Tanusha Raniga, Gordon Vincenti, Rina Visser and May Økland of the Mont Fleur group for stimulating discussions, enthusiasm and support for the idea. A special thanks to Kjell Henriksbø for being a pillar of strength and for his support and contribution throughout the process.

Following the Mont Fleur research meeting, a seminar on participatory approaches in community work was arranged in Bergen, Norway in 2009. This provided fertile ground for further discussion among the three editors and for the development of the synopsis for the book. As any academic or person with a book project would know, getting published is no easy business. The processes can be as arduous and tedious as they can be exciting. We are indebted to Grace McInnes, senior editor from Routledge for believing in this project and allowing the idea to flourish into this book, and to James Watson from Routledge for his responsiveness, support and timely advice throughout the writing process.

We are thankful to all the authors and reviewers for their significant contributions to the successful completion of this book. We have chapter contributions from eleven countries, across five continents. Each chapter has undergone two independent review processes. Our reviewers have come from different parts of the world and we express our deepest appreciation for their valuable contributions.

Thanks to our students for contributing to our knowledge through their participation in the mutual learning process.

Without the strong convivial relationship and team spirit among the three editors this book would perhaps have not come to fruition. We are grateful for that.

We also credit our institutions, Bergen University College and University of KwaZulu Natal for providing the environmental conditions, the time and opportunity to complete this task.

The book is directed towards students, practitioners, educators and researchers in the fields of social and community work, community psychology and health care or any other professional group or person interested in grassroot welfare and human development. We do hope that the book provides inspiration to become engaged, to tune into the life worlds of people and to ensure their full and unequivocal participation at all times. If we respect human agency we must then, of necessity, respect people's right to participate in decisions and processes that affect their lives, and that help them realize their highest possible capabilities.

Anne Karin Larsen, Vishanthie Sewpaul and Grete Oline Hole (editors)

ACKNOWLEDGEMENTS

Here we wish to thank those people close to us who have made sacrifices to ensure that we had the time and space to complete the book.

To the following, thank you for being the inspiration for us:

Ingvar Grastveit and Silje Larsen Grastveit
Preshanthi Sewpaul and Vannessa Naidoo
Steffen Eide, Sigvat Hole Eide, Brynjar Hole Eide and Bård Gustav Hole Eide.

LIST OF ABBREVIATIONS

ABCD	Asset-Based Community Development
AI	Appreciative Inquiry
ARV	Antiretroviral drugs
BIOPICCC	Built Environment and Older People
CINAHL	Cumulative Index to Nursing and Allied Health
ECTS	European Credit Transfer System
EU	European Union
FO	Social Workers' Union in Norway
GDP	Gross Domestic Product
GEAR	Growth Employment and Redistribution
HEI	Higher Education Institutions
IASSW	International Association of Schools of Social Work
ICT	Information and Communication Technology
Medline	Database for health related research
NGO	Non-Governmental Organizations
NOU	Official Norwegian Reports from the Government
NPO	Non-Profit Organization
OECD	Organization for Economic Co-operation and Development
PAAR	Participatory and Appreciative Action
PAG	Pacific Islands' Advisory Group
PAL	Participatory Action Learning
PAR	Participatory Action Research
PDS	Public Distribution System (an Indian food security system)
PICUM	Platform for International Cooperation on Undocumented Migrants
PISPP	Pacific Islands' Safety and Prevention Project
PLA	Participatory Learning and Action

PRA	Participatory Rural Appraisal
PREP	Planning for Resilience and Emergency Preparedness
PsycINFO	Database for peer-reviewed literature in the behavioural sciences and mental health
RRA	Rapid Rural Appraisal
SCP	Swiss Cultural Program
SEZ	Special Economic Zones
SJA	Sarvahara Jan Andolan; a people's organization of tribes in Indian
SW-VirCamp	Social Work-Virtual Campus
TAC	Treatment Action Campaign
UDHR	Universal Declaration of Human Rights
UDI	The Norwegian state office for handling asylum applications
UKZN	University of KwaZulu Natal
UN	United Nations
UNDP	United Nations Development Programmes
UNICEF	United Nations Children's Fund
VCoP	Virtual Community of Practice
WTO	World Trade Organization

1

INTRODUCTION

Anne Karin Larsen, Vishanthie Sewpaul and
Grete Oline Hole

A participatory approach to community work

This book highlights the idea that participation is central to community work and that the theory-practice-research nexus is an important one, not only with foregrounding research but also with practice that provides fertile ground for theorizing about community work. We have thus included chapters of a theoretical/ conceptual nature as well as chapters that are rooted in the experiential work of the authors. Some of the chapters reflect a combined approach, incorporating research, theory, teaching and community based interventions. We have deliberately focused on community work engaging groups and societies, with the principle of participation being central in all chapters. The focus is not on community work methods in general because several other textbooks cover this theme (Ledwith 2011; Minkler 2006; Minkler and Wallerstein 2005; Swanepoel and De Beer 2007; Tesoriero 2010; Twelvetrees 2008; Dominelli 2002). We highlight the importance of bottom-up, grassroots approaches through participation in community work both from a theoretical and an empirical view.

The book critically engages with the theoretical and conceptual underpinnings of the concept 'participation' in community work. Discourses on participation must of necessity include other aspects of global discourses, such as human rights, direct democracy, the power of contexts, social justice, social inclusion and social cohesion, and related discourses on poverty, exclusion, marginalization and oppression as well as highlight the power of dreams, hopes and visions for change, all of which are dealt with in the various chapters.

Our introductory chapter begins with a short glimpse into the history of community work from an international perspective, and then teases out our understanding of core concepts: community, community work, participation and critical reflection and we conclude with a presentation of the structure of the book.

A short history of the roots of community work

While indigenous forms of community practices have existed for time immemorial across the globe, the roots of professional community work are grounded in social movements, as religious, women's rights and liberation, or political based movements. The modern history of community work in the western world had its beginnings in the industrialization of the eighteenth century with people moving from the countryside to the cities to get jobs in the new industries. Industrialization brought in its wake increased suffering and poverty as well as lack of social security. Labour districts and neighbourhoods suffered from lack of cohesion and poor housing and living conditions. To meet the needs of people living in these areas settlements were established, first in England and later in the United States and other countries in Europe. This was also the time when social work education had its beginnings in Europe and the USA.

Community work is said to have started in Chicago by Jane Addams.[1] She was an academic living at the same time as important sociologists and philosophers, like George Herbert Mead and John Dewey who influence approaches to social work education and practice to date. The critical tradition of social work started with Addams (Healy 2012). She believed that changes had to start from below with the influence of people who suffered, and with support and solidarity from people 'better off' that moved into and lived in the deprived districts. Using the same strategy as the founder vicar Barnett of the 'Toynbee Hall' in London, she and Ellen Gates Starr established the Hull House in Chicago in 1889. They invited researchers and academics to live in the area to work for better living conditions by mobilizing people for public schooling, health care, leisure activities for children and other activities later related to public welfare. As an academic Addams published books and, through her practice and writing, inspired social workers all over Europe and the USA. In 1931 she was given the Nobel Peace Prize (Turunen 2004: 51–4).

Another important person that influenced participatory approaches in community work is Paolo Freire.[2] His book 'Pedagogy of the oppressed', which was published in 1968 (2006) has been translated into diverse languages and is on the curriculum lists of many universities today. His emancipating and empowering theories, based on combining education and culture with conscientization and politicization, has contributed to the way we think about and use participatory methodologies in community work and the pedagogical strategies that we adopt in teaching. His idea was to present questions that provoked and stimulated independent thinking based on egalitarian relationships. The value of Freire's work lies in his linking micro–educational methodologies to theories of social change. This understanding combined with his emphasis on the integrative processes of action, critical reflection, theoretical knowledge and participatory democracy, support the contention, as reflected by several authors in this text, that the micro–macro dichotomy is a fallacious one (Sewpaul 2003).

In Asia, Mahatma Gandhi and his movement for independence influenced not only India, but also the rest of the world, to mobilize people in peaceful action for democracy.[3] Gandhi lived in the beginning of 1900 in Transvaal in South Africa and his philosophy about peaceful non-violent resistance inspired local people, including Nelson Mandela,[4] in the political struggle for emancipation, democracy and justice for the people of South Africa. The ideas of critical thinking and participation became global, and have inspired community workers all over the world to focus on the importance of participation and involvement of indigenous people in democracy building and in challenging and changing oppressive structural conditions of life. As pointed out clearly in some of the chapters in this book the philosophy of participation, peaceful action and the struggle for democracy, welfare and human rights are closely related to politics, the way countries and communities are organized and the types of welfare systems that exist.

Conceptualizing 'community'

The concept 'community' is variously conceived of (Craig 2007; Dominelli 2004; Leonard 1997). Sewpaul consolidated these into the following two views that have gained primacy in community social work:

> A community may be conceived of as groups of people, who although diverse, live in and share a specific geographic space within common mezzo level infrastructural development. Community has also been defined in relation to a group of people that share a common interest where people may be spatially separate and indeed may never physically meet.
>
> *(Sewpaul 2008: 98)*

A recent powerful example of the latter is the Occupy Movement. Another example is the Treatment Action Campaign (TAC) in South Africa. The TAC consists of an association of people at local and national levels, who have successfully networked with like-minded NGOs on an international level to exert pressure on the South African government and on the multi-national drug companies to make anti-retroviral treatment accessible. Leonard (1997: 155) speaks of *imagined communities* as social movements 'which consist of those who *apply* for the rights and responsibilities of belonging, whose subject positions include a certain commitment to a set of ideas, even though some of them may be internally contested'. He points at the strengths of such communities compared to communities in which membership is automatic or taken for granted. These imagined communities are generally issue or interest based, with engagement in social activism, lobbying and advocacy whether the reach and influence is local, national, regional and/or international.

Sewpaul (2008) argued that the concept community is generally imbued with positive connotations of: a common solidarity; people coming together to work towards common goals; altruism, sharing and benevolence; and social and economic interdependence. Dominelli criticized Toennies's conception of *Gemeinshaft* as 'communities as unifying forces' (Dominelli 2004: 203) with the argument that such conception contributes to suppression of diversities and to the dynamics of inclusion and exclusion. However, Dominelli concludes:

> Communities provide spaces in which people seek and gain approval, are reaffirmed in their interests or sense of who they are and what they stand for, participate in key decisions, and negotiate with others around issues of change and stability. [...]. Dignity, reciprocity, interdependence and solidarity provide the ties that bind communities and disparate people together.
>
> *(Dominelli 2004: 204)*

Borrowing on Toennies's typology of *Gemeinshaft* and *Gesellschaft* (see chapter thirteen by Dominelli in this book) Pawar and Cox (2004: 10) differentiate between traditional and modern communities, with the former characterized by a locality base, common culture, sense of identity and sense of belonging and the latter as geographically dispersed, multi-cultural and one that provides a partial sense of identity where belongingness depends on common interests. Traditional communities should not be idealized or rarefied; negative attributes also abound (Sewpaul 2008). Pawar posits that humanistic postmodernism with its focus on human orientation, reflexivity, sensitivity for the aesthetic, the particular and the excluded, holds potential to constrain or eradicate the 'mean spirited, superstitious, religious, constraining, authoritarian and backward' (Pawar 2003: 256) characteristics of traditional communities. Humanistic post-modernism also holds potential to counter the negative aspects of modernism in relation to the alienation, individualism, increased consumerism, greed, the creation of weapons of mass destruction and environmental degradation in the wake of modern technological and scientific advancement.

Community work, community organization and community development

In this book authors from different parts of the world describe how the global structural systems of oppression, poverty and inequality affect people at micro levels. Communication technology has brought the global situation into our homes and we cannot claim to be ignorant about what happens in other parts of the world. Neither can we remain indifferent to how our epistemologies influence world-phenomena. The growing use of the Internet and social media with the creation of online communities have imbued the concept 'community' with new meanings, evocative of Leonard's 'imagined community' mentioned above.

Community work is a multi-professional approach to addressing community related issues aimed at improving the living situations of marginalized groups, either through the conventional community organizational approach or the more radical developmental approach, with its focus on participation and challenging structural barriers to the realization of human capabilities and well-being.

Community work constitutes a way of addressing socially related problems on a community level. An often-cited explanation of community work, which we think succinctly expresses its intentions, purpose and aims is the one by Taylor and Presley:

> Community work is not a profession like any other. It is a profession dedicated to increasing the expertise of non-professionals; to increasing the capacity of people in difficult and disadvantaged situations, getting more control over their collective circumstances. Community workers stimulate and support groups of people working to improve conditions and opportunities in their own neighbourhoods. The immediate aims are often concrete – better amenities, housing, job-opportunities; the underlying aim is an increase in confidence, skill and community self-organising power which will enable the participants to continue to use and spread these abilities long after the community worker has gone.
>
> *(Taylor and Presley 1987: 2)*

The concept of community work has not remained consistent; it has changed over time along with changes in the way community work has been initiated and practised. However, there are two main thrusts to community work: community development and community organization. In different parts of the world these concepts have been attributed different meanings. While in Australia and Europe community development has been the overall term for community-strategies, community organization has been the overall term in the US and Canada (see Turunen 2004: 43–4). In the Nordic countries, as in many other parts of the world a pluralistic approach to community work has been characterized by grassroot community work within neighbourhoods, community organization mobilizing self-help groups, and social planning on the municipal and national level. While community work had been a method used for years in many parts of the world, the first time the concept 'community work' was mentioned in a Norwegian White Paper was in 1979 (St.meld. 16, 1979–80: 49). It was defined as 'a method for problem solving where problems for the individual or groups are related to situations in their living environment' (translation by author). A similar definition is presented by the Danish scholar in community work, Hermansen (1985: 11). The need for a new approach was a result of a new housing and living pattern in the cities and suburbs contributing to the need for new network building through the use of community work methods to make sustainable living areas. Community work was divided into three sub methods: 'grass-roots' community work, 'community organization' and 'social planning' at local, regional and country level (Hermansen 1991; Hutchinson 1999). Grassroots community work can be either an aim or a process for change. As an aim it is used by pressure groups to achieve something or to hinder an unwanted action from taking place in their surroundings. As a process for change, it is important that community work create a sense of community feeling in a local area and develop responsibility among the people in a neighbourhood to identify common needs. As the word indicates grassroots community work builds on people's own initiative and action and constitutes a bottom-up approach. Community development had its origin in developing countries, but as a result of the urbanization following the industrialization the method was found useful also in the industrialized part of the world. Community development is a process where locals define their needs and aims and participate in collective actions to achieve them (Hermansen 1985: 21–3).

Community organization can be initiated by either official or private institutions. In contrast with community development initiatives, community organization is generally associated with a top-down approach to initiate changes in a community either with or without the participation of the inhabitants. Community organization usually involves changes taken on a political level to increase the cooperation among different institutions aiming to provide better services to people and/or to reduce the costs. When social planning, linked to community work, is designed to include the voices of people concerned it can negate some of the bureaucratic and top-down influences of community organization.

Bracht, Kingsbury and Rissel (1999: 86) define community organization as 'a planned process to activate a community to use its own social structures and any available resources to accomplish community goals that are decided on primarily by community representatives and that are generally consistent with local values'. The question that this definition must raise is: who plans the processes to activate the communities? As discussed later in this chapter participation of local people in planning processes can have a symbolic effect and be experienced more as merely tokenism than real influence.

A participatory approach in community development can have a pluralistic and a critical radical content. Raising consciousness about oppressive forces in the community and mobilization of people's own ability for change through support, education and organizational changes can increase the level of self-esteem and empowerment both on an individual and a community level. The level of resistance of the disempowering forces in the community or within the group of people will decide which strategy, social action or neighbourhood development is needed (Tesoriero 2010).

The wide complexities of social and environmental issues confronting many societies need to be addressed by stimulating bottom-up, participatory initiatives. While acknowledging the place of community organization strategies used in various contexts, our preferred approach to community work is community development underscored by a radical/critical epistemology aimed at challenging and changing structural conditions that impact the living conditions of people through their active engagement and participation. Community development addresses community work as a bottom-up approach as sustainable changes are best achieved when people concerned participate in an active way, bringing to the development process their knowledge, skills and experience (see chapter two by Hugman and Bartolomei).

The concept participation

Each chapter in this book emphasizes and provides examples of how participatory approaches to community work are, or can be implemented and what it involves. In this introduction we provide a short outline of our understanding of this concept, and the different typologies of participation that can create a backdrop to the reading of the chapters and to the reflection on the questions at the end.

Cornwall (2008) made an effort to unpack the concept 'participation' where she presents different models, meanings and practice. She discusses the most popular typologies of participation that have been developed. The most well known of these is the ladder of participation by Arnstein (1969; 2011). Taking the stand of the citizens as the end receivers Arnstein describes the level of participation from non-participation, through tokenism up to full participation represented by citizen's power. At the level of non-participation she includes manipulation and therapy. As tokenism she mentions placation, informing and consultation, and as the characteristics of citizens' power she includes partnership, delegated power and citizen control. Pretty (1995) presents another ladder of participation, starting his scale with manipulative participation which is simply pretence of involvement of people, and at the other end of the scale is self-mobilization where people take their own initiative without any external interference (see Cornwall 2008: 272) (see Table 1.1).

Participation is always related to power; who is in position and who has the power to give others access to participation, or who has the power to choose and demand their participation in decision-making or in cooperation. Participation is both a means and an end. It is a means to make one's voice and opinions heard; to achieve and to work for change; and a means for a community or a group to reach their objectives. Often it implies the use of citizen involvement to achieve some predetermined goal or objectives, e.g. initiatives taken by the government or local authorities. Used as means, participation is often of short duration, and can appear as a passive form for taking part. As an end, participation is a result of long-term

TABLE 1.1 Arnstein's and Pretty's typologies of participation

Level of participation	Arnstein's ladder of participation	Pretty's typology
High level of citizen participation	Citizens control Delegated power Partnership	Self-mobilization Interactive participation
Tokenism	Consultation Information Placation	Functional participation Participation for material incentives Participation by consultation
Non-participation	Therapy Manipulation	Passive participation Manipulative participation

involvement, engagement and contribution, sharing of ideas and willingness to take part in the development process. It is a process of empowering people to participate in their own development in a meaningful way (Oakley cited in Tesoriero 2010: 144–5).

Participation can be seen as interaction in a learning process, or by self-mobilizing in action groups where people themselves take action for social change, both of which are discussed in several of the chapters in this book.

Many initiatives taken from authorities when involving groups of interests or groups with special needs to take part in planning processes end up as tokenism or decoration (Hart 1992) with no real influence of the people at stake. The issue of power and the inability to know the rules of the game make it difficult to be involved in settings that are unfamiliar. When engaging in community development one of the challenges is to get to know the community well enough to be able to engage the groups of people that will be affected by the changes and should take part in the process from the beginning to the end. To make sure that the voices of the most affected groups are heard is something that community workers should work hard for. Getting in touch with and finding viable entries into the different groups is important and presents challenges. Often lack of time and money to ensure citizens' involvement can result in more expedient non-democratic solutions.

Many factors can make participation difficult. Self-exclusion from taking part in decisions and projects can be a result of different things like meetings held at a time of the day when other commitments need priority, or meetings held at places where people feel uncomfortable coming to. It can be caused by lack of self-confidence that their opinions would be met with laughter and not taken seriously, often because of previous experiences. Another reason for self-exclusion can be an outcome of previous participation without results so participation is perceived to be worthless (Cornwall 2008). To trigger participation and involvement of people in their local community people must feel that their participation is important and desired. The issues at stake have to be essential for them and they need to believe that their actions will make a difference. Not all people can participate in the same way and people have to feel that what they can contribute is appreciated and valued, even if such participation is minimal. Some people will also need help to be able to take part, for example, for transport or babysitting. Not all people feel comfortable with strict meeting structures and speaking lists and this must be taken notice of by setting an alternative, more informal organization of meetings (Tesoriero 2010: 150–1). An inclusive participation means raising questions about what people need, want, how they can contribute, what are their dreams and wishes, and what hinders their action for a good life.

Ledwith and Springett (2010: 30) present participation as a worldview with these characteristics: 'A participatory worldview is founded on cooperation not competition, on diversity not disempowerment; it is a belief that we can coexist in the world in harmony and diversity in ways that enable everyone and everything to flourish'. This is an idealistic stand that demands hard work and critical education fostering empowerment, theory building, social justice and democracy, as well as acceptance of and respect for biodiversity.

Ideological foundation for change from below

Focusing on community development, change from below is a crucial action to take, being founded on the ideology of democracy building, human rights, empowerment and social-ecology. Bottom-up approaches can make change more sustainable when it is set up by the local knowledge of people living in the area. Examples of problems seen when local knowledge in India has been devaluated or not taken into account is shown in the examples presented in chapter fifteen by Singh and Tirmare.

Change from below is based on the principles of participation and citizens' involvement. Examples of how industrialism and capitalism have overruled local communities and destroyed the original foundation for locality-based living are numerous and have been going on through colonization and through contemporary forms of globalization and exploitation of indigenous people. The power of capital has been good for the very rich few and a disaster for the many marginalized groups of people living in poverty. We need to work against authoritarian and oppressive governmental push and corporate greed and reclaim our commitment to human rights and social justice (Ferguson and Lavalette 2006; Ferguson 2008; Wronka and Staub Bernasconi 2012), and adopt radical and emancipatory approaches in our education, research and practice.

Increasing global warming, diminishing natural resources and destruction of the earth's biodiversity call for radical lifestyle changes from each one of us, especially in the rich part of the world, but also from those living in countries striving to reach western living standards. Valuing and drawing on local resources and skills, while ensuring that external resources are provided where needed, constitutes the foundation for sustainable community development and self-reliance. 'Sustainability requires that structures be developed that are able to be maintained in the long term, by minimizing the extent to which they draw on and consume external resources and the extent to which they create polluting and harmful product or outcomes' (Tesoriero 2010: 128). Facing the huge challenges as a consequence of air-pollution and heating of the global atmosphere, lack of water supply in parts of the world, AIDS, homelessness, hunger and poverty, financial crises and wars, means that a more holistic approach to problem solving in social work is necessary. In many situations local problems cannot be solved without global actions. The melting of the glaciers and the polar ice are causing problems that will affect the whole globe. This means that social workers need to recognize the importance of inter-dependence, and they need to possess the values, knowledge and skills to intervene at community levels within and/or across national borders. In her latest book on *Green Social Work* (2012) and in chapter thirteen in this book Dominelli reveals how environmental issues are an integral part of social work's responsibility and emphasizes its relevance to the social issues that societies have to deal with.

Tesoriero (2010) focuses on the Green perspective in his book on *Community Development* where the ecological perspective based on holism, sustainability, diversity and equilibrium is closely related to the ethical imperative of social justice and human rights for all people. Turunen (2004: 7) in her dissertation on community work in Nordic countries, mentions 20 concepts related to community work; one of these is ecosocial work. Gitterman and Germain first presented this perspective in social work in 1980, and their third edition of the book on *The Life Model* was published in 2008 (Gitterman and Germain 2008). In their model for action the community worker addresses the stressors that influence people's life especially in poor and deprived neighbourhoods. The community worker acts together with the inhabitants, not necessarily living in the same area as Jane Addams did, but by mobilizing their strength and ability to cope, in addition to work for allocation of more resources to the neighbourhood. While there are merits to this approach, ecosocial work places no moral imperatives on the community worker to engage people in Frierian-Gramscian strategies of consciousness-raising to challenge and change those structural conditions that retain people in disadvantaged, marginalized, excluded and disadvantaged positions.

Critical reflection

Critical reflection and reflexivity is an important part of community work both for the community worker and for the people involved in projects. To raise questions about established or ongoing practice, the issues at stake and what contributes to the challenges that people meet in their community is crucial as a starting point for community change. Critical reflexivity means to question one's own practice as a community worker/social worker, to understand on what ground one's decisions are taken and what ideas and concerns are leading to one's actions. Critical social work means to be conscious about the knowledge that informs our practice and actions and what this knowledge is based on (Payne and Askeland 2008). As part of the effort at developing reflexivity it is important that we critically interrogate all our taken-for-granted assumptions (Gramsci 1977) about ourselves, the people that we work with, and the world that we live in. In its simplest form we need to question the sources of our values, knowledge and beliefs and how we have come to know what we know, value and believe.

As stated earlier our preferred approach to community work is based on critical theory and radical, structural and anti-oppressive approaches. Fook summarized the following basic elements of a critical approach in social work:

- A commitment to a structural analysis of social, and personally experienced problems, i.e. an understanding of how personal problems might be traced to socio-economic structures, and that the 'personal' and 'political' realms are inextricably linked;
- A commitment to emancipatory forms of analysis and action (incorporating both anti-oppressive and anti-exploitative stances);

- A stance of social critique (including an acknowledgement and critique of the social control functions of the social work profession and the welfare system);
- A commitment to social change.

(Fook 2002: 5)

Structure of the book

This book is divided into four sections. The focus in the first section is on 'participation, ethics and co-construction of knowledge in community work' and includes four chapters. Chapter one outlines core concepts related to community work, participation and critical reflection and provides a background for the following chapters in the book. In the second chapter, ethical issues are related to participation being valued as both a means and an end in community work. Hugman and Bartolomei examine participation in relation to the core principles of social justice, human rights and virtue ethics, the latter referring to the professional integrity of the community worker. They conceive participation as a fundamental human rights issue as it relates to human agency and autonomy. In chapter three Astray, Gonzalez and Alonso take an epistemological, historical and critical perspective on professional knowledge and practice in community work and discuss the co-construction of knowledge in the light of pre-modernist, modernist and postmodernist epistemologies. In chapter four Hole, Harris and Larsen describe and discuss how findings from a strategic literature review enlightened what happened in the Social Work-Virtual Campus project. By analyzing the concept of co-construction of knowledge and virtual communities of practice they reflect upon how these concepts have been understood and operationalized to help teachers and students to co-construct meaningful knowledge to address practice issues.

Section two focuses on participatory learning and action research (Reason and Bradbury 2004). Participatory action research as a method of developing knowledge together with the participants in projects is commonly used for evaluation and research in community work initiatives, securing participation in the research process from the planning and analysis of the data and ownership of the results. The first chapter in this section, chapter five, provides an overview of participatory learning and action techniques and outlines their potential uses in community work. In this chapter Bozalek explains how these tools can open up engagement and ensure participation and be useful techniques for community workers facilitating involvement of community members. Chapter six presents perspectives on the asset-based community development model as it offers key strategies to mobilize and sustain economic development initiatives. Using participatory action research methodology, Raniga presents empirical evidence from the experiences of fifteen community members who were involved in a garden project in a low-income community in KwaZulu-Natal, South Africa. Three themes emerging from the data analysis are discussed: enhancing capacity, building partnerships for change and linking resources from outside the community as strategies to mobilize and sustain economic development initiatives and the implementation of asset-based community development in practice. In chapter seven Larsen and Hole present participatory learning of community work in an e-learning course. The authors present how teachers and students have been involved in development and evaluation of the course by the use of participatory action research. By analyzing the results in the light of the roles a community worker can adopt, the students' learning outcomes are discussed.

Section three focuses on power and participation in community work presenting examples of participatory community work projects from different parts of the world. This section starts with chapter eight where Sewpaul, Østhus and Mhone present a community based practice and research project with children and youth living on the streets of Durban. It details an approach to community development that combines teaching, supervision, field practice education and research informed by critical theory. In chapter nine Browne and Adelman present the ideas, worldviews and approaches that informed the development of Imagine Chicago, an idealistic organization that, over the last twenty years, has inspired a self-organizing global Imagine movement of social innovation, and has informed community participation efforts in government, business, education, culture, health, youth and community development. In chapter ten Hutchinson focuses on Norway and the possibilities for doing community work in a country with a strong welfare state, and in chapter eleven Henriksbø and Grimen present experiences from a neighbourhood project in the city of Bergen, Norway. In chapter twelve Visser and Marques elucidate how art work can be an effective tool to enhance community engagement and change.

Section four focus on new global challenges and here local and indigenous issues are presented addressing capitalism, and environmental and gender specific issues. The ecological/green perspective is introduced as important for sustainable development by Dominelli in chapter thirteen. The challenges related to global warming, war, poverty, lack of water, economic crisis, and housing problems are important issues to be addressed by community workers. In chapter fourteen, Passells discusses how colonialism and imperialism have impacted indigenous communities in New Zealand, with a particular focus on gender-based violence. Chapter fifteen by Singh and Tirmare present the paradigm of indigenous community work with powerful examples of grassroot projects in India to face global challenges. In chapter sixteen Sewpaul addresses the challenges of neoliberalism and new managerialism and the influence of the global economy on local communities. What we have seen is how modern technology can escalate small-scale protest action in one country/city into actions in other countries to consolidate in the form of the latest international 'Occupy Movement'. All these chapters remind us that development is not gender neutral, and that one of the biggest global challenges of our times is the impact of globalization on women and children, particularly the girl child, and finding ways to curb the high levels of violence against women.

In the concluding chapter Sewpaul and Larsen draw on the sixteen chapters to highlight the power of context in shaping conceptualizations of community and community work. Following critiques of conventional definitions and some of the existing models of community work they proffer alternative definitions of community work, community organization and community development, and a radical ecological approach that accord with their emancipatory philosophy. They highlight the importance of understanding and undoing power and oppressions linked to social criteria such as race, class, gender and sexual orientation. They argue that the calls for autonomous action by communities without external resources are reflective of liberal, individualistic discourse of self-reliance that deny the impact of structural conditions in maintaining people in poor and disempowered positions. Based on their understanding of the power of ideological hegemony on the collective identities of people, they challenge popular notions that rarefy community development from within. They argue that skilled facilitators (organic intellectuals of the Gramscian ilk) play a profound role in engaging people in consciousness raising exercises, enabling them to reflect on the external structural sources of oppression and/or privilege, and on the constraints of their own thinking. Such praxis validates people and it makes them appreciate that they are much more than that defined by their social circumstances; it enhances their sense of self, increases self-confidence, belief in themselves, and instills hope that change is possible, which are all requisites for constructive engagement and participation.

QUESTIONS FOR REFLECTION

- What does participation mean to you?
- Who and what determines your level of participation in different settings?
- When participating in a group/organization what kind of position do you take? Which factors influence your way of participation?

Notes

1. Addams lived from 1860–1935.
2. Freire lived from 1921–1997.
3. Gandhi lived from 1869–1948.
4. Mandela was born in 1918.

Suggestions for further readings

Cornwall, A. (2011) *The participation reader,* London/New York: Zed Books.
For ladders of participation go to 'Staying for Tea'. Online. Available HTTP: http://stayingfortea.org/2011/06/13/participation-ladders-101/ (accessed 2 February 2013).

References

Arnstein, S.R. (1969) 'A ladder of citizen participation', *Journal of the American Institute of Planners*, 35(4): 216–24, republished in A. Cornwall (2011) (ed.) *The Participation Reader*, London, New York: Zed Books.

Bracht, N., Kingsbury, L. and Rissel, C. (1999) 'A five-stage community organization model for health promotion', in N. Bracht (ed.) *Health Promotion at the Community Level: New Advances*. 2nd edn. Thousand Oaks, California: Sage Publications, pp. 83–104.

Cornwall, A. (2008) 'Unpacking "Participation": models, meanings and practices', *Community Development Journal* 43(3): 269–83, Oxford University Press.

Craig, G. (2007) 'Community capacity-building: something old, something new ...?' *Critical Social Policy*, 27(3): 335–59.

Dominelli, L. (2002) *Anti-oppressive Social Work Theory and Practice*, Basingstoke, Hampshire, UK: Palgrave Macmillan.

——(2004) *Social Work: Theory and Practice for a Changing Profession*, Cambridge: Polity Press.

——(2012) *Green Social Work. From Environmental Crises to Environmental Justice*, Cambridge, UK: Polity Press.

Ferguson, I. (2008) *Reclaiming Social Work: Challenging Neoliberalism and Promoting Social Justice*, Los Angeles: Sage Publication.

Ferguson, I. and Lavalette, M. (2006) 'Globalisation and global justice: towards a social work of resistance', *International Social Work* 49(3): 309–18.

Freire, P. (2006) *The Pedagogy of the Oppressed*, trans. Myra Bergman Ramos, 30th anniversary edition, New York, London: Continuum.

Fook, J. (2002) *Social Work, Critical Theory and Practice*, London: Sage Publications.

Gitterman, A. and Germain, C.B. (2008) *The Life Model of Social Work Practice*, New York: Columbia University Press.

Gramsci, A. (1977) *Selections from Political Writings 1910–1920*, London: Lawrence and Wishart.

Hart, R. (1992) *Children's Participation from Tokenism to Citizenship*, Florence, Italy: UNICEF, Inoccenti Research Centre.

Healy, K. (2012) 'Critical perspectives' in M. Gray, J. Midgley and S.A. Webb (eds) *The Sage Handbook of Social Work*, London: Sage Publications.

Hermansen, O.F. (1991) 'Historisk beskrivelse av socialrådgiveruddannelsen i Danmark', [History of social work education in Denmark] *Nordisk Sosialt Arbeid. Nordisk Sosialhøgskolekomite 25 år. Jubileumsskrift.*

——(1985) *Socialt arbejde i de lokale fællesskaber*, 2nd edn [Social work in the local communities], Socialpædagogisk Bibliotek.

Hutchinson, G.S. (1999) *Samfunnsarbeid i sosialt arbeid*, Oslo: Universitetsforlaget.

Ledwith, M. (2011) *Community Development. A Critical Approach*, 2nd edn, Bristol: The Policy Press.

Ledwith, M. and Springett, J. (2010) *Participatory Practice: Community-based Action for Transformative Change*, Bristol: The Policy Press.

Leonard, P. (1997) *Postmodern Welfare: Reconstructing an Emancipatory Project*, London: Sage Publications.

Minkler, F. (2006) *Community Organizing and Community Building for Health*, London: Rutgers University Press.

Minkler, M. and Wallerstein, N. (eds) (2005) *Community Based Participatory Research for Health*, San Francisco, CA: Jossey-Bass.

Pawar, M. (2003) 'Resurrection of traditional communities in postmodern societies', *Futures*, 35(3): 253–65.

Pawar, M. and Cox, D. (2004) *Community Informal Care and Welfare Systems: A Training Manual*, Centre for Rural Social Research, Charles Stuart University, New South Wales.

Payne, M. and Askeland, G.A. (2008) *Globalization and International Social Work. Postmodern Change and Challenge*, Aldershot: Ashgate.

Pretty, J. (1995) 'Participatory learning for sustainable agriculture', *World Development* 23 8), 1247–63.

Reason, P. and Bradbury, H. (eds) (2004) *Handbook of Action Research Participative Inquiry and Practice*, London, Thousand Oaks, New Delhi: Sage Publications.

Sewpaul, V. (2003) 'Reframing epistemologies and practice through international exchanges: global and local discourses in the development of critical consciousness', in L.D. Dominelli and W.T. Bernard (eds) *The Value Base of Social Work and Social Care*, Berkshire: Open University Press.

——(2008) 'Community intervention and social activism', in A. Barnard, N. Horner and J. Wild (eds) *The Value Base of Social Work and Social Care*, Berkshire: Open University Press.

Swanepoel, H. and de Beer, F. (2007) *Community Development – Breaking the Cycle of Poverty*, Landsdowne, SA: Juta & Co Ltd.

St.meld. 16 (1979–80) *Nærmiljømeldingen*, [White Paper from the Norwegian Government about local communities].

Taylor, M. and Presley, F. (1987) *Community Work in the UK 1982–6*, ed. G. Chanan, London: Library Association Publishing in association with Calouste Gulbenkian Foundation.

Tesoriero, F. (2010) *Community Development, Community-based Alternatives in an Age of Globalisation*, French Forest: Pearson Education Australia.

Turunen, P. (2004) *Samhällsarbete i Norden. Diskurser och praktiker i omvandling*, [Eng. Community work in Nordic countries. Discourses and practice in change], Acta Wexionensia no. 47/2004, Växjö University Press.

Twelvetrees, A. (2008*) Community Work,* Basingstoke: Palgrave.

Wronka, J. and Staub Bernasconi, S. (2012) 'Human rights', in K. Lyons, T. Hokenstad, M. Pawar, N. Huegler and N. Hall (eds) *The Sage Handbook of International Social Work*, London: Sage Publications, pp. 70–84.

PART 1

Participation, ethics and co-construction of knowledge in community work

2

THE ETHICS OF PARTICIPATION IN COMMUNITY WORK PRACTICE

Richard Hugman and Linda Bartolomei

Introduction: participation and ethics

It could be said that participation has been a central aspect of community work for a long time. It is placed centre stage by the work of Addams (2002 (1907)) through Alinsky (1971) and Arnstein (1969) to Ife (2010). Participation, quite simply, is the practice of grounding community work in the active involvement of those people who benefit from and are affected by it, in every aspect including problem definition, strategy, action and intervention, and review. It seeks community control of community work, with a genuine partnership between community members and practitioners (Kenny 2006; Ife 2010: 40).

Participation can be seen as an approach to practice (a means) and a goal of practice (an end) in community work. So it is both a method and an objective: it is what community work seeks to achieve and at the same time how it intends to get there. So, right from the start it can be a complicated task to be clear about what is under consideration here. This complexity is not made any easier by the range of more specific forms of community work practice that have developed over time in different contexts (see other chapters in this volume).

It must also be recognized that the relationship between means and ends is both practical or technical (concerning what works) and moral (concerning what ought to happen). Arguments for participation are grounded in claims about its effectiveness in achieving the objectives of community members in developing their lives *and* in the way in which it is valued as an end in itself because it embodies a core aspect of what is necessary to live a truly human life. So, participation in community work cannot be considered without thinking about these aspects together.

All of these arguments point to the centrality of ethics in the way in which participation should be understood. Put simply, ethics is 'the conscious reflection on our moral values' (Hinman 2008: 5). This is the process through which people consider what matters most to them in how they live their lives, in their relationships within families, neighbourhoods and the wider society. Ethics is what people do every day in thinking about what is good and what is right. It can be mistaken for externally imposed sets of rules, especially in the professions (Hugman 2005). Yet, although ethics becomes formalized in some circumstances, such as in codes of ethics (and so in situations of unacceptable practice can be used as ways of seeking redress for people who have been dealt with inappropriately by professionals), what makes practices acceptable or not is based not so much on rules as on shared values. This is what ethics is really all about.

So, what are the ethical issues that need to be considered when examining participation in community work? We can distinguish between three main approaches to ethics that are widely discussed in the professional literature and which underpin relevant professional statements of ethics such as those of the international social work organizations (IFSW/IASSW 2004; Hugman 2005). These are: social justice; human rights; and virtues. Each of these ethical approaches is based on a different way of thinking about what is good and right. Ideas about justice come from considerations of the balance to be achieved between competing interests, which can be understood as 'fairness'. Rights are derived from thinking about what it is to be human, those things without which people cannot be said to be able to live a truly human life. Virtues concern the way in which the character of a person might be directed towards human flourishing, both of that person and of others. Although there are points at which these ethical approaches may conflict in their demands, looked at together they provide a powerful basis for asking critical questions about social life. Furthermore, although there are many debates about the ways in which ethics differ in various cultures, the over-arching ideas of justice, rights and virtues are applicable to asking ethical questions in the wide range of cultural contexts in which community work is practised. In all such contexts, these ethical concepts enable the exploration of the idea of participation in community work, as a means, as an end and in terms of the connections between means and ends.

Participation and social justice

Questions of social justice relate to how we understand justice not only as a quality of individuals but also of our wider societies. Although the ancient sages of East and West offered quite markedly divergent answers as to how we might achieve such societies, they were at least in harmony on this underlying point (Kupperman 2004). Between the Eastern and Western traditions there is also a common point that justice is to be understood in terms of *balance*, in the achievement of those things that enable all members of a society to live as fully human a life as possible. Thus the competing interests, needs, rights and so on of all parts of a society should be taken into consideration. This places a limit on the claims made by any one person or group, because of the impact such claims might then have on others. It also places responsibilities on those who have power in any situation (whether this is the power of decision, control, influence or resistance) to use that power to achieve a balance that takes the interests, needs and rights of everyone into account. In the modern world, this is often taken to imply paying specific attention to those who otherwise are disadvantaged or marginalized, as they require more attention than others in order to achieve the same from the society (see, for example, Nussbaum 2003: 35).

For community workers, social justice is a core element of human development. The idea of 'development' carries with it the notion that the capacity of people to achieve the things that they value in life can be extended and enhanced. For example, material resources can be distributed more equitably, or obtained where they were not previously available or new ways of interacting within a community may produce more effective outcomes (Drucker 2008). What lies at the heart of the pursuit of human development is recognition that in order to achieve a good life, all people have needs that must be met. A society in which opportunity to achieve a truly human life is not fairly distributed is one in which it is highly likely that not all people will be able to achieve the things that the society values. Kenny (2006: 339) lists many needs that are of concern to community workers. From this list it is clear that the way in which a society is organized and functions can affect the way in which people can meet their needs, either individually or collectively. So what is of concern to community workers is how such needs are identified and then how they are addressed (also see Ife 2010, 2012).

The importance of participation by community members in how needs are identified and addressed must, realistically, be seen in terms of effectiveness (Bak 2004; Weyers and van den Berg 2006; Drucker 2008). (We will return below to questions of 'right'.) Quite simply, there is ample evidence that when those people whose needs are being considered have the opportunity to express their own understanding and priorities, then there is a demonstrably better outcome from the efforts of those who work to achieve change, whether these are the efforts of community members or the professionals assisting them. Moreover, when community members are involved directly in the efforts towards meeting their needs the effectiveness of programs also tends to be much better. For example, Weyers and van den Berg's (2006) study in South Africa demonstrates that the active involvement of both formal and informal community leaders and the motivation and action of community members were among the most significant factors in the success of community programs that they studied.

This is crucial: against those who argue against participation as simply an ideological fixation, the empirical evidence is that participatory practice works better as defined by the results (Bak 2004; Kenny 2006; Weyers and van den Berg 2006; Drucker 2008). But why is this an ethical issue? The most straightforward answer is that in so far as human development is a primary value of a fair society, then to be able to achieve this goal must be seen as 'good'. Beyond that, in a world with finite resources (both material and social) to act in ways that are unlikely to achieve such goals would be wasteful, taking resources away from others who also have needs, which would be 'bad'. In this way, we can see that ecological and economic questions are as much part of the ethical considerations that must be given to how we undertake practice as are issues of social and cultural impact (Hugman 2005).

Another important question to be asked about any community work is that of sustainability: how durable are the outcomes of a program? While this also carries with it the implications of environmental and economic sustainability, the ongoing social and cultural implications of any program must not be forgotten. What is gained, therefore, is not only the immediate and tangible outcomes of a program, such as an improvement in policy and services or a gain in material resources available to a community, but also the longer term benefit of people gaining experience in participation. So, the capacity to participate in the community can be considered as a 'good', something of value both for what it can be used to create but also in itself. The debates of the last two decades about 'social capital' have shown that the twin values of participation, as a means and an end, together contribute to stronger communities in which people experience greater social well-being (Putnam 2001; Winter 2000).

Ife (2010: 48) reminds us that one of the key concerns of a social justice approach is about changing social relationships in order to address structural inequalities, such as gender, class and ethnicity. In looking at participation and social justice it is not possible to ignore the underlying fact that this is about power. For example, power is often exercised by those who control communities from outside, such as governments, corporations and indeed academic researchers on the basis of structural inequality. All too often the rhetoric of community engagement and participation espoused by many such institutions remains at a purely superficial level denying communities the opportunities to actively engage in the process of defining their own needs and of identifying solutions. The authors have published extensively on these challenges in their own community based research work among refugee and displaced populations (Pittaway et al. 2010; Hugman et al. 2011a; Hugman et al. 2011b). This work documents and explores the participatory model of action research entitled 'Reciprocal Research' which was developed in partnership with refugee communities in order to ensure their meaningful and active participation in all research activities as well as to ensure that the learning generated by the research was both accessible and useful to the communities involved (Pittaway and Bartolomei 2009a, 2009b). Community workers possess knowledge and skills that are useful for community members, which places them in a powerful position (Hugman 1991; Ife 2010). The problem is not whether to exercise power, but in how to use it. Thus a participatory approach, both as a means and as an end in working towards social justice, is ethical as well as technical. Seen in this way, with acknowledgement to the evidence for great effectiveness and sustainability, it is hard to see how practice that does not embrace participation could be regarded as just.

Participation and human rights

Many commentators on community work emphasize the importance of connecting participation, empowerment and human rights (for example: Ife and Fiske 2006;

Kenny 2006; Ife 2010, 2012). This understanding begins from the position that meeting human needs cannot fully be achieved unless the means to do so are regarded as human rights. Because the lack of these means prevents people from living a fully human life, they are not simply choices or preferences but are core aspects of what it is to be human and so must be seen as entitlements. To prevent people from gaining access to such 'goods' mean to deny them something of their very humanity. It is, quite literally, dehumanizing. Following this, so far as it seeks to assist people in gaining empowerment and achieving access to these goods, a primary goal of community work clearly is to promote human rights (Ife 2008).

However, we can go further than this. The traditions in Western philosophy that provide the foundation for human rights are those that are concerned with the idea of 'human agency' (Hinman 2008). To be human is to be able to exercise autonomy and moral responsibility, and so be capable of understanding right and wrong. Within this perspective, all human beings are worthy of respect and dignity, for no other reason than that they are human; there are no qualifications or exceptions. Based on this understanding, human agency then has to be seen as a right. That is, if people are denied the opportunity to act on their capacities to exercise autonomy and moral responsibility, then they are being denied a foundational aspect of their humanity. On this basis, participation is a right, in and of itself, precisely because it embodies human agency. From a human rights perspective, participation therefore cannot be regarded simply as an option. It must explicitly be incorporated in theory and practice.

Ife (2008) discusses three different aspects of human rights. Because these have developed in sequence historically, they are referred to as 'generations' of rights. The first of these concern civil and political rights, such as equality before the law, being able to choose who governs the country in which we live, not to be prevented from acting freely in who we associate with or what we say (provided that we do not harm anyone else in doing so) and to a fair trial if we are accused of breaking the law. Ife (2008: 31) argues that these rights are formalized in laws and can be seen as 'negative', in that to achieve them requires that others do not stand in a person's way. The second group consists of social, cultural and economic rights. These concerns whether we can enjoy health, become educated, have appropriate housing and so on. Such rights are more 'positive', in that in addition to being free to pursue them people also have to have the necessary involvement of others in being able to achieve them. For example, education and health require shared organization because they go beyond the capacities of most people to achieve them on their own. The third type of rights is even more collective, in that it consists of 'community rights'. By this Ife means the right to clean water and clean air, to have a culture recognized and to achieve social and community development. Such rights 'only make sense if they are defined at a collective level' (Ife 2008: 27).

As Ife also notes (2008: 33, 75), there are parts of the world in which civil and political rights are contested, notably by some political leaders as well as by defenders of 'traditional culture', but in which there is a strong claim to recognizing community rights. In these social and cultural contexts civil and political rights as conceived of in the global North may be rejected as irrelevant or even as destructive of culture. However, this objection must be considered very carefully. It often appears as a rejection of the 'interference' of global Northern countries in the global South, especially as this applies to the actions of governments or corporations. The history of colonialism shows that many of the problems faced in the global South currently have their roots in the damaging impact of colonial rule (Asad 2000; Ife 2008). However, at the same time, it is important also to be cautious as to whether the rejection of civil and political rights always arises from this cause. As Annan observed when he was the Secretary General of United Nations, '[i]t is never the people who complain about human rights as a Western or Northern imposition. It is too often their leaders who do so' (Annan 1997). The implication is that some objections to human rights on grounds of culture can be for self-interested reasons, in that those who deny the rights of others usually have much to gain by doing so.

Nussbaum (2000, 2003) proposes a way of thinking about these questions that seeks to move beyond this debate. She argues that what lies behind human rights are those things that we need to achieve in order to live a good human life. Without the capacity to do so, which she calls 'capabilities', a person is less than fully human (for the full list see Nussbaum 2000: 77–80). There is no culture about which Nussbaum has found relevant information 'in which people do not ask themselves what they are able to do' (2000: 100). While the detail of her empirical list has developed over time, the important point is that for Nussbaum these capabilities are common across cultures and all express the exercise of human agency in different ways. It is the detail that varies between cultures.

A similar argument advocating the cross-cultural relevance of human rights principles is that of Ebadi who declares 'however different they may be, all cultures embrace certain common principles […] so cultural relativity should never be used as a pretext to violate human rights' (in UNDP 2004: 23). It may be noted, ironically, that the assertion of cultural relativity is ultimately self-defeating, in that it claims an inviolability that it then denies to others (usually, Ebadi implies, in the interests of those who hold power against 'the weak'). For example, in our own practice we have seen how knowing more about human rights can empower people in vulnerable communities (Pittaway et al. 2010: 244–5). For example, work conducted with displaced women in Sri Lanka following the 2004 Asian Tsunami which aimed to ensure their active engagement in the recovery process resulted in both a new UN Resolution on Gender Sensitive Disaster responses and the establishment of 27 community led women's centres (Pittaway et al. 2007).

For all of these reasons, community work must be concerned with human rights, whether this is perceived in terms of the 'three generations' of rights or as 'human capabilities'. The ethics of participation necessarily addresses the issue of human agency and as with social justice (although from different premises) this points to the integration of means and ends in practice. So the discussion now turns to the question of good practice and the 'virtuous' practitioner.

Participation and virtuous practice

Much of the preceding discussion has focused on principles and ideas, especially those concerning the broad goals of community work. At the same time the connection with the ways in which community workers practice has been implied repeatedly. But if we are to achieve the integration of ends and means, then we need to address explicitly the question of how participation is undertaken. For that reason, a discussion of 'virtuous practice' is vital and is not simply a matter of conceptual neatness (Webb 2010).

Discussions of participation in community work emphasize that there are various ways that it may be used (Arnstein 1969; Kenny 2006; Ife 2012). For Arnstein (1969), the idea of participation may lead to practices as varied as token consultation, in which community members are asked to comment on pre-determined plans, through to full control by community members of all aspects of a project or program. The forms of 'non-participation' that make up part of Arnstein's 'ladder' are excluded here. [This is presented in chapter one (editor's note)]. As Ife (2012: 202) makes clear, supporting citizen participation is often a far from straightforward process and one which challenges community workers to seek a range of diverse methods to ensure that the voices of the marginalized are heard. Community workers also need to be aware of and responsive to the diversity within communities, as well as issues around factors such as gender, and to be able to act in ways that enable diverse voices to be heard.

From this understanding, it can be seen that participation is a practice skill. It concerns 'competence', which has an ethical as well as a technical meaning. Indeed, it can be argued that this is a point at which the ethical and the technical can be shown to be interwoven and not separable concerns. For community workers to be able to facilitate participation to the fullest possible extent, which has been discussed above, is good both because it is the better way to achieve the outcomes sought by communities but also that in itself it achieves other benefits, such as the empowerment of experience and knowledge gained from participating. Examples provided by Weyers and van den Berg (2006) and Drucker (2008) demonstrate that through the development of processes that were higher up the 'ladder of participation' (see above) not only were better outcomes achieved in terms understandable to professionals and governments but also people gained confidence in their own capacities and a sense of ownership over projects so that benefits were sustained. For example, in practice involving one present author (LB) we have seen how the focus on human rights in gender-based post-tsunami community work in Sri Lanka in 2005 led to women from the affected districts lobbying directly for themselves at the United Nations to seek better protection against sexual and gender-based violence (Pittaway et al. 2007).

The other major way in which participation concerns virtuous practice lies in the way in which it forms the basis for the responsive and responsible use of 'professionalism' (Drucker 2008: 58; Tesoriero 2010: 153; also see Hugman 1991, 2005). Professionalism, seen here as the possession of distinct knowledge and skills that have been gained through education and training, inevitably brings with it social power, which may be through influence, respect, authority, control of resources or of the agenda. It is important to note that this list is not uniformly negative. Furthermore, as Kenny notes (2006: 162) power resides in every sort of social interaction. It is the capacity to shape events and influence outcomes. It is also not possible for professionals to avoid exercising power (Hugman 1991). From this perspective the virtuous practitioner is not one who tries to avoid power but the one who uses it in partnership and collaboration with others, in ways that promote these others' capacities to understand and use the power that is available to them. This is empowerment in practice (Adams 2008).

If, then, the good practitioner is the one who can use power positively, and part of that process must involve promoting participation both as a means and as a goal, it follows that the good practitioner must be competent in doing so. We do not get one aspect without the other. This is what is meant by 'integrity', which is a virtue that has long been recognized as crucial in the links between being the sort of people that we might wish to be and the types of practice that we have to pursue in order to become that sort of person – in this case, a 'good' community worker (compare with Banks 2006: 54–8). This in turn carries with it implications for other virtues, such as acting in good faith, honesty, respectfulness or conscientiousness. Simply promoting a particular model of participation, such as the higher levels of Arnstein's ladder (1969) as a technique while failing to address these other qualities, will not make for good practice. It might also be expected that community members would quickly 'see through' such an attempt as lacking integrity and reject it as deceitful or manipulative.

So the ethics of virtues can be seen as having something to say to a consideration of participation and community work, as necessary for the way in which we connect ideas and actions and link social justice and human rights as goals that must be integrated with the practices through which participation is achieved.

Means-ends connection

One of the recurring themes in this discussion so far has been the way in which means (practices) and ends (goals) are linked. This integration goes beyond the idea of virtues and relates also to social justice and human rights. That is, in each case it must be asked whether it is reasonable or even possible for any of these broad values to be achieved if in the process an injustice is perpetrated or someone's rights are denied. On face value the answer must immediately be 'no, of course not' – but these are very complex issues and it can often be very difficult in concrete situations to draw a line between limiting someone's perceptions of what they should be allowed to do and what others might find acceptable. This is not simply to complicate or avoid the matter (compare with Kenny 2006: 384), but to recognize that there are particular obligations on professionals, officials and others with particular forms of power to focus on the needs and interests of community members, as community members experience them, and not simply to tell people what they need or can have for reasons of professional dogma or bureaucratic convenience.

In his classic work on community action, Alinsky (1971) appears to take the view that ends always justify means. This stance is a fairly basic utilitarianism, seeking one view of the 'greater good for the greatest number', justified by the way that Alinsky was confident that he could recognize 'the enemy' (those who oppress others, usually for material gain). While this approach can be seen in the context of its time and place (as Alinsky himself noted) it can be criticized as being internally inconsistent. Tesoriero (2010: 164–5) notes that Alinsky's 'rejection of ethics' was based on a military metaphor, moreover one that judges good and bad solely by reference to particular outcomes. It is difficult to see that this is the best way to proceed, ethically or technically, as while it may result in an outcome that is considered 'successful' for some it does not result in sustainable community building precisely because it separates process from outcomes. It also creates an image of the community worker as the powerful expert, even the heroic warrior, which is an image in conflict with participation as both means and end and is curiously similar to Drucker's description of a health professional asserting their own skill instead of equipping community members to understand and act for themselves (Drucker 2008: 58).

We can allow Alinsky this, that if participation was to be shown as being ineffective (say, if it had no impact one way or the other) or it was actually negative in its effects (made matters worse) then even if it were philosophically attractive there would be no basis for seeing it as important in the relationship between means and ends in community work. Indeed, under those circumstances then it should be avoided. Conversely, if it were technically effective but regarded widely as morally abhorrent then it would also be unacceptable. However, as Kenny (2006), Weyers and van den Berg (2006), Drucker (2006) and Tesoriero (2010) among many others all demonstrate, participation is not only consistent with core principles that are widely valued, such as social justice and human rights, but it also contributes to better community work outcomes.

Conclusion

This chapter has examined the ethics of participation in community work in relation to the core principles of social justice, human rights and virtues. Arguments from all three approaches to ethics have together supported the idea and the practice of participation as the basis for good community work. First, it was argued that participation of community members in the projects and programs that affect their lives assists in the achievement of a more just society. This is a conclusion that hinges, at least partly, on the practical impact of participation in achieving better outcomes for communities. Second, participation was shown to be not only a way of enabling people to achieve human rights more effectively but also in itself to be a right. Participation is an aspect of human agency and therefore part of what it is to be human. This applies across cultural contexts. Third, the relevance of participation to thinking about what it is to be a good practitioner was suggested in a brief consideration of 'virtuous practice'. Here questions of competence were explored and the capacity to work participatively was seen to be interwoven with the reflective use of professional power.

From this analysis it can be concluded that the importance of participation has to be understood in terms of the integration of technical skill and ethics. It is not simply that participation as a practice does not conflict with core ethical values, rather it is the case that it positively contributes to their achievement as part of the goals a community might have for better services, a greater say in its own affairs or more broadly to long-term development. Thus participation has to be seen as necessary for good community work.

QUESTIONS FOR REFLECTION

- Is it possible to achieve good community work practice without seeking the participation of community members?
- Can ends ever justify means in community work, as Alinsky claimed, or is it necessary always to integrate goals and the methods by which they are achieved?

References

Adams, R. (2008) *Empowerment, Participation and Social Work*, 4th edn, Basingstoke: Palgrave-Macmillan.

Addams, J. [2002 (1907)] *Democracy and Social Ethics*, ed. C. H. Siegfried, Chicago: University of Illinois Press.

Alinsky, S. (1971) *Rules for Radicals: a Primer for Realistic Radicals*, New York: Random House.

Annan, K. (1997) 'Ignorance not knowledge … makes enemies of man', *UNHCRH*. Online. Available HTTP: http://www.unhchr.ch/huricane/huricane.nsf/view01/EF16892B9B9D46ABC125662E00352F63? (accessed 20 February 2013).

Arnstein, S. (1969) 'A ladder of citizen participation', *Journal of the American Institute of Planners*, 35(4): 216–24.

Asad, T. (2000) 'What do human rights do? An anthropological inquiry', *Theory and Event*, 4(4), electronic journal. Online. Available HTTP: http://muse.jhu.edu/journals/theory_and_event/v004/4.4asad.html (accessed 23 February 2013).

Bak, M. (2004) 'Can developmental social welfare change an unfair world? The South African experience', *International Social Work*, 47(1): 81–94.

Banks, S. (2006) *Ethics and Values in Social Work*, 3rd edn, Basingstoke: Palgrave-Macmillan.

Drucker, D. (2008) 'Ask a silly question, get a silly answer: community participation, entry points and the demystification of planning', *Smith College Studies in Social Work*, 7(4): 53–72.

Hinman, L. H. (2008) *Ethics: a Pluralist Approach*, 4th edn, Los Angeles: Wadsworth-Thomson.

Hugman, R. (1991) *Power in Caring Professions*, Basingstoke: Macmillan.

——(2005) *New Approaches in Ethics for the Caring Professions*. Basingstoke: Palgrave-Macmillan.

Hugman, R., Bartolomei, L. and Pittaway, E. (2011a) 'Human agency and the meaning of informed consent: reflections on research with refugees', *Journal of Refugee Studies*, 24(4): 655–71.

Hugman, R., Pittaway, E. and Bartolomei, L. (2011b) 'When "do no harm" is not enough: the ethics of research with refugees and other vulnerable groups', *British Journal of Social Work*, 41(7): 1271–87.

Ife, J. (2008) *Human Rights and Social Work: Towards Rights-Based Practice*, 2nd edn, Port Melbourne VIC: Cambridge University Press.

——(2010) *Human Rights from Below: Achieving Rights Through Community Development*, Port Melbourne VIC: Cambridge University Press.

——(2012) *Human Rights and Social Work: Towards Rights-Based Practice*, 3rd edn, Port Melbourne VIC: Cambridge University Press.

Ife, J. and Fiske, L. (2006) 'Human rights and community: complementary theories and practices', *International Social Work*, 49(3): 297–308.

International Federation of Social Workers/International Association of Schools of Social Work (2004) *Ethics in Social Work: Statement of Principles*, Berne: IFSW/IASSW.

Kenny, S. (2006) *Developing Communities for the Future*, 3rd edn, South Melbourne: Thomson.

Kupperman, J. J. (2004) 'Tradition and community: formation of the self', in K-L. Shun and D. B. Wong (eds) *Confucian Ethics: a Comparative Study of Self, Autonomy and Community*, Cambridge: Cambridge University Press, pp. 103–23.

Nussbaum, M. (2000) *Women and Human Development*, New York: Cambridge University Press.

——(2003) 'Capabilities as fundamental entitlements: Sen and social justice', *Feminist Economics*, 9(2): 33–59.

Pittaway, E., Bartolomei, L. and Rees, S. (2007) 'Gendered dimensions of the 2004 tsunami and a potential social work response in post-disaster situations', *International Social Work*, 50(3): 307–19.

Pittaway, E. and Bartolomei, L. (2009a) 'Innovations in research with refugee communities', *Refugee Transitions*, 21, NSW Service for the Treatment and Rehabilitation of Torture and Trauma Survivors (STARTTS). Online. Available HTTP: http://www.startts.org.au/media/Refugee-Transitions/Refugee-Transitions-Issue-21-innovations-in-research-with-refugees.pdf (accessed 1 March 2013).

——(2009b) 'Reciprocal research: aiming for empowerment not exploitation'. Paper presented at *Migration Methodologies: Researching Asia* National University of Singapore (NUS), Seminar Room Auditorium, 8–9 March 2010.

Pittaway, E. and Bartolomei, L. and Hugman, R. (2010) '"Stop stealing our stories": the ethics of research with vulnerable groups', *Journal of Human Rights Practice*, 2(2): 229–51.

Putnam, R. (2001) *Bowling Alone: the Collapse and Revival of American Community*, New York: Simon & Schuster.

Tesoriero, F. (2010) *Community Development*, 4th edn, French's Forrest NSW: Pearson Australia.

United Nations Development Program [UNDP] (2004) *Human Development Report 2004: Cultural Liberty in Today's Diverse World*, New York: UNDP.

Webb, S.A. (2010) 'Virtue ethics' in M. Gray and S.A. Webb (eds) *Ethics and Value Perspectives in Social Work*, Basingstoke, Palgrave-Macmillan, pp. 108–19.

Weyers, M.L. and van den Berg, A.M. (2006) 'The success factors in community work services. A critical incident study', *International Social Work*, 49(2): 177–87.

Winter, I. (2000) *Social Capital and Public Policy in Australia*, Melbourne: Family Studies Institute.

3

COMMUNITY KNOWLEDGE AND PRACTICES AFTER THE POSTMODERN EPISTEMIC FRAMEWORK

Towards a second modernity

Andrés Astray, David Alonso and Andoni Alonso

Introduction

In this chapter, we adopt an epistemological perspective to analyze what has been and may be considered as the knowledge and practice base in community work. Community workers have always tried to promote the development and use of the 'best' available local and professional knowledge and practice in the communities they work with (Teater and Baldwin 2012: 44; Hardcastle et al. 2011: 6; Ledwith 2011: 11; Meenai 2007: 64) but this is not an easy task. On the one hand, decisions about knowledge and action do not occur in a vacuum. They depend on various factors: contextual (approaches that particular organizations strengthen), political (ideology adopted by governments at a particular time), legal (depending on the legal system in which the social work is embedded and to which it is answerable), economic (which material possibilities are available at a given time) and ethical (principles and values), among others. On the other hand, the value of knowledge and action depend on the epistemological framework professionals embrace. They may use a particular framework explicitly but often do so implicitly. An epistemological framework informs the way professionals grasp reality and how they evaluate the claims of others in knowledge making. This framework is part of a greater understanding or 'Weltanschauung' (the general understanding of the world) which includes ideas about what reality is (ontology) and how to change that reality (practice).

We have delineated four epistemological frameworks that reflect the broad stances historically adopted toward knowledge. These four frameworks describe the potential positions held by those who have a role in the welfare of communities. They are: pre-modern, modern, postmodern and today's situation which can be called 'after-postmodern'.

Our contribution is a brief sketch and maybe an oversimplification of a more complex issue. The proposed frameworks can be understood as ideal types in the

Weberian sense or a simplification of actual/empirical knowledge positions (Weber 1949 (2011: 41)). Each successive framework that depicts distinctive, though overlapping, historical periods emerges from and constitutes a reaction to dissatisfaction with preceding frameworks. Although the pre-modern, modern and postmodern emerged at particular times in history, residues of their characteristics tend to survive into contemporary society. So, it is possible to recognize traits belonging to different frameworks in contemporary social scenarios (e.g. prevalence of traditional/orthodox religious discourse in some communitarian settings). Each framework represents an integrated whole where conceptions about knowledge, reality and practice are inextricably linked. It could be said that these frameworks provide answers to three central questions which humanity in general and philosophers in particular have always pursued: what reality is, how we can grasp that reality and how the current reality can be transformed into something better. In the realm of community work this would imply providing answers to questions like: (1) What is a community and what kind of issues, problems, needs and aspirations does it present? (2) How can we apprehend these community phenomena? (3) Who is responsible for the fate of the community or who can intervene, and how, to improve that fate?

In this chapter, we describe the four proposed frameworks using the same structure and conductive thread. The prototypical answers to the three questions above are presented and, in doing this, we describe the characteristics of the subjects or entities identified as being responsible for the fate and welfare of the communities. We identify the major discourses in each of these frameworks in relation to: those who take the leading roles in defining community problems; needs and aspirations; the specific ways in which these might be detected; and desirable ways to address community needs and problems.

Pre-modern framework

From the earliest times to the Renaissance in Europe, the possibility of knowing anything with certainty, even the existence of reality itself, was explained, with very few exceptions, through invoking a divine and unquestionable order (Howe 1994). There were many variations on this basic idea, which can be discerned even in the secular discourse of the great philosophers of Antiquity. For instance, Plato (1992) would say that only a deep look into true nature reveals what the idea of the good is and not everybody is equally equipped to grasp such a thing. Those who do not access the ultimate reality must believe and obey those who do. In fact, phenomenal reality may lead to misjudgements and true reality is posed beyond earthly facts, so only those privileged by birth or divine calling are truly able to see reality. In Plato's case, only philosophers and intellectual authorities could achieve that knowledge, which inheres of something divine. The certainty that characterized this period was that only a few 'experts' could dictate what was good and what should be done or interpreted. Another example is, surprisingly, Aristotle (1924), the great philosopher who attributed a divine character to that part of the soul (the agent intellect) that allows us to know reality.

But surely, the exemplar of the pre-modern framework is the thinking of the Scholastic philosophers and the ways of life in medieval Europe. Here, God is the ultimate reality and guidance for action. Human communities and their particular social arrangements (*bellatores, oratores* and *laboratores* – warriors, priests and workers) are created by divine will. Human need and misery are not seen as problems but as circumstances that allow the beggar, the widow or the blind to be closer to God. Rich and wealthy people must use charity as a way to reach God and salvation and to preserve the divine natural order. Only those who follow the dictates of God may act in an appropriate way. Each thing or person has a particular and fixed place in the world. This is so because everything is part of a hidden divine plan that shows meaning from 'above'. In such ontology, fortunate people have the opportunity to become good people and achieve grace by helping the disfavoured, who are, by definition, closer to God (Mathew 19: 24, ESV): 'Again I tell you, it is easier for a camel to go through the eye of a needle than for a rich person to enter the kingdom of God.' These are the particular meanings attached to charity, hospitality and poverty at that time. Also, poor or disfavoured people are like children who must be guided: they do not understand why they should act in this or that way or why they belong to such disfavoured class (Ecclesiastes 1: 18 ESV): 'For in much wisdom is much vexation, and he who increases knowledge increases sorrow.' That belongs to the economy of grace and salvation. In the end, everybody will understand and everything will be explained but to reach that end individuals must follow divine authority, as represented primarily through the clergy and aristocrats. The idea of community was central for this vision of the world. Individuals could not conceive of themselves as detached from a larger group and were part of a parish, guild or village. Having a defined place among others, each person would find a sense of life articulated in relation to others. On the other hand, different communities would define and regulate themselves. As Rubin (1987: 292) points out, these communities would try to become 'a familiar and trustworthy community of piety'. In fact, this piety implied a complex system of relationships within communities. The economy beyond Christian charity at this time was a gift economy, implying not just an altruistic or devotional element but an expectation of return and debt. Communities were crisscrossed with these givers and takers in many directions and different senses. As a result, individuals outside communities, such as non-Christians and foreigners, were the real poor people (Rubin 1987: 6). One of the main criticisms of this understanding of the world centred precisely on the place individuals should occupy. Poverty was considered to be a destiny rather than a situation that could be resolved or eliminated. Impoverished and disfavoured people existed in their own right; in the economy of salvation they are as necessary as prosperous or able people. Foreigners are deemed to be outsiders and they manifest part of the invisible theological reality no matter how painful or incomprehensible the consequences might be. The major limitation of the paradigm is the acceptance of a revealed truth that organizes the world. When the framework changes, the nature of concepts changes as well, but some elements remain. It is true that altruism, charity and help are shaped by all major world religions to a great extent even nowadays. Charity must be for free; there should be no charge for helping people. Charity cannot be transformed into a commodity. Community is the result of a Divine will. Each caste in a society has a fixed role to carry out. God's representatives on Earth have to preserve that social order. Therefore other types of communitarian intervention, that do not guarantee divine order, are ruled out. It was against these beliefs that the emerging bourgeois struggles of the eighteenth and nineteenth centuries, heralding the modern era, were directed.

Modern framework

It is repeatedly maintained that the Enlightenment represents a turning point in Western intellectual history, maybe the most important, because it still defines our society to a great extent. Now, what characterizes a human being best is their ability to be rational. Modernity holds that it is rational thought and systematic enquiry that allow us to make sense of the world (Sewpaul and Hölscher 2004). Rationality represents not only the cultivation of a faculty but also the main source of independence, freedom and autonomy. The movement in favour of individual autonomy and rationality involved a long process beginning with Descartes (1985) and ending with Kant (1781 (1996)). What matters now is not only truth but also certainty: how can I be certain that something is true? In this context, reality presents itself as problematic to humans. It is a question of having the right method rather than having a superiority preordained by divinity. Rational activity works against privileged individuals because reality is open to anyone who is able to look rationally and has the proper method to proceed. In fact, rationality has a twofold value: it is what makes each of us an autonomous and valuable individual, and at the same time it makes us equal. When Kant speaks about the transcendental subject, who remains a human being in essence, he does not refer to particular individuals but to a sort of generic human being in each of us. So anyone can interpret, follow nature and act socially if rationality guides them. Ethics derive from reason. Therefore this is a movement from theory to practice. So welfare, justice and solidarity must have a rational nature to be certain and true. It is interesting to note that true freedom does not consist of spontaneous acts, of getting rid of norms and laws. On the contrary, legalized and formalized behaviour is the essence of freedom. Rational methods impose norms and guidelines and only by following them can an individual be autonomous. National states acquire an important feature in this paradigm. Individuals become citizens and states are those who provide such status. From a political point of view, the French Revolution applies Enlightenment findings to constitutions, regulations and new codes. Basically, the idea behind this movement is the existence of a humanity where all the members are equal, free and must help one another. It is true that, because of empirical or historical circumstances, not every human being succeeds in reaching adequate standards of welfare. Those who do not reach such standards must be helped. This is the kernel of the Universal Declaration of Human Rights that was formulated for the first time in 1948. Poverty and exclusion are illnesses, misfortunes that must be corrected. Social justice is the main goal for politics and, here, social work finds its place detached from religious practices (Statham 1978; Knight 1993).

Now the question is what happens with those individuals who are not able to act rationally, or who are outside these rational guidelines? In a world where reason and rationality are raised to ontological status, these individuals lack 'proper' humanity. This is a great difference compared with pre-modern times: now there is no 'natural' place for outsiders. How can rationality help them if they are not fully rational? The first step is to consider them as an exception, a problem in and for the community. They lack proper rationality and therefore must be guided and tutored. They become part of what states and laws must prevent, solve and manage. Only in an enlightened society can the idea of social engineering acquire sense. The Industrial Revolution allows engineering to be the framework for conceiving of reality; from the production of goods ('Taylorism' and 'Fordism') to the solution of social problems. Now, those who are on the fringes of the community, those unable to prosper and find a place are part of state management. States must provide happiness, justice and wellbeing for their citizens. Now citizens become people in need of education, health, security, transport, etc. – all things which states must provide. Gradually, individuals become needy consumers. In order to achieve this, states must manage those who are on the fringes. Managing means transforming citizens into resources or into mere numbers to be administered. Individuals outside standards are oddities that must be reprocessed. Seed (1973) sees a movement in social work in this direction. Adopting the framework of justice and human rights, according to Seed, social work tries to differentiate itself from religious and political points of view and to transform into something independent and more managerial, regardless of ideologies and beliefs. The question is not power or creed but progress in basic issues such as justice, solidarity and inclusion. Progress explains the Enlightenment as a whole and somehow social work is a force in that direction. Inclusion and empowerment are different ways to help those who have been left behind catch up.

From a conceptual framework and in its more radical version, communitarian practices could only have one direction. The scientific method would indicate where we really want to go. This method would be the only way to define proper communitarian work. Only experts can handle the method, only they have the voice and the power to decide. They are the only ones able to represent the true communitarian needs, interests and aims with no mistake or bias. Experts are those who define the best ways to reach welfare standards and, at the same time, these experts are the only ones able to assess if those standards have been accomplished.

The Social Planning model, as referred to by Rothman (1974), is the application of this modern concept of the scientific method to community work. External experts define goals and procedures suited to communities and at the same time these experts guarantee social order. An example of such a model would be colonial communitarian practices. But almost every top-down practice obeys the same strategies. Even other approaches, such as models for social reform, take as their initial reference point the logic of modernity, although they try to produce a deeper transformation of communities. These approaches are indicative of a unique work method designed and guided by experts that postulate, from outside the communities they are studying, what changes should take place and how they must be done. Given the influence of positivism, modernity went beyond the rise of the human subject; it turned the subject into the object of its own rational scientific enquiries (Leonard 1997).

Conceptually, the modern framework has something really valuable: all human beings are equal and have basic rights. To fulfil those elementary needs is a collective responsibility that states must meet and therefore that task goes beyond small local communities. However, as Sewpaul and Hölscher (2004: 19) argue 'modernity, as a paradigm – while pursing equality among autonomous subjects – has on the basis of its claim to perfection, development and progress led to the *practice* of exclusion and marginalization of the *Other*'. There are other setbacks, such as the creation of uniformities, standardization and categorization (Leonard 1997). The universal goals, practices and criteria characteristic of modernity are in fact local standards created in a particular historical and geographical moment. Those standards reflect a Western hegemony, based on the model of a middle class, white male and not on the diversity of individuals in the world.

After-modernism and the postmodern framework

The philosophy of language (Nietzsche; Wittgenstein) showed how reason itself is limited and cannot provide for our understanding of the world (Apel 1980). Modernity, Enlightenment and rationalism were under attack after the Second World War.

Foucault criticized the physics of micro-power, included in the role of professionals, practitioners and expert's authority (Foucault 1970; Rabinow 1984). Also the idea of a transcendental-citizen-subject is thrown into question as an invention of the Enlightenment that hides a rough ontology that dictates how individuals must be – it does not explain how they really are. This also accords with structuralism and post-structuralism. If the subject vanishes, where is the object for community workers? Strong criticism of institutions and modern societal systems (education, health system, technology) also reflected how systemic practices may be counterproductive because they generate more harm than good. Illich used the concept iatrogenesis for this counterproductivity. The problem of iatrogenesis has to do with scale. The Enlightenment has favoured large institutions – health care systems, education, social work – that cannot identify the different situations, individuals and communities that exist in the world. According to Illich (1970), bureaucratization of care institutions transforms 'what is a good into an evil'. This is one of the main complaints in social work: the growth of a bigger and bigger bureaucracy where resources disappear (Illich et al. 1977).

Postmodernism began as an aesthetic, architectural enterprise. As a reaction to rationalism and international style in architecture, postmodern architects asked for a more diverse, rooted and 'relativistic' architecture. They sought the rhetorical and playful instead of utility and function (Morgan 2012).

Postmodernism tried to deconstruct the Enlightenment because of the idea of authority and management and the limits of rationality itself (O'Donnell 2003). Modernity holds that those who do not use rational laws become a sort of anomaly; they are in the realm of the aberrant. Therefore, they must be treated differently – as the *other* – and thus unequally. This inequality becomes a way of management that transforms individuals into problematic objects for whom services must be standardized even against their will. These individuals do not have a proper place; they belong to the wilderness, the incomprehensible. Secondly, rationality has its own limits. Therefore, any ontology derived from the Enlightenment, and its essentializing discourses based on meta-narratives and truth, does not allow us to account for uncertainty and diversity. What can be said about the world applies to humans, so there is not a unique way to deal with individuals. If human beings are part of nature, then it is logical to assume that the same universalizing laws apply to them (Sewpaul and Hölscher 2004). If we accept the primary tenets of modernity, then rationality dictates all of human and societal functioning. Using deconstruction, Derrida (Wolfreys 1998) tried to show how a biased white patriarchal discourse controls both the world and societies: a modern world where 'Western capitalism leads to the attempted homogenization of a world of diverse cultures, beliefs and histories' (Leonard 1997: 7). What lies behind the Enlightenment is social engineering, a type of oppression generated because differences that exist in the world must be reduced to ones we are able to manage rationally. Gender problems, diversity and the 'other' have no place in society unless they are recycled and standardized. Reason becomes a force to repress what is different.

Postmodernists assert that, to solve this, first it is clear that rationality has to admit its limitations in favour of communities, contextual or relative codes and rationalities (Wolfreys 1998). There is not a fixed, unique ontology to understand and act upon reality. The world is seen to be opaque and our actions uncertain. Ontologies and epistemology become also plural. Even in scientific theory, there are calls for relativity (Shapin 1995) anarchist epistemologies (Feyerabend 1975) and the transformation of social sciences into narratives and literature (Gilbert and Mulkay 1984).

From an epistemological point of view, postmodernity tries to deconstruct many oppressive elements in our society such as homophobia, patriarchy, ethnocentrism and sexism that exist in old communitarian practices (Sim 2012). The centre should be the community where identity and differential features are crucial. Differentiation and identity fight against the limits of Modernity, of a univocal and uniformed bureaucratized wellbeing. Postmodernity now places on communitarian even an individual identity to achieve wellbeing as something produced by individuals and communities themselves. But in that postmodern context, communitarian practices are fragmented and dispersed. The State, as an 'oppressor', should eventually disappear, losing its role of integrating society and individuals. Civil society is fragmented into competing groups trying to gain advantage from the political system. There is no universality understood as Modernity proposed and therefore fundamentalism, relativism and exclusivist nationalism take over society.

After the postmodern framework or what now: towards a second Modernity?

Postmodernism built strong criticisms against Modernity and the Enlightenment. But at the same time, it did not satisfactorily answer many problems: how to understand the world, how to act and how to define an ontology that could avoid harming human welfare at the same time. Ife (1999) claims that postmodernity does not provide insight into how society should be. Postmodernists criticize values such as humanism, solidarity, development and inclusion. Yet, these values are an essential part of how community work is understood. While postmodernists attempt a deconstruction of society through their critiques of the limits of Modernity, they do not provide for a reconstruction left in its wake. This leads to a sort of theoretical paralysis and a correlating lack of guidance for practitioners. But real problems are still pressing, such as extreme poverty, gender inequality and exclusion and this is happening at a time when politics and the economy are changing profoundly and when institutions are being strongly criticized without being able to give answers to these vital demands.

In the last few decades, there have been many criticisms of postmodernism. Some Marxists consider postmodernism as a trap where no important or crucial questions can be raised (Zizek 2012; Laclau 1996; Negri 1999; Mouffe 2005). Maybe the most important criticism is that there is a need to fight formal democracy and to understand that the welfare state is not a negotiable goal. Even more, we should say that social work is a form of politics and not only a question of professional activity. However, there is a neo-liberal bias against social welfare. Professional politicians consider the welfare state as something which is impossible to sustain and which, therefore, must be dismantled. In the extreme, postmodernism does not provide any firm ground for supporting social work in its criticism of oppression, inequality and injustice. In sum, human suffering is not a matter of relativism. Reality demands action and criteria on which to base that action (Howe 1994; Ife 1999). The present situation appears to be worsening and neo-liberalism and neo-conservatism give less and less room for equality, so the very idea of community social work in particular and social work in general is continually questioned. Pseudo group and pseudo communitarian work are false alternatives presented as solutions. What we have instead is a diminished social work which lacks the basic economic and material resources to cover the most elementary needs for people's autonomy and welfare. The result of this rearrangement hides the dismantling of welfare systems.

There is a need to find a more stable epistemology from which to build an ontology that is able to give guidance. There are different possible answers. The notion of rooted knowledge tries to take into account diversities, while avoiding relativism. Contextual knowledge is also a term that tries to explore plural answers without falling into relativism. All of these accept criticisms of the Enlightenment, avoiding the postmodern trap. For instance, MacIntyre (2007) proposes a communitarian approach to give sense both to knowledge and action. Communitarian philosophy is a quite recent trend that tries to recover basic ideas about ethics and action. According to communitarians, morality or the ethos depends on an ethnos: moral values are rooted in communities. Another possible approach lies in social constructivism, which proposes a vision of the world that defines theories as something provisional up to the moment when a controversy is closed by a community of knowers or practitioners. Latour (1987) and Harman (2009) try to understand reality in this comprehensive way. From their perspective, humans, reality and understanding theories must reach a definitive agreement to close controversies.

Now politics is at the centre of the debate. Maybe as neo-Marxists and other critics point out, we have to question the complete economic system (Statham 1978). This is a possibility where social work presents a force against a market that is completely hostile to excluded people. This is a 'social work of resistance' (Lavalette and Ferguson 2007) where social work must move into communities and try to build from the bottom-up instead of from the top-down as before. Now all the actors are important: society, communities, churches and institutions.

The problem is that the subject of knowledge has been considered as an individual and not a communitarian subject of knowledge. We propose that a communitarian subject could co-construct our knowledge about our needs, aims and desire. This kind of subject would allow true democratic and participative processes when producing knowledge and developing social actions. At the same time, that knowledge would condense the images of individuals and society determined democratically by the members of communities. The roles for the community worker would be to mediate and to facilitate so that people can co-build their communities by determining when and how they participate. For that role, professionals have to rely on the possibilities offered by technology. Information technologies allow modern and postmodern individuals to transform into networked, collective and communitarian subjects.

The co-construction of knowledge will be then the result of participatory and democratic processes and be seen as an ethical duty for all those sincerely interested in the development of community work practices that promote human and social welfare. We should rescue from pre-modern times the need to be a part of a whole, from modern times the need for welfare standards and social responsibility and from postmodernism the need to preserve identities and differentiated realities. That should form part of what we propose as an after-postmodern stage where a future co-building of knowledge on communitarian practices can be produced.

QUESTIONS FOR REFLECTION

* What responsibilities have the community members in each period of time to achieve a better welfare?
* As a practitioner, how do you build the concept of community? Can you relate that concept with some of the depicted stages?
* What elements of the stages mentioned above do you consider still exist? Can you think of any example?

References

Apel, K. (1980) *Towards a Transformation of Philosophy*, London and Boston: Routledge & Keegan Paul.

Aristotle (1924) *Metaphysics*, trans. W.D. Ross, Oxford: Clarendom Press.

Descartes, R. (1985) *The Philosophical Writings of Descartes,* trans. J. Cottingham, R. Stoothoff and D. Murdoch, Cambridge: Cambridge University Press.

Ecclesiastes 1: 18 *English Standard Version (ESV) of the Christian Bible.*

Feyerabend, P. (1975) *Against Method: Outline of Anarchistic Theory of Knowledge*, London: Verso.

Foucault, M. (1970) *The Order of Things: An Archaeology of the Human Sciences*, London: Tavistock Publications Ltd.

Gilbert, G. N. and Mulkay, M. (1984) *Opening Pandora's Box*, Cambridge: Cambridge University Press.

Hardcastle, D. A., Powers, P. R., and Wenocur, S. (2011) *Community Practice: Theories and Skills for Social Workers,* Oxford: Oxford University Press.

Harman, G. (2009) *Prince of Networks: Bruno Latour and Metaphysics*, London: Routledge.

Howe, D. (1994) 'Modernity, postmodernity and social work', *British Journal of Social Work,* 24(5): 513–32.

Ife, J. (1999) 'Postmodernism, critical theory and social work', in B. Pease and J. Fook (eds), *Transforming Social Work Practice: Postmodern Critical* Perspectives, St.Leonards, New South Wales: Allen & Unwin, pp. 211–23.

Illich, I. (1970) *Deschooling Society,* New York: Harper & Row.

Illich, I., Zola, I.K., McKnight, J., Caplan, J. and Shaiken, H. (1977) *Disabling Professions,* London: Marion Boyars.

Kant, I. (1781) *Critique of Pure Reason,* trans. W. S. Pluhar (1996) [*Kritik der reinen Vernunft.* Unified edition], Indianapolis: Hackett Publishing Company.

Knight, B. (1993) *Voluntary Action,* London: Home Office.

Laclau, E. (1996) *Emancipation(s),* London: Verso.

Latour, B. (1987) *Science in Action: How to Follow Scientists and Engineers through Society,* Cambridge, MA: Harvard University Press.

Lavalette, M. and Ferguson, I. (eds) (2007) *International Social Work and the Radical Tradition,* Birmingham: Venture Press.

Ledwith, M. (2011) *Community Development: A Critical Approach*, Bristol: The Policy Press.

Leonard, P. (1997) *Postmodern Welfare: Reconstructing an Emancipatory Project*, London: Thousand Oaks.

MacIntyre, A. (2007) *After Virtue*, 3rd edn, Notre Dame, IN: University of Notre Dame Press.

Mathew 19: 24, *English Standard Version (ESV) of the Christian Bible.*

Meenai, Z. (2007) *Participatory Community Work*, New Delhi: Concept Publishing Company.

Morgan, D. (2012) 'Postmodernism and architecture', in S. Sim (ed.) *The Routledge Companion to Postmodernism*, London: Routledge, pp. 61–9.

Mouffe, C. (2005) *The Return of the Political*, London: Verso.

Negri, A. (1999) *Insurgencies: Constituent Power and Modern State*, Minneapolis: University of Minnesota.

O'Donnell, K. (2003) *Postmodernism*, Oxford: Lion.

Plato (1992) *The Republic,* trans. G.M.A. Grube, Indianapolis: Hackett Publishing Company.

Rabinow, P. (1984) *The Foucault Reader*, New York: Pantheon Books.

Rothman, J. (1974) 'Three models of community organization practice', in F. Cox, J. Erlich, J. Rothman and J. Tropman (eds), *Strategies of Community Organization*, Ithaca, IL: Peacock Publishing, pp. 25–45.

Rubin, M. (1987) *Charity and Community in Medieval Cambridge,* Cambridge: Cambridge University Press.

Seed, P. (1973) *The Expansion of Social Work in Britain*, London: Routledge & Kegan Paul.

Sewpaul, V. and Hölscher, D. (2004) *Social Work in Times of Neoliberalism: A Postmodern Discourse*, Pretoria: Van Schaik Publishers.

Shapin, S. (1995) 'Here and everywhere: sociology of scientific knowledge', *Annual Review of Sociology*, 21(1): 289–21.

Sim S. (ed.) (2012) *The Routledge Companion to Postmodernism*, 3rd edn, London: Routledge.

Statham, D. (1978) *Radicals in Social Work*, London: Routledge & Kegan Paul.

Teater, B. and Baldwin, M. (2012) *Social Work in the Community: Making a Difference*, Bristol: Policy Press.

Weber, M. (1949) *Methodologie der Geschichts-und Sozialwissenschaften*, trans and ed. E. Shils and ed. H.A. Finch (2011) *Methodology of Social Sciences*], New Jersey: Transaction Publishers.

Wolfreys, J. (ed.) (1998) *The Derrida Reader. Writing Performances*, Edinburgh: Edinburgh University Press.

Zizek, S. (2012) *Less than Nothing: Hegel and the Shadow of Dialectical Materialism*, London: Verso.

4

THE CO-CONSTRUCTION OF KNOWLEDGE

Reflection on experiences of developing an online international community work course

Grete Oline Hole, Janet Harris and Anne Karin Larsen

Introduction

In 2008 a group of partners from Higher Education Institutions in Europe came together to develop a curriculum for a 15 ECTS credits online course in community work as a part of the Social Work-Virtual Campus Project (SW-VirCamp).[1] The development of the online course in 'community work from an international perspective' was motivated by phenomena such as immigration, changing family structures and the decline of social networks in Europe. The European Union must deal with challenges of social exclusion and ethnocentrism while trying to realize its goals towards social inclusion. In addition, welfare systems in Europe are changing. These challenges affect the social work profession and their approach to work. Social work approaches have traditionally focused on meeting the needs of individuals, primarily through casework. If the welfare state and family networks cannot take care of the individual one must develop new approaches and take collective initiatives based on people's needs (Larsen 2009). Training in community work is needed so social workers can develop skills in the planned process of assisting people to improve their own communities and undertake autonomous collective action.

The process of participation in curriculum development was important in terms of sharing knowledge about community work, obtaining agreement on the pedagogical framework, and creating ownership and commitment to the content of the curriculum plan. The idea of constructing a course through a participatory approach became an important guideline for the teachers in developing the community work module (Larsen et al. 2011; Edmark 2010; Hole et al. 2010). (For more information about the project see http://www.vircamp.net and chapter seven in this book.)

Although curriculum is commonly created by teachers working together as a team, little is written about the process, and there are few examples of participatory approaches to curriculum development. From the start in 2005, Lave and Wenger's (1991) concept of 'communities of practice' have been used as a guiding framework in the development of the courses. Communities of practice is defined as the process of letting newcomers become members of a professional working unit through gradually learning the specific skills needed by initial 'legitimate peripheral participation' (Lave and Wenger 1991: 29). During this learning process knowledge is constructed together with the aim of solving problems that arise during the work.

Over the years, one has seen that communities of practice can take place through online communication (Johnsen 2001) and via international collaboration (Hildrith et al. 1998). But little is known about how one can promote a virtual community of practice (VCoP) among an international group of teachers and students where the aim is to create a curriculum which fosters participatory learning among all partners.

This chapter presents the educational concepts that guide the online international community work course – the SW-VirCamp project. We briefly describe the review process where we found research exploring the core concept of communities of practice, and how we used the findings from the review to reflect on the conditions needed for 'co-construction of knowledge' to take place. We wanted to find out how virtual communities of practice could be used to help students and teachers to co-construct meaningful knowledge to address practice issues. The aim of this chapter is to discuss how findings from a literature review on community of practice/virtual community of practice can enlighten the process of fostering co-construction of knowledge among participants. Findings from the review supported the participatory action research/participatory action learning process which followed the development of the SW-VirCamp project (for more information about this process see chapter seven).

Central educational concepts within SW-VirCamp

From the late 1980s, health and social care educators have used theories of social-constructivism (Brown et al. 1989) and social-cultural learning (Bruner 1996) to bridge the gap between 'theory at school' and 'real life practice' (Carr and Kemmis 1986). Learning is seen as a process where knowledge is actively constructed in a social context – a process of learning together (Dewey 1938/1963). Students make sense of the world through participation in learning, enabling them to construct meaningful knowledge from abstract facts and theories that can be applied in practice. The underlying assumptions are that hands-on and task-oriented approaches, 'learning by doing', can improve learning outcomes. Such study methods require more engagement from the students during the learning process than more passive, didactic learning approaches (Biggs 1999). Social constructivist approaches also create opportunities for educators to align learning situations with future working practice for students (Brown et al. 1989). In other words, applying social constructivist and social learning theories to curriculum development can promote participatory learning for students who are either training for, or actively practising, in the health and social care disciplines.

The concept of 'communities of practice' is closely associated with such social constructivism and social learning theories (Lave and Wenger 1991; Wenger 1998). Communities of practice arise when there is a need to solve problems together in 'real-world' situations, referred to as 'situated learning'. Both 'communities of practice' and 'virtual communities of practice' have been used since the 1990s within health and social care sectors as a strategy for sharing professional knowledge with new workers who are learning 'the tools of the trade' as part of a 'master-apprentice' relationship. Diverse approaches to communities of practice in the fields of business, education, health and social care has led to claims that it is an 'evolving concept with a lack of uniform operating definitions' (Li et al. 2009b). We wanted to explore the fundamental elements of both communities of practice in order to identify the components that were relevant to curriculum development. We were particularly interested in the relationship between communities of practice and the process of co-constructing knowledge in curriculum development. The phrase 'co-construction of knowledge' appears from the mid-1990s in the educational literature that focuses on the constructivism/social constructivism learning paradigm (Gunawardena et al. 1997; Koschmann 1996), but descriptions of the concept are diverse, and further information is needed on how to create learning environments that makes this happen.

The literature review

Our initial question for the literature review was 'Does online support promote a (long-distance) community of practice?' A systematic search for literature that explored the concepts of communities of practice/virtual communities of practice in electronic databases (CINAHL, Medline and PsycINFO) was conducted. We also did a scoping review of the literature on communities of practice and combined the results of this search with the fields of community work, health and social care, limited initially to online or distance learning. The search strategy was developed with the help of a skilled librarian. The search terms included all relevant key words[2] related to 'online learning' with text words[3] for 'communities of practice'.

In the initial phase papers were divided between two of the authors (Hole and Harris). Abstracts were screened to see if they explicitly used the concept of communities of practice. Concepts related to virtual communities of practice were identified in each paper, and criteria were developed from the first reading to enable decisions about relevant papers to include in the review.

Included communities of practice papers were then screened to determine whether they addressed online teaching and learning. Studies were included if they discussed groups coming together to learn something related to their specific professional roles and practices, including both bachelor level and continuing and post-graduate education. Studies examining on-campus education were excluded.

Of the 232 initial hits, 23 papers were seen as potentially relevant, while 13 papers were subjected to further scrutiny. Four papers that addressed communities of practice and co-construction of professional knowledge in online learning environments were used as 'seed articles' for further conceptual searching. Ancestor referencing produced seven additional studies. A further 11 studies were included in the review; several of them were systematic reviews exploring communities of practice or other tenets we found to be relevant for understanding the relation between communities of practice and co-construction of knowledge, and altogether 22 studies were included in the review.

In the following, we discuss how our findings enlighten what happened during the process of developing the SW-VirCamp course.

Situated and social learning in virtual communities of practice

The concept of communities of practice originally focused on the transition 'from-novice-to-expert' learning (Lave and Wenger 1991), but recently the focus has shifted to the use of communities of practice as a managerial tool for organizational development (Ranmuthugala et al. 2011). Our review revealed that for both individuals and organizations, communities of practice/virtual communities of practice provide an environment for three types of learning: situated learning, social learning and organizational learning. We focus here on how situated learning and social learning are used in education, and how they have been applied to the development of online courses. Organizational learning focuses on how an organization actively promotes and facilitates collective learning among its members (Argyris and Schön 1978; Nonaka et al. 2000). Although this dimension of communities of practice may be important for sustainability in community work projects, we did not include papers on organizational learning because we were interested in how teachers could work together across diverse organizations, as opposed to learning within a single organizational setting. We illustrate how the concepts of communities of practice/virtual communities of practice were specifically used in SW-VirCamp to promote participation in both curriculum development and online learning.

Situated learning as an educational concept

Situated learning occurs in real life environments when people see that there is a problem that needs to be solved. Groups come together to address the problem, and disband when the problem has been resolved (Wenger 1998). These learning groups, communities of practice, differ from traditional classroom learning environments as the learning takes place in the actual situation – in a setting functionally identical to that where the knowledge will be applied. Learning in situ occurs in a very different context from traditional classroom learning, which tends to isolate knowledge from practice (Li et al. 2009a; 2009b). The situated learning needs to take account of the context surrounding the problem to be solved, the common underlying practices and the traditions of working together. Learning is participatory, and dependent on social interaction (Johnson 2001). The interaction is based on traditional practices and working relationships and the process that arises from the interaction is a co-construction of knowledge. People develop a shared understanding of the issue that needs to be addressed, and contribute their various perspectives and expertise in order to transform information into meaningful knowledge.

In order to foster situated learning, the online learning environment must provide a setting similar to that which the learner will encounter in real life. For example, the online learning environment can identify 'domain specific' needs for learning, and recreate real life problem scenarios. Opportunities to form small groups are offered online, thereby creating a structure for situated learning. Students may have different institutional expectations as they try to acquire knowledge and skills. Successful online learning environments will recognize this institutional tension, collect information on the expectations that are placed on the learner and try to align the online material with the institutions. Case studies are one strategy that is used to facilitate learning that is directly relevant to institutional practice (Soubhi et al. 2010). Such cases and the practice experience that derives from them are made into interactive web-based e-cases, to support active participation and promote team learning in a virtual environment. Students value the opportunity to learn from real life situations and find this approach relevant for future practice (Carroll et al. 2009; Greenhalgh and Russell 2006; Larsen et al. 2007; Larsen et al. 2011).

Social learning as an educational concept

Social learning was the second concept identified in the literature review, and although it was presented as a distinct concept across different papers in reality it overlaps with the concept of situated learning and communities of practice. Social learning theorists suggest that communities provide a foundation for sharing knowledge within a social context. Individuals observe and model other people's behaviour within the community, which allows for a safer and more efficient way of acquiring complex behaviours or skills than learning by trial and error (Li et al. 2009b). Social learning contains four related elements: social interaction; knowledge sharing; knowledge creation and identity-building (Li et al. 2009a). Social interaction is critical because knowledge can only be constructed where a social network exists, and the quality and the strength of relationships facilitate knowledge sharing (Bate and Robert 2002). Through relationships, people also acquire 'the ability to act in the world in socially recognized ways' (Brown and Duguid 2001: 200), and an identity of belonging to this community evolve. Participation in the community triggers a process of collective sense-making where meaning is negotiated in the social context where knowledge is created.

The challenge for an online community of practice is to develop and enrich professional practice by sharing and pooling complementary knowledge (Henri and Pudelko 2003) in a virtual environment. The interests are therefore the transmission of codified knowledge through the interaction and communication between individuals, as people in the group learn from one another and solve problems together. The success of online social learning rests on the ability to form virtual social relationships where 'experts' and learners can engage in rich and effective construction of knowledge (Greenhalgh and Russell 2006). Relationship building and trust are central, and a learning community must develop a high level of trust among participants in order to be functional (Li et al. 2009b). For health and social workers the identity as a professional is seen as a central tenet of learning outcomes, as well as learning the tools of the trade. Any online education within these disciplines should aim towards enhancing such identity-building (Lie et al. 2009b; Cook-Craig and Sabah 2009; Henri and Pudelko 2003; Moule 2006; Tolson et al. 2005).

In the next section, we briefly present the educational project SW-VirCamp and show how the concepts we found in our review helped us to define the desired outcomes, the development of a community of practice as well as a virtual community of practice which fostered co-construction of knowledge among first the partners of the project, and later among the students who participated in the new course.

The SW-VirCamp educational project

As stated in the introduction, the SW-VirCamp consortium received in 2008 a grant from the EU-lifelong learning program to develop an online course in community work for social work bachelor students. The new course was used to realize the possibilities for international collaboration which encouraged the participants to adopt a critical stance towards different approaches in community work, enabling them to apply these principles to problem solving conditions in their respective environments. A priority for collaboration was to ensure that the new partners in the project should be included in the established network of partners. Another goal was to make sure that all partners, with their diverse knowledge of social work education and community work theory and methods, were given opportunities to share their knowledge and learn from each other. The main idea was to create a milieu which fostered 'co-construction of knowledge' among all participants.

As one of the aims of community work is to make change possible by 'assisting people to improve their own communities by undertaking autonomous collective action' (Twelvetrees 2008: 1), the project group intended that this should be reflected both in the curriculum plan, the structure of the course and in the ways the future students should work with the study material. This stimulated discussion and reflection on how to collaborate on developing a virtual campus using the core principles of community work, and was followed up by research using the principles of participatory action research (PAR) (Kemmis and McTaggart 2000) and participatory action learning (PAL) (Pedler and Burgoyne 2008). The underlying idea was that the dialectical and reflective methods of PAR/PAL during the development process would give the teachers a hands-on experience with this way of working, and thereby be better equipped to teach and supervise their future students. The literature review was carried out in tandem with the SW-VirCamp project, to explore to what extent virtual community of practice could promote these outcomes.

Situated and social learning in the SW-VirCamp team

As a part of the PAR/PAL process following the development process of the pilot course, four group interviews were conducted with the teachers during the project. The sessions became an arena for discussion and reflection upon how to create, initiate and sustain the course, and created an opportunity to share more practical aspects of teaching community work online. By working with such cycles of reflection on what had happened so far as well as adjusting the planned schedule, an open and trusting environment was created. (For more information about the process, see chapter seven).

The teachers became a community of practice in the sense that they came together for a specific task, which was to create the community work course which would be based on the principles of situated learning. The idea of community work is that methods are adapted to a particular place and context. There is a process of 'recreating' context online in order to simulate a real life setting for the student to develop practice skills. Early in the project the teacher group decided to make a virtual case with diverse situations where the students could explore the situations when creating their own community work project. It was envisaged that the case should be 'very broad, so every student can have an own choice about what he/she wants to construct. The case must be so every country can use it' (Hole et al. 2010). Therefore, a virtual community called the Green Park Community was created that reproduced a real life environment.

The virtual case and the tasks connected to it aimed to enable students to link the theoretical knowledge embedded in the course and the practice part of being a community worker. The virtual case also demonstrated the potential of web-based learning environments for giving access to multiple perspectives and culturally diverse resources (Greenhalgh and Russell 2006). All tasks for the students were carefully created to represent real life tasks which would promote the development of the desired CW skills.

The participants involved in creating the learning resources were experienced social work teachers, with diverse knowledge of community work. They came from different countries, which helped them to reproduce the common cross-cutting international community work themes. At the same time, the variations in community work practice in different countries were identified, and this diversity was represented in SW-VirCamp by preserving different contexts. The teachers also had different knowledge and experiences of community work approaches. For example, some used the strength-based approach of community development (see i.e. chapter 9) and 'appreciative inquiry' (Ledwith and Springett 2010: 146–7) with its focus on positive change in their work while others used art as a tool for community development (see chapter 12). The variety of experiences created a process where teachers 'co-constructed' the situated learning environment. This was a rewarding process for the teachers, as they learned different approaches from each other. Their diverse knowledge and skills enriched the learning opportunities for the future students.

The process of developing the reading list for the course is another example of how shared knowledge within the group benefitted all participants, and enhanced their views of how to help students to understand the principles of community work. The discussion of potentially relevant text books, papers and handbooks for the Green Park case made the participants aware of many diverse resources which were useful for the campus-based courses at the partner institutions. In the second group interview just before the course started, a teacher reflected:

> Yes, it is interesting how much we learn from planning and making the course. It is really a learning arena. Like the reading-list we have been working with: we all bring in literature, we share it, and we discuss it – so it is really a 'co-construction area'.
>
> *(Hole et al. 2010)*

The benefits for the teachers were expressed on many levels. 'We have really a lot to learn from each other' as one teacher expressed in the external report, referring to inspiring meetings with colleagues from different countries and exciting exchange of knowledge. The external reviewer cites one teacher who stated:

> I have become more European. You take a lot of things for granted in your own country, now you have to think it over. I had to explain why. I learned a lot. You even learn a lot about your own country. That is really interesting and a big challenge for both me and the students.
>
> *(Edmark 2010: 25)*

The process of co-construction required teachers to share their experiences with each other. As a result, trust was developed and a process of social learning among the teachers evolved. Teachers accustomed to using teacher-centred approaches were introduced to how to be a 'guide on the side' to help them support student-centred learning. Teachers were encouraged to step back from their usual role of expert, and to act instead as facilitators and co-participants who can display ignorance as well as knowledge. The 'transparent classroom' – where everyone can see what others are doing in the virtual learning environment – enabled teachers to learn through observation of how other teachers with more experience in social-cultural teaching online guided their students and facilitated social learning via discussion. The openness of sharing how teachers worked with students created a trusting learning environment for teachers. In the third teacher interview, halfway through the pilot course one of the teachers said: 'I find it very interesting to read the teacher reflections in the teacher blog […] it is very useful.'

The equalization of roles between teachers and learners in a community often maximized the participation of everyone, but can create a sense of discomfort and insecurity. Research has indicated that Internet courses with discussion are seen as more effective than Internet courses that do not promote discussion. In courses where there was opportunity for discussion, participants felt more of a sense of belonging (Carroll et al. 2009) and expressed frustration about non-participating students. During the development of the course the learning tasks for the Green Park case were created in order to promote engagement. Emphasis was placed on developing tasks which fostered collaboration between students, where they needed to share knowledge and exchange opinions. These activities made them 'learn together' in a social process, where everyone had to participate in order to realize the course outcomes. It also aimed toward building a 'community-worker identity'; giving the student the needed skills and competences as well as the essential attitudes of a community worker. A teacher said at the teacher meeting just before the pilot-course started:

> As a teacher in this course we must think about the role of a community worker. This is a catalytic role, and we will stimulate the learning process among the students. When I think back to what Freire said about teaching, this is not the 'banking role' of teaching, but a stimulating role.

Another teacher followed this up later in the interview:

> It is interesting […], the students will be responsible for their own learning, but they are also responsible for what their peer students learn. We must tell them that this course has a new student-role, that we all are expected to have a catalytic role!

After the course had started, midways through the pilot course, a teacher reflected over how he/she acted when some students were delayed in their tasks; which had consequences for their peer-students' work:

> In my role as a teacher … I'll try to act a bit more like a community worker, because I do not want to give too much structure or too much instruction to the students. I want them to give the examples, to find the project, search for information, to talk about it, chat about it! But it is not so easy to have that role, as they don't always see what they have to do.

Later in this session one discussed the controller role of the teachers; and the same teacher said:

> I do not feel like a controller! I observed what they were doing in the role-play; and asked them questions afterwards, to let them think about what they were doing and help them to find their role as a community worker. For example: 'Did you use appreciate inquiry?' or 'How did you feel about ...?' But not as a controller!

The competence-based curriculum, with its focus on learning outcomes (Kennedy et al. 2007) gave the teachers an opportunity to emphasize the connection between theory and practice, as well as learning how to mentor students within this framework. As a teacher, experienced in working with competency-based curriculum, said in the first group-interview at the very start of the project:

> It is not only me as a teacher who makes the construction of the knowledge [...] I do this together with the students. How can I trigger them to take part in the whole process? Not to ask about specific things related to the content of the module, but give them the challenge of themselves bringing in the ideas [...]. How can the students be triggered to be a part of the construction of knowledge?

By participating in this discussion, the reflection from the experienced teacher gave useful inputs to the teachers not used to this way of working.

Conclusion

The project group from 12 higher education institutions all over Europe managed to create a learning environment with material which enabled the students to bridge the gap between theory and practice, as well as give them hands-on experience of the core principles of community work. The teachers' involvement with important elements of online learning, as well as the core principles of community work during the development process, enabled them to promote situated and social learning both in the development process as well as in the online courses. The dialectical and reflective process of participatory action research/action learning promoted the wanted outcomes. Through the teachers' engagement with a bottom-up perspective they got first-hand knowledge of the importance of participation as well as of reflection during the learning process.

As shown elsewhere (Larsen et al. 2011; Hole et al. 2010), the decision to conduct the SW-VirCamp project with a participatory action research framework stimulated the sharing of information and promoted co-construction of knowledge among participants. The epistemological and ontological ideas underlying the project lead to an awareness of participation, reflection, sharing of experiences and construction of new knowledge which contributed to the success of SW-VirCamp. The two-year project, following the principles of situated and social learning, enabled the participants to create an arena which fostered co-construction of knowledge not only for the future students but also for the participating teachers.

QUESTIONS FOR REFLECTION

- Reflect on the different roles you see in your teaching and learning institutions: to what extent do you think one can create a learning environment with equal roles between teachers and students?
- To what extent do you think such equal roles will promote participation and foster learning?

Notes

1. From 2004 first VIRCLASS, later the The SW-VirCamp Consortium, offered online courses in social work in Europe. During the years there have been different partners. For the period described here, 2008–2010, the SW-VirCamp Consortium consist of 12 HEI from Europe: Bergen University College, Norway; Jönköping University, Sweden; Inholland University of Applied Sciences, the Netherlands; K.H. Kempen University College, Belgium, University of Complutense, Spain; Miguel Torga University College, Portugal; Mannheim University of Applied Sciences, Germany; Bodø University College, Norway; University of Liepaja, Latvia; Lusofona University, Portugal; Swansea University, United Kingdom and Mittweida University of Applied Sciences, Germany.

2. Medical Subject Heading (MESH-terms) have for more than 50 years been a thesaurus with descriptors for indexing articles with keywords with both an alphabetical and a hierarchical structure. The phrase you search for will be 'translated' to the relevant search term. For example the MESH terms 'Computer Assisted Instruction' and 'Educational Technology' covers all search terms as 'e-learning'; 'online learning'; 'electronics learning'; 'virtual learning'; etc.

3. To find articles not indexed with relevant keywords; we also used text-words; that includes all words and numbers in the title, abstract, journal name etc.

References

Argyris, Ch. and Schön, D. (1978) *Organizational Learning, a Theory of Action Perspective,*   AQ?
    Reading, Mass.: Addison-Wesley.
Bate, S.P. and Robert, G. (2002) 'Knowledge management and CoP in the private sector: lessons for modernizing NHS', *Public Administration,* 80(4): 643–63.
Biggs, J.B. (1999) *Teaching for Quality Learning at University: What the Student Does,* Buckingham: Society for Research into Higher Education.
Brown, J. S., Collins, A. and Duguid, P. (1989) 'Situated cognition and the culture of learning', *Educational Researcher,* 18(1): 32–42.
Brown, J.S. and Duguid, P. (2001) 'Knowledge and organization: a social-practice perspective', *Organization Science,* 12(2): 198–213.
Bruner, J. (1996) *The Culture of Education,* Cambridge, Mass.: Harvard University Press.

Carr, W. and Kemmis, S. (1986) *Becoming Critical: Education, Knowledge and Action Research*, London: Falmer Press.

Carroll, Ch., Booth, A., Papaioannou, D., Sutton, A. and Wong, R. (2009) 'UK health care professionals experience of online learning techniques', *Journal of Continuing Education in the Health Professions*, 29(4): 235–41.

Cook-Craig, P. and G. Sabah, Y. (2009) 'The role of virtual communities of practice in supporting collaborative learning among social workers', *British Journal of Social Work*, 39(4): 725–39.

Dewey, J. (1938/1963) *Experience & Education*, New York, N.Y./Canada: Macmillan Publishing Company.

Edmark, H.L. (2010) Over the Borders – Building and Launching the Virtual Campus – SW-VirCamp, an external evaluation report, Lund, Sweden: Lund University. Online. Available HTTP: http://vircamp.net/old/ep_tmp/files/20519805874cf761a3b543c.pdf (accessed 8 March 2013).

Greenhalgh, T. and Russell, J. (2006) 'Promoting the skills of knowledge translation in an online MSc course in Primary Health Care', *The Journal of Continuing Education in the Health Professions*, 26(2): 100–8.

Gunawardena, C.N., Lowe, C.A. and Anderson, T. (1997) 'Analysis of a global online debate and the development of an interaction analysis model for examining social construction of knowledge in computer conferencing', *Journal of Educational Computing Research* 17(4): 397–431.

Henri, F. and Pudelko, B. (2003) 'Understanding and analysing activity and learning in virtual communities', *Journal of Computer Assisted Learning* 19(4): 474–87.

Johnson, Ch.M. (2001) 'A survey of current research on online communities of practice', *Internet and Higher Education* 4(1): 45–60.

Hildrith, P. M., Kimble, Ch. and Wright, P. (1998) 'Computer mediated communication and international communities of practice', *Proceedings of Ethicomp '98*, March 1998, Erasmus University, The Netherlands, pp. 275–86.

Hole, G.O., Olsson, K.G. and Wouters, W. (2010) *Development of an E-learning Course in Community Work within an International Perspective*. Evaluation report from the pilot course, SW-VirCamp project. Online. Available HTTP: http://vircamp.net/old/ep_tmp/files/8771376314d008f8b40ab7.pdf (accessed 8 March 2013).

Kemmis, S. and McTaggart, R. (2000) 'Participatory action research', in N.K. Denzin, Y.S. Lincoln (eds): *Handbook of Qualitative Research*, 2nd edn, Thousand Oaks, California: SAGE, pp. 567–605.

Kennedy, D., Hylan, A. and Ryan, N. (2007) *Writing and Using Learning Outcomes: A Practical Guide*, University College Cork, Ireland.

Koschmann, T. (1996) *CSCL: Theory and Practice of an Emerging Paradigm*, Mahwah, N.J: Lawrence Erlbaum Associates.

Larsen, A.K. (2009) 'Open distance learning as instrument for teaching and learning social work in a changing Europe', in E. Kantowicz (ed.), *Role of Research in Education for Social Work in Europe*. EUSW report, Olsztyn, Poland: Wydawnictwo UWM.

Larsen, A.K., Hole, G.O. and Fahlvik, M. (2007) 'Developing a virtual book – material for virtual learning environments', *Seminar.net. Media, technology and lifelong learning*, 3(3).

Larsen, A.K., Visser-Rotgans, R. and Hole G.O. (2011) 'Teaching and learning community work online: Can e-learning promote competences for future practice?' *Journal of Technology in Human Services*, 1(29): 13–32.

Lave, J. and Wenger, E. (1991) *Situated Learning: Legitimate Peripheral Participation*, Cambridge: Cambridge University Press.

Ledwith, M. and Springett, J. (2010) *Participatory Practice, Community Based Action for Transformative Change*, Bristol: The Policy Press.

Li, L.C., Grimshaw, J.M., Nielsen, C., Judd, M., Coyte, P.C. and Graham, I.D. (2009a) 'Use of CoP in business and health: A systematic review', *Implementation Science*, 4(27). Online. Availalble HTTP: http://www.implementationscience.com/content/4/1/27 (accessed 20 January 2013).

——(2009b) 'Evolution of Wenger's concept of communities of practice', *Implementation Science*, 4(27). Online. Availalble HTTP: http://www.implementationscience.com/content/4/1/11 (accessed 20 January 2013).

Nonaka, I., Toyama, R. and Konno, N. (2000) 'SECI; *Ba* and leadership: a unified model of a dynamic knowledge creation', *Long Range Planning*, 33(1): 5–34.

Moule, P. (2006) 'E-learning for health-care students developing the communities of practice framework', *Journal of Advanced Nursing*, 54(3): 370–80.

Pedler, M. and Burgoyne, J. (2008) 'Action learning' in P. Reason and H. Bradbury (eds) (2008), *The SAGE Handbook of Action Research Participative Inquiry and Practice*, London: SAGE, pp. 319–22.

Ranmuthugala, G., Plumb, J.J, Cunningham, F.C., Georgiou, A., Westbrook, J.I. and Braithwaite, J. (2011) 'How and why are communities of practice established in health care sector? A systematic review of the literature', *BMC Health Services Research*, 11(273). Online. Available HTTP: http://www.biomedcentral.com/1472-6963/11/273 (accessed 20 January 2013).

Soubhi, H., Bayliss, E.A., Fortin, M., Hudon, C., van den Akker, M., Thivierge, R., Posel, N. and Fleiszer, D (2010) 'Learning and caring in communities of practice: using relationship and collective learning to improve primary care for patients with multimorbidity', *Annals of Family Medicine*, 8(2): 170–7.

Tolson, D., McAloon, M., Hotchkiss, R. and Schofield, I. (2005) 'Progressing evidence based practice: an effective nursing model', *Journal of Advanced Nursing*, 50(2): 124–33.

Twelvetrees, A. (2008) *Community Work*, London: Palgrave.

Wenger, E. (1998) *Communities of Practice. Learning, meaning and identity*, Cambridge: Cambridge University Press.

PART 2

Participatory learning and action research

5

PARTICIPATORY LEARNING AND ACTION (PLA) TECHNIQUES FOR COMMUNITY WORK

Vivienne Bozalek

Introduction

In order to be able to engage meaningfully with communities, social and community work practitioners working in this field need knowledge of useful approaches and techniques with which to engage people and ensure their participation. A central goal of community work, or community development and social work practice more generally, is to work towards social justice by addressing inequalities and facilitating the inclusion of marginalized and vulnerable groups of people (Sewpaul and Jones 2004). Social justice and the achievement of economic, cultural and political inclusion can only be achieved if there is what the political theorist Nancy Fraser has referred to as 'participatory parity' between people – which is the ability to interact socially as peers on an equal footing with each other (see Bozalek 2012a, 2012b; Fraser 2008, 2009, 2012 for a fuller discussion of participatory parity). A good way of working with people to achieve participatory parity is to use Participatory Learning and Action (PLA) techniques. These techniques can provide a means of people interacting with each other in an equitable way to achieve political and social change.

PLA techniques have their roots in the Gramscian and Freireian approaches to community work, which writers such as Ledwith (2001, 2011) and Mayo (2004, 2008, 2012) have written extensively about. These approaches to community work focus on the conscientization of people by various means of enabling them to consider how their personal concerns are related to sociopolitical and economic contexts. This conscientization would be regarded as the first step of praxis, which would lead to collective action to achieve transformation with regard to the identified issues (Freire 1970). PLA techniques, in short, provide the means by which people in communities can participate together in learning and then act on the learning.

Ledwith (2001; 2011), using Gramscian-Freireian ideas, sees community work as pedagogy of difference and transformation. Her analysis transcends a dichotomous view of oppression which Gramsci and Freire tended to fall into, identifying in its place a three-dimensional model of community work incorporating the interweaving of *difference* (age, gender, race, ability, sexual preference etc.), *context* (economic, cultural, environmental, historical, spiritual etc.) and *level* (local, regional, national, continental, global), to locate the complexity of thought and action and to be able to identify sites of resistance. PLA techniques fit well into this three-dimensional model in that they address issues of difference (see Bozalek 2011, for a fuller discussion of how this may be achieved through PLA techniques), context – the techniques focus on particular contextual issues, and level – mostly a local level is foregrounded as the techniques are practised in small groups in local communities. However, with the advent of social media and the World Wide Web, it is possible for these techniques to be practised across geographical contexts (see Leibowitz et al. 2012; Yusuf-Khalil et al. 2007 for examples of how PLA techniques have been used in an online course).

This chapter provides an introduction to and an overview of PLA techniques for community work. It is divided into the following subsections: firstly PLA techniques are defined and compared to other similar approaches, after which the history of PLA is elucidated. A section looking at common PLA techniques, what they are and how they could be used then follows and the final section deals with the limitations and advantages of using PLA techniques.

What are Participatory Learning and Action techniques?

PLA techniques are open ended, flexible visual methods which are used in the learning process (Bozalek 2011; Bozalek and Biersteker 2010; Chambers 2002a, 2002b, 2008). These techniques are used in a process which makes it possible for learning by doing in an incremental manner, using participation in small groups to build on people's capacities for becoming catalysts and change agents themselves in their communities of practice. These techniques would involve community members in the assessment, analysis and action of a problem themselves, rather than having an outside expert or social worker coming to investigate the problems and acting on this expert knowledge.

One of the foremost proponents of participatory learning and action (PLA) techniques, Robert Chambers, describes these techniques in the following way:

> A growing family of approaches, methods, attitudes and behaviours to enable people to share, enhance and analyse their knowledge of life and conditions and to plan, act and monitor, evaluate and reflect.
>
> *(Chambers 2002a: 3)*

The above definition alerts us to the fact that these techniques can be used throughout the community work process – for assessment, action, evaluation, planning and monitoring. Levels of participation and the roles and responsibilities of those involved may change throughout these processes, with some being more involved in various stages.

PLA techniques are well suited to community work in that they provide a means for people themselves to identify issues of concern to them about which they can pursue social action. These techniques can encourage community workers to empathize with the people they are working with, to understand the influence of social structures and individuals' own cultural assumptions, and for community members to be agents of social change. PLA techniques are helpful for democratic practice in that they regard community members as experts of their own lives. The role of the community worker would be one of learner and enabler. The community worker would be required to be a skilled facilitator, who is committed to engaging in quality interaction, as well as being self-reflexive and enculturated into issues of difference and social inclusion (Chambers 2008; Cornwall 1999; Leibowitz et al. 2012). Working towards participatory parity by giving everyone, but particularly those who have been marginalized, an opportunity to voice their concerns and then to act on these concerns, is made possible with PLA techniques.

Participatory Learning and Action techniques can be seen as similar to emancipatory, decolonizing and indigenous methodologies as ways of resisting dominant discourses (see Bozalek 2011 for a fuller discussion of these method-ologies). In all these approaches, relationship and trust between all parties involved is of primary importance. There is a need to consider which techniques are suitable for which groups in terms of gender, age, social class, educational levels etc. and it is good to use a range of techniques rather than just one. One also needs to take into account the workloads and livelihood commitments of participants in the process when designing the timelines and programmes using PLA techniques. It is best when people can incorporate doing the techniques into the rhythms of their daily lives, rather than making unrealistic demands on people. For example, one could work with people in rural areas to accommodate times when seasonal work is not being done.

In the Western Cape in South Africa, PLA techniques have been used as part of the social work research curriculum, where students have been taught how to use these techniques for their final year research projects. Final year undergraduate social work students at the University of the Western Cape (UWC) are also required to use PLA techniques for their community work assessment practice in their fieldwork placements. PLA techniques have been used in postgraduate modules as well, such as the Women's Health and Well-Being course which was run across five countries (see Yusuf-Khalil et al. 2007 for more details of this course).

A history of the development of PLA techniques

Participatory action research (PAR) was initiated and developed in Africa and South America in the 1970s by Southern activists and academics concerned with addressing effects of colonization and poverty using social investigation, political conscientization or education and action. The educational aspect of PAR supports the development of critical consciousness, and encourages an examination of issues from political, social and economic perspectives (Freire 1970; Hall 1979, 1981; Tandon 1981; Maguire 1987; Mbilinyi 1982, 1993).

Participatory action research starts from a critique of dominant ideologies which place the blame for problems such as poverty or racism on the persons involved rather than on social structures or the behaviour of dominant groups. It aims to undermine the patterns that make members of oppressed groups identify with this ideology and see themselves as being responsible for their own situations of personal deficit. In this way it is similar to a Freireian approach to community work, where the process of conscientization is used to alert people to the structural causes of their personal problems, rather than blaming themselves and interiorizing negative regard produced by dominant discourses. Through the process of participation in the research process, they start to view their situations from alternative perspectives (Hall 1979, 1981; Maguire 1987; Mbilinyi 1993). This view of knowledge in the participatory research paradigm articulates well with the arguments of Sen (1995) and Nussbaum (1995, 2000), in that they all assume that those who are marginalized have internalized discursive practices which naturalize their disadvantaged positions. The process of working through the social, political and economic issues is thus necessary to engage critically with such interiorization of disadvantage.

PLA techniques have also grown from a community development process which started off being known as Rapid Rural Appraisal (RRA), which evolved to Participatory Rural Appraisal (PRA) in the late 1980s and 1990s and transformed into a process where local people themselves became involved in appraising, analyzing and acting on their situations through participating in drawing of maps, diagrams etc., typically in small groups. This spread to many countries in the North and the South and many organizations. The term Participatory Learning and Action (PLA) techniques was developed in 1995 and was similar to PRA but included a broader range of approaches and methods. The terms are sometimes used interchangeably however, as the RRA/PRA/PLA methodologies (Chambers 2008). PLA/PRA techniques, which are participatory and enabling for community members, can also be used with other research methodologies, such as interviewing or survey research in order to gain a broader view of local circumstances.

The section above has given a brief understanding of what PLA techniques are, how they have been used and how they developed. In the following section, some examples of these techniques will be provided, with a brief explanation of how to do the techniques and an illustration of how they have been used.

Some examples of PLA techniques

Visioning

With visioning, people come up with their vision for how things might be and it can widen their thinking as well as indicating the things that are important to them.

This could be drawn, modelled, acted or sung. It serves as a starting point for discussion of what actions could be taken.

In a community work project with teachers at a preschool in Queenstown in the Eastern Cape, South Africa, they drew their vision of what they would want in a preschool. Each teacher drew their own vision and this initiated a discussion about what was lacking in the schools and what could be done about this. Other examples of visioning have been used for students to indicate their vision of a university which would enhance their learning, children's vision of a society where children's and human rights are valued, and higher educators' vision of the resources they would need to achieve change in teaching and learning at their institutions.

Visual mapping

Mapping includes mapping of social, demographic, health and service issues, opportunities or resources. Maps can be drawn on the ground or on paper, models can be made and natural resources, such as leaves and sand, can be used. Mapping is useful in community work as it can provide a starting point for discussion or for prioritizing issues for change.

Visual community mapping

Community mapping has been used with social work, psychology and occupational therapy students, students in general, higher educators and NGO staff members in South Africa to examine the conditions in their communities and to discuss the issues they would like to change. Social work students have used mapping in their community work placements as a means of doing needs assessments and following up on actions with community members on the basis of the identified social issues needing change in the communities (see Rohleder et al. 2008a and 2008b for more information on the use of community mapping in this project). The following set of instructions can be given to people to initiate a drawing and discussion of a community map:

Step 1:   Draw a picture/map of your home and neighbourhood including the resources that are there.

Step 2:   Identify and label three things that you would like to change (could be physical or relate to attitudes, social issues). Put these in order by choosing to give the one you feel is most important the most tokens.

Step 3:   Share in your group, explaining your picture/map and the reasons for wanting things to change.

The community map drawing in Figure 5.1 was done by a social work student at the University of the Western Cape, depicting the lack of resources in her community and the social problems that exist. The circumstances in which a student from the University of the Western Cape is living are made explicit. These

FIGURE 5.1 Community map drawing

are the sorts of issues about which community members could rally together regarding further action in a community work project. One of the students from the course on Community, Self and Identity remarked on what she learnt from doing the mapping exercise:

> Through mapping my own community and the available (and blatant scarcity of) resources, I got the opportunity to reflect on my community not only in terms of resources, but also communal ethos (including prevailing prejudices, attitudes towards gender, and even racism).

Visual body mapping

Another kind of mapping that can be used is body mapping, where community members draw their own bodies and indicate their knowledge about the kinds of conditions that people in the community are suffering from. An example of how body maps were used in a community work project is the Bodymaps for Khayalitsha Hospital Art Project 2011 (Figure 5.2). The project was initiated in 1999 by psychologist and narrative therapist, Jonathan Morgan (see http://art2bebodymaps.com for more details of body mapping), who used body mapping in his group work with adults living with HIV/AIDs. This group then became an activist community group, engaging in many different community projects.

Body mapping is now widely used in countries such as Kenya and the UK to provide a safe space where people living with HIV/AIDs can reflect on and communicate their life experiences, form communities of practice and engage in further action in their own geographical communities. Figure 5.2 is an image of a body map drawn in Jonathan Morgan's original work with the Bambanani Women's Group which has now been recorded in a book (see Morgan and the Bambanani Women's Group, 2003) and which appears on the Memory Box website (www.memorybox.co.za).

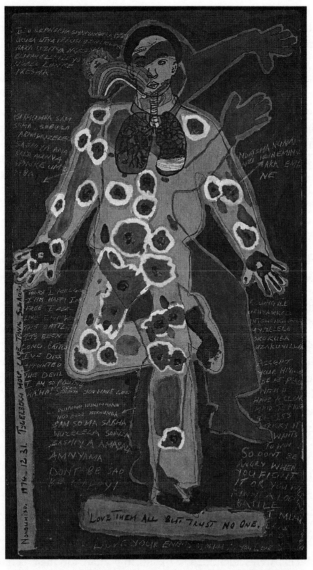

FIGURE 5.2 Body map of a community member living with HIV/AIDS

The artist, Nondumiso Hlwele, kindly gave permission to use this image and in an email to me explained how the Bambanani Group's work has been taken forward. On the Memory Box website she explains her body map thus:

> On my picture I drew the virus – it's the small blue dot. The red circles are the ARVs eating the virus and the virus is going down. The white is my blood. The ARVs are strong. Look what I have written under my left hand.
>
> *(www.memorybox.co.za)*

According to her, in June/July 2011 seven members of the Bambanani Group took part in a three-day workshop to create body map images that will be done in mosaic at the nurses' stations in some of the wards of the new Khayelitsha Hospital in the township of Khayelitsha, Cape Town. In this workshop an adapted version of the initial body mapping process with Jonathan Morgan in 1999 was used as a way for participants to reflect on their lives, health, living with HIV and well being over the past nine years and share this with the group in a safe space.

The group are also keen to share what they have learnt about antiretroviral (ARV) drugs with others by including this information on their bodymaps and possibly feeding this information into further research around ARVs in South Africa. The Bambanani Group are an activist group running workshops using the body map tool in poorly resourced communities in Cape Town.[1]

Matrix ranking

Matrix ranking can be used in community work when one wants to establish which issues take priority such as which services are used and what aspects of them are valued. For example, various health care services such as hospitals, clinics, private providers and traditional healers could be identified. The group would then brainstorm what it thinks is important in relation to a particular issue and then group members use counters to vote on which they think are the most important issues or characteristics of the service. For instance, health care facilities could be evaluated against the staff being skilled, staff being friendly and kind, medication being available, cost being low, accessible in terms of distance etc. A two-way matrix would then be drawn up with the health care services along one axis and the qualities sought along another, and then group members would be given 10 counters each with which to vote for which they thought to be the most important qualities. The idea is that the group develops some sort of action plan for dealing with poor services and for alerting service providers about their needs.

An example of a simple one-way matrix is one which was drawn up by parents of a preschool in Queenstown, South Africa, where they identified what things they thought children should gain from preschool and then voted on how important each of these were for child development. The matrix in Table 5.1 shows the qualities which parents identified as being important for their children in the preschool education. The numbers next to the qualities indicate the number of

TABLE 5.1 Things which children gain from preschool.

Ukuzimela	Independence	16
Ulwazingokhuseleko	Knowledge about safety	8
Ukubuza xa bengaqondi	Asking when you do not understand	9
Bakhulile ngokwasenkolweni	Growing spiritually	11
Banolwazi ngococeko	Knowledge about hygiene	7
Baqeqeshekile	Discipline	9
Banolwazi ngabakufundayo	Knowledge about learning	10

Matrix generated by parents of children at Yipakamisa Preschool, Ezibeleni, Queenstown, Eastern Cape, South Africa

votes each quality received – thus independence was rated most highly and spiritual growth the next highly etc. The next step would be for the parents to interact with the school regarding their expectations and to develop some collaborative plans about how the expectations could be met.

Transect walks

In this PLA technique, local people in the community walk the facilitator around, showing issues which are pertinent to them. This is a useful technique in community work as it allows the community members to take the lead and the community worker to learn from them about the local environment and experiences which are important for them. For example, a child at a crèche could show a community worker which are the special places for her, girls in the community could show where they do not feel safe when walking around etc.

Proportional piling

This is a quick way of assessing proportions of things like how different groups of community members spend their time or income. You could ask people to draw a diagram or give them a pile of beads – say 24 beads to show what they do in a day. It can show gendered differences of how income and time is spent.

Mood or lifelines

Mood or lifelines are where people can track their experiences and events over a time period. The exercise can be done individually or as a group. An example of a lifeline is the River of Life exercise which students from the University of the Western Cape and Stellenbosch University did in the Community, Self and Identity course. They were given the following instructions:

Step 1: Draw the river of your life that has brought you to your current choice of profession/discipline. Go right back to the source of the river (your early years), the different periods in your life, such as quiet peaceful times (smooth flow) or wild difficult times (waterfalls, rough water). Important influences which grew your river can be shown as tributaries and labelled. Add little drawings along the side of important people, events and experiences. Use different colours to show different moods.

Step 2: Share in groups of three.

In Figure 5.3, it can be seen that this can be a powerful tool, revealing many issues in people's lives, which they then discuss in groups. Because sensitive issues may be revealed, mood and lifelines need to be used with caution.

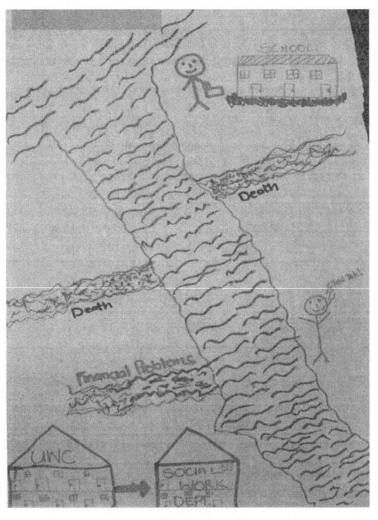

FIGURE 5.3 River of Life showing the difficult circumstances leading to the choice of social work as a profession at UWC

Venn diagrams

These are also referred to as Chappati diagrams and are similar to diagrams used in mathematics and can be used to show the importance of resources or issues in the community and how they relate to each other. For example, they have been used in higher education to show the influences of higher education issues and resources on teaching and learning in South Africa. (For example of Venn diagrams used in PLA community work, see Mukherjee 2002: 247.)

Flow and impact diagrams

These diagrams show the impact of particular issues such as programmes which have been started in the community; they may indicate the positive and negative consequences of these programmes. For example, in South Africa, public works programmes were evaluated by community members using flow and impact diagrams. They identified that one positive impact of the public works programme was greater employment leading to less crime, but a negative impact was that not many people could benefit from these programmes, leading to community conflict, which can be seen in Figure 5.4.

The PLA techniques described in the section above are only examples of what can be used in working with community members to allow them to express their

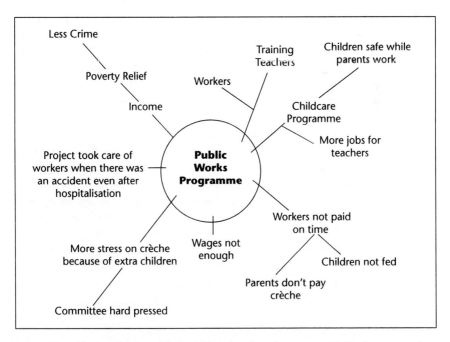

FIGURE 5.4   Flow and impact diagram showing the advantages and disadvantages of public works programmes in South Africa

opinions and experiences, to reflect upon these, discuss them and decide upon the best courses of action to engage in. The techniques cannot be used to indicate the pervasiveness of problems or issues in the community, as they relate only to people's subjective experiences of these issues.

The techniques which have been described provide some examples of how practitioners can use them in community work to conscientize community members regarding what they may interiorize as personal issues but which have structural-sociopolitical and economic causes. They can also be used to highlight issues of difference, context and level, where local issues can be identified as having global roots as in the unemployment situation of clothing workers due to cheap Chinese products being available in South Africa. This was discussed in the introduction and can be seen to emerge from the process of engagement with the various PLA techniques.

Limitations and advantages of using PLA techniques

PLA techniques can be time consuming because initiating and managing a participatory process in community work takes time. It can be critiqued also because it only has the possibility to reach small numbers of people that require special training and support. On the other hand, change is more sustainable when strength and capacity is developed within the community of practice, enabling the members to consider their positions, initiate action, become more self-reflexive and potentially assume greater control over their circumstances. PLA techniques reflect subjective experiences and act as a springboard for discussion and analysis. Engaging in PLA techniques can be unsettling or discomforting (Leibowitz et al. 2010a, 2010b), and this may need management by the social or community worker. The facilitation skills of the community worker are enormously important with PLA techniques, as one needs to behave in a democratic and respectful way towards participants. Some participants may also be resistant to engaging with PLA techniques, especially when there are power differentials at play.

Despite the disadvantages outlined in the paragraph above, PLA techniques have been found to be powerful tools to accomplish change with participants in communities. They are inclusive techniques, allowing for participatory parity in the community work process. They provide alternative ways of expressing need – especially useful for those who cannot express themselves verbally or in writing such as smaller children. They can be seen as non-threatening and playful techniques (see Bozalek and Biersteker 2010). The techniques are a good reflective tool which often allows people to develop new insights into their situations and to collectively discuss common concerns and also differences. PLA techniques have the potential to bring to the fore strong emotions about issues of difference (Bozalek 2011). They also provide opportunities to challenge and to deepen knowledge about issues.

For the community worker, the facilitation of PLA techniques can model for community members democratic and respectful forms of practice. People have the opportunity to be more self-reflexive, to have fun and learn – engaging in what Ledwith (2011) calls a pedagogy of difference and transformation. Democracy is more achievable with these methods as power relations can be reversed as the role of the expert is changed into one of learner and facilitator, with the community members being able to express and analyse complex phenomena in their communities themselves (Chambers 2008).

QUESTIONS FOR REFLECTION

- How could you apply PLA techniques in your own community work practice? Which techniques would work best in your particular context?
- What are the advantages and disadvantages of PLA techniques?
- How do these techniques differ from other types of research and community work methods?

Note

1. For more information on this project, see the website http://www. memorybox.co.za or contact the project leader Nondumiso Hlwele, email address: nondumiso.h@gmail.com.

Suggestions for further reading

Other examples of how PLA techniques can be used in community work and community development projects can be found on the Institute for Development Studies website where many books and papers are available on projects which have used these techniques and where papers on how to use the techniques can be found. Online. Available HTTP: http://www.ids.ac.uk/ (accessed 1 March 2013).

Another very useful reference on a project that has used PLA techniques in community work is: Shrumm, H. and Jonas, H. (eds), (2012) *Biocultural Community Protocols: A Toolkit for Community Facilitators*, Natural Justice: Cape Town.

The website *Reflect* gives examples of participatory tools. Online. Available HTTP: http://www.reflect-action.org/how (accessed 1 March 2013).

References

Bozalek, V. (2011) 'Acknowledging privilege through encounters with difference: Participatory Learning and Action techniques for decolonizing methodologies in Southern contexts', *International Journal of Social Research Methodology*, 14(6): 469–84.
——(2012a) 'Recognition and participatory parity: students' accounts of gendered family practices', *The Social Work Practitioner-Researcher*, 24(1): 66–84.
——(2012b) 'Interview with Nancy Fraser', *The Social Work Practitioner-Researcher*, 24(1): 136–51.

Bozalek, V. and Biersteker, L. (2010) 'Exploring power and privilege using participatory learning and action techniques', *Social Work Education*, 25(5): 551–72.

Chambers, R. (2002a) 'Relaxed and Participatory Appraisal: notes on practical approaches and methods for participants in PRA-PLA familiarisation workshops', Institute of Development Studies: University of Sussex. Online. Available HTTP: http://worldteachcambodia.org/File/Development%20Doc/docs/ID11513.pdf (accessed 24 February 2013).

——(2002b) *Participatory Workshops*, London: Earthscan.

——(2008) *Revolutions in Development Inquiry*, London: Earthscan.

Cornwall, A. (1999) 'Introduction to PRA visualisation methods', in The Participation Group (1999) *Introduction to PRA and Health: A Reader*, Brighton: Institute of Development Studies, University of Sussex.

Fraser, N. (2008) 'Reframing justice in a globalizing world', in K. Olson (ed.) *Adding Insult to Injury: Nancy Fraser Debates her Critics*, London: Verso.

——(2009) *Scales of Justice: Reimagining Political Space in a Globalizing World*, New York: Columbia University Press.

——(2012) 'Social exclusion, global poverty and scales of (in)justice: rethinking law and poverty in a globalizing world', in S. Liebenberg and Q. Quinot (eds) *Law and Poverty: Perspectives from South Africa and Beyond*, Cape Town: Juta.

Freire, P. (1970) *Pedagogy of the Oppressed*, New York: The Seabury Press.

Hall, B. (1979) 'Knowledge as a commodity and participatory research', *Prospects*, 9(4): 4–20.

——(1981) 'Participatory research, popular knowledge, and power: a personal reflection', *Convergence*, 14(3): 6–17.

Ledwith, M. (2001) 'Community work as critical pedagogy: re-envisioning Freire and Gramsci', *Community Development Journal*, 36(3): 171–82.

——(2011) *Community Development. A Critical Approach*, 2nd edn, Bristol: Policy Press.

Leibowitz, B., Bozalek, V., Carolissen, R., Nicholls, L., Rohleder, P. and Swartz, L. (2010a) 'Bringing the Social into Pedagogy; Unsafe learning in an uncertain world', *Teaching in Higher Education*,15(2):123-133.

Leibowitz, B., Bozalek, V., Rohleder, P., Carolissen, R., and Swartz, L. (2010b) ' "Whiteys Love to Talk About Themselves": Discomfort as a pedagogy for change', *Race, Ethnicity and Education*, 13(1):83-100.

Leibowitz, B., Swartz, L., Bozalek, V., Carolissen, R., Nicholls. L. and Rohleder, P. (eds) (2012) *Community, Self and Identity: Educating South African Students for Citizenship*, Cape Town: HSRC Press.

Maguire, P. (1987) *Doing Participatory Research: A Feminist Approach.* Amherst: Centre for International Education, University of Massachusetts.

Mayo, P. (2004) *Liberating Praxis: Paulo Freire's Legacy for Radical Education and Politics*, Rotterdam: Sense Publishers.

——(2008) 'Antonio Gramsci and Paulo Freire: some connections and contrasts' in C.A. Torres and P.A. Noguera (eds) *Social Justice Education for Teachers: Paulo Freire and the Possible Dream*, Rotterdam: Sense Publishers.

——(2012) *Echoes from Freire for a Critically Engaged Pedagogy*, New York: Continuum International Publishing.

Mbilinyi, M. (1982) 'My experience as woman, activist and researcher in a project with peasant women', in M. Mies (ed.), *Fighting on Two Fronts: Women's Struggles and Research*, The Hague: Institute of Social Studies.

——(1993) 'Transformative adult education in the age of structural adjustment: a Southern African Perspective', paper presented as keynote address to the *CACE University-Based Adult Education Conference*, Cape Town, 14–16 April.

Memory Box. Online. Available HTTP: http://www.memorybox.co.za (accessed 1 March 2013).

Morgan, J. and the Bambanani Women's Group (2003) *Long Life. Positive HIV Stories,* Cape Town: Double Story Books.

Mukherjee, N. (2002) *Participation, Learning and Action with 100 field methods,* New Dehli: Ashok Kumar Mittal Concept publishing company.

Nussbaum, M.C. (1995) 'Human capabilities, female human beings', in M.C. Nussbaum and J. Glover (eds) *Women, Culture and Development. A Study of Human Capabilities,* Oxford: Clarendon Press, pp. 61–104.

——(2000) *Women and Human Development: The Capabilities Approach,* Cambridge: Cambridge University Press.

Rohleder, P., Swartz, L., Bozalek, V., Carolissen, R. and Leibowitz, B. (2008b) 'Community, self and identity: participatory action research and the creation of a virtual community across two South African universities', *Teaching in Higher Education,* 13(2): 131–43.

Rohleder, P., Swartz, L., Carolissen, R., Bozalek, V. and Leibowitz, B. (2008a) '"Communities isn't just about trees and shops": students from two South African universities engage in dialogue about "community" and "community work"', *Journal of Community and Applied Social Psychology,* 18(3): 253–67.

Sen, A. K. (1995) 'Gender inequality and theories of justice', in M. Nussbaum and J. Glover (eds) *Women, Culture and Development. A Study of Human Capabilities,* Oxford: Clarendon Press, pp. 259–73.

Sewpaul, V. and Jones, D. (2004). *Global Standards for the Education and Training of the Social Work Profession,* adopted at the General Assemblies of IASSW and IFSW: Adelaide, Australia. Online. Available HTTP: http://cdn.ifsw.org/assets/ifsw_65044-3.pdf (accessed 8 March 2013).

Tandon, R. (1981) 'Participatory research in the empowerment of people', *Convergence* 24(3): 20–9, University of Massachusetts.

Yusuf-Khalil, Y., Bozalek, V., Staking, K., Tuval-Mashiach, R. and Bantebya-Kyomuhendo, G. (2007) 'Reflections on a collaborative experience: using ICT in a transcultural women's health module', *Agenda,* 21(71): 54–65.

6

MOBILIZING COMMUNITY STRENGTHS AND ASSETS

Participatory experiences of community members in a garden project

Tanusha Raniga

Introduction

In contemporary times, globally social workers engaging in communities are faced with dire crises of poverty, inequality, disease and social divisions. Paradoxically, this creates an opportune time for community work to redefine its agenda and to focus on understanding the relationship between the community, the practitioners' knowledge, skills and attitudes and the context, if it wishes to contribute meaningfully to development practice (Raniga 2011). Kretzmann and McKnight (1993) advocate that communities are able to drive the development process themselves by identifying and mobilizing existing (but often untapped) resources and assets, thereby responding to and enhancing community economic development initiatives. Asset-based community development (ABCD) offers a set of practices to assist individuals, community groups and institutions to increase social networks and relationships within a community (Pan et al. 2005). South Africa's apartheid ideology was based on the premise that the integration of races in society could not ensure peace, freedom and prosperity for all and thus a system of institutionalized racial discrimination ruled South Africa for 46 years (Patel 2005). In the post-apartheid era, a focus on social capital, a concept used by Putnam (2000) to describe the power of social networks through building reciprocity and trust in communities, has been enshrined in the White Paper on Social Welfare (Department of Welfare and Population Development 1997). Empirical evidence from research in development has demonstrated associations between characteristics of social capital and sustainability of community economic development projects (Mathie and Cunningham 2005). Social capital is believed to influence development in communities by increasing access to social and emotional support as well as knowledge, leadership influence on development and access to shared resources and material goods. Given the positive relationship between social capital and community development, it is widely acknowledged that if social capital can be increased in a community, it may result in improved social and economic development of those living in low-income communities (Ife and Tesoriero 2006; Mathie and Cunningham 2005; Ledwith 2005). In other words through mobilizing individual community members, voluntary associations and organizations, asset-based community development provides a valuable framework to strengthen community building, increase social capital and enhance development of local economic opportunities in communities.

This chapter draws attention to the connections between ABCD strategies and current interest in community economic development. Using participatory action research methodology, a key objective of this study was to gain insight into community members' reflections of ABCD in the implementation of a garden project in Bhambayi, North of Durban, KwaZulu-Natal. Three key themes distilled from the data are deliberated: enhancing capacity, building partnerships for change and linking resources from outside the community as strategies to mobilize and sustain community economic development and the implementation of ABCD in practice. This contributes to the body of knowledge in two foundational ways: providing a nuanced understanding of community work practice from the perspectives of community members and secondly by encouraging academic debate about the significance of ABCD in social work practice.

The chapter begins with a review of some of the current debates related to participation in communities. The second section deliberates ABCD as a critical organizing practice framework. Section three outlines the research methodology, followed by the presentation and discussion of the three key themes. The final section of the chapter synthesizes the community members' reflections and highlights key implications of the research for social workers and development practitioners in employing ABCD in practice.

Current debates related to community participation and the context for the current project

In the post-1994 era, taking into account colonial and apartheid legacy, South Africa continues to grapple with deep levels of poverty, deprivation and immense disparities of wealth and opportunities (Chikadzi and Pretorius 2011; Frye 2007; Desai 2007). Proponents of leftist thinking aptly argue that in contemporary times, neoliberal globalization which emphasizes 'comparative advantage, free trade, the social and spatial divisions of labour and absolute exploitation of resources by multinational corporations' (Fisher and Ponniah 2003:28) has contributed to skewed income and high rates of poverty and inequality in the world (Sewpaul 2006). Furthermore, a pivotal consequence of neoliberal globalization is not just economic domination of the world but the imposition of a Western worldview that permeates every facet of political, cultural, gendered, sexual, ecological and epistemological spaces within and between countries, leading to diminished solidarity and increased fragmentation in communities (Ledwith 2005; Stephney and Popple 2008). In fact Ledwith (2005) asserts that in this context, poverty and inequality tend to become increasingly convoluted and concealed making social exploitation and oppression distant and infrequently challenged. As development practitioners, it is impossible to embrace critical organizing strategies in community work practice without taking into account an analysis of power and discrimination in society (Ife and Tesoriero 2006).

Hence the practice of a more just society starts through the active involvement and participation of local people in activities related to development improvement and change of an existing situation (Swanepoel and de Beer 2006; Ledwith 2005). Community participation and its potential for positive impact on development projects have always been subject to manifold interpretations. In part, the reason for this is the misperception that governments, organizations and development practitioners had all the answers to solve community problems, in Africa in particular (Raniga and Simpson 2002; Swanepoel and de Beer 2006). This was partly due to development projects being blueprinted and imported from other failed project experiments by national governments and development agencies (Korten 1980) without being adapted to local conditions and situations.

Swanepoel and de Beer (2006) argue that development projects were used to indoctrinate local people into subscribing to Western values. It is thus not surprising that projects have been known to have alienated and marginalized the very people for whom such strategies were meant to help (Ife and Tesoriero 2006). This colonial approach with non-participation of local people in project development and treating them as passive subjects devoid of any knowledge, values and skills except for those acquired from formal educational institutions has been a key contributing factor in the failure of community projects (Swanepoel 2002; Ife and Teseriero 2006; Swanepoel and de Beer 2006; Mtshali et al. 2012). Consequently, the 1980s and 1990s were characterized as an era of development crisis arising from policy failures (Leach, 1995; Swanepoel and de Beer 2006) which resulted in very little faith being expressed in the Western, 'external agency' model of development imposed from the top both by national governments and international development agencies.

The United Nations (1981: 5) set the tone for an ideological shift in the development field with the definition of participation: 'as the creation of opportunities to enable all members of a community to actively contribute to and influence the development process and to share equitably in the fruits of development'. This definition conceptualizes community participation as liberating where there are more conscious efforts made by organizations and development practitioners to authentically involve local people in project planning, implementation and evaluation (Raniga and Simpson 2002; Swanepoel 2002; Ife and Tesoriero 2006; Swanepoel and de Beer 2006; Weyers 2011). In this sense development projects can become transferable and transformative (Ledwith 2005).

In this context local people self-mobilize, are actively involved in decision making and transformative action and contribute meaningfully to the development process. Taking into account such participatory rhetoric, Mathie and Cunnigham

(2005) questioned 150 community members about spontaneous self-mobilization and their role in the initiation and implementation of development projects with little or no outside assistance from external organizations. What stands out in their stories is the strong base of social networks and mobilization of various community assets to bring about positive changes as key practices to sustain community economic development.

Asset-based community development (ABCD) as a community organizing practice framework

As a critique of needs-based approaches to development, ABCD offers a set of practices in which local people can act to increase social networks at an individual and/or institutional level (Mathie and Cunnigham 2005). ABCD represents participation as a self-mobilization process that happens with minimal or no involvement from an external change agent or organization. Research conducted by Kretzmann and McKnight qualitatively analysed stories about community development projects that were initiated and implemented by members of low income communities in the United States, drawing on the community's own resources with little or no involvement from external organizations. This ground-breaking study culminated in their book: *Building Communities from the Inside Out: Asset-based Community Development* (1993). The central premise of this book is that communities have the capacity to drive their own development process by identifying and mobilizing existing (but often untapped) assets and resources, thereby creating opportunities for local economic projects. Such unrecognized assets may include human resource capacity and skills as well as the bonds and relationships among local people that fuel voluntary associations and social networks. Kretzmann and McKnight (1993) identified five major assets that contribute to building stronger and socially cohesive communities. The first asset is the skills and capacities of local people who reside in the community. Ife and Tesoriero (2006) refer to this as 'valuing local skills' as an underlying principle that should be embraced by social workers and development workers. The second major asset is the social bonds and associations that exist within communities. Pan et al. (2005: 1186) define associations as 'the organizing venues in which residents and others can contribute their talents and skills and provide a forum for networking and social support'. Putnam (2000) refers to this as bonding social capital and states that the power of social networks constitutes a valuable part of the community environment. The third asset includes what Swanepoel and de Beer (2006) refer to as manufactured resources which includes governmental, non governmental agencies and public service institutions (hospitals, clinics, schools, local businesses etc.) who employ paid staff to provide professional expertise for increasing service delivery and infrastructure in communities. The fourth asset is economic development potential and the fifth asset includes natural resources such as land and other physical assets (Swanepoel and de Beer 2006). Sheehan (2003) discusses the importance of tapping into the economic potential of manufactured resources such as schools and hospitals and turning physical assets such as abandoned buildings and vacant land into assets to build stronger communities. Mathie and Cunningham (2005) indicate that mobilizing such physical and social assets can lead to more formal investments and linkages being formed with organizations interested in contributing to development in the community. As such the development process is not only increased but sustained while it continues to recognize local networks and associations as the key driving force through which community assets can be identified and linkages formed to multiply their power and effectiveness (Kretzmann and McKnight 1993).

ABCD offers a set of practices such as interviews to identify unrecognized assets; asset-mapping which includes documenting the full range of assets in a community and which local people can draw on; mobilizing a core group of community organizers; initiation of a community activity that requires no outside assistance and progressively increasing the linkages of these activities with organizations which are tapped on to invest in the community-driven development activity (Mathie and Cunnigham 2005). Smit (2006) makes an important point that in informal settlements, economic development projects and social networks are strategies for poorly resourced communities to increase food security, well-being and to reduce vulnerability.

Bearing these deliberations in mind, this study was an endeavour to address a renewed interest for an alternative approach to development that emphasizes a more evolutionary, flexible, rigorous approach to planning and evaluating community economic interventions on the part of community members (Ledwith 2005; Mathie and Cunningham 2005). I have been actively involved in co-ordinating a student training unit in the Bhambayi community since 2007 as part of the University of KwaZulu-Natal Community Outreach and Research initiative. It was then that a research partnership was formed with the local civic structure namely, the Bhambayi Reconstruction and Development Forum to investigate the effects of poverty and HIV and AIDS in households in the area. The University of KwaZulu-Natal Research Ethics Committee provided the mandate to conduct the study in June 2007. Phase one of this broader study comprised a quantitative audit of 351 households, which revealed that 67 per cent of the economically active people were unemployed and food insecurity was rife in the area (Raniga and Simpson 2011). As an outcome of this broader study, 42 residents who formed part of a senior citizens club called Siyazama invited the researcher and social work students to pilot a community economic development initiative in 2009, namely a garden project using asset-based community development as a framework for intervention. What was valuable about the success of the project is the positive networking relationships with the local civic structure and which has been nurtured over 16 years of the university's presence in this community.

This paper presents empirical evidence from the experiences of 15 community members who were involved in the facilitation, implementation and evaluation of the garden project. The foundational objectives of this study were to:

FIGURE 6.1 A typical informal dwelling built by a resident using mud in Bhambayi

- Examine the community work experiences of local members involved in the implementation of a garden project using ABCD.
- Gain insight into community members' reflections of the practices of ABCD in the implementation of a garden project.
- Make suggestions about how social workers can apply ABCD strategies to community economic development projects.

Methodology

Participatory action research

Consistent with the objectives of this study, participatory action research (PAR) methodology guided the data collection process as it 'offers an alternative that is possibly more empowering, participatory and sustainable for the community itself' (Pyles 2009: 108). Proponents of transformative methodologies note that PAR endeavours to alleviate some of the concerns that research may be exploitative and tends to marginalize participants in the process (Baines 2007; Stringer 1999; Pyles 2009). This study endeavoured to remedy power dynamics by engaging participants (student social workers, staff from the Department of Social Work, UKZN and community members) in the research design, data collection and evaluation phases of the research process. Stringer (1999: 21) indicates that this method 'provides researchers with the opportunity to change the social and personal dynamics of the research situation and to provide solutions to problems encountered'. In so doing, the research process in this study focused on building capacity and skills of all stakeholders (students, community members and academic) thereby enhancing self-determination, planning and co-ordination of the garden project in the Bhambayi community.

Participants

The garden project using ABCD provided the scope for reflection beyond technical-rational responses and provided the ethos for community members to engage critically with their knowledge and skills utilized in their practice context. As Pyles (2009: 108) notes 'PAR offers an alternative belief that research skills should be in the hands of organizers themselves'. Purposive, availability sampling was used to guide the selection of the participants for this study. Every year academic staff and final year social work students complete a three-month field placement from the beginning of August until the end of October as part of the Advanced Practice Module. For the period August 2009 to October 2011 10 students and 15 community members from the Siyazama support group were involved in the initiation, implementation and evaluation of the garden project using ABCD practices.

Data collection

Four key phases comprised the research process. The research process was guided by Pyles' (2009) organizing framework for conducting participatory action research. As outlined in Table 6.1, phase one comprised knowledge from concrete experience, which entailed three four-hour training workshops with students and community members on asset-based community development practices. A further purpose of the workshops was engagement with key stakeholders in the community, such as the councillor, executive committee members from the Bhambayi Reconstruction and Development Forum (BRDF) and 42 members of the Siyazama support group to explore the development issues and challenges faced in the community. Phase two entailed organizing a core group to be involved in the garden project and considering its significance for meeting the economic needs of the community. This process culminated in the selection of 15 members who were keen to be involved in the planning, implementation, monitoring and evaluation of the garden project. Phase three comprised mainstream experimentation where ABCD practices (collecting stories, asset-mapping and linking assets for economic development) were tested out through the implementation of the garden project over a period of 18 months. Phase four comprised the evaluation phase which consisted of 15 in-depth interviews with the Siyazama members and three focus group sessions (including students) to reflect on community work experiences of implementing the garden project using ABCD practices.

TABLE 6.1 Outline of the research process

Phases	Intervention	Focus
Phase one: knowledge from concrete experience	Monthly training workshops with students and community members in Bhambayi on ABCD practices	Overview of objectives of the study, brainstorm developmental needs in community and asset mapping exercise
Phase two: organizing a core group	Meetings with stakeholders in the community (councillor, BRDF members, 42 Siyazama support group members)	Clarifying the purpose of the study with stakeholders and building a vision and plan for the garden project with little outside assistance
Phase three: mainstream experimentation	ABCD practices were included in implementation of the project	Students and community members were required to test out the ABCD practices such as collecting stories, asset-mapping and linking garden activities with organizational resources to add value to the project
Phase four: evaluation	Joint evaluation of the garden project	15 in-depth interviews were held with community members. Three focus group sessions (including students) were held to reflect on experiences of implementing the garden project using ABCD practices

Four qualitative methods were used to collect the data: minutes of team meetings, participant observation, in-depth interviews with community members and focus group sessions held with students and Siyazama members. Permission was sought from participants to tape record interviews and focus group sessions. This was combined with secondary data from literature reviews and policy analyses.

Data analysis

The training workshops, in-depth interviews and three focus group sessions held with community members were used as data for analysis of the empirical data presented in this chapter. Consistent with PAR, the researcher endeavoured to democratize the research process by making the data analysis tools (transcripts of interviews and focus group sessions, field reports and training material) available to the participants. Pyles (2009) states that it is imperative that those individuals who are most affected by developmental issues are at the centre of the research process. As an on-going study, this is the first of a series of articles in which descriptive results are reported.

Ethical issues

At the orientation meeting held in August 2009, community members from the Siyazama support group approached the researcher about the lack of food security and high levels of unemployment in Bhambayi. This was confirmed by quantitative audit undertaken by Raniga and Simpson (2011) which revealed that 67 per cent of the economically active members of the community were unemployed and that 62 per cent of people sustained on one meal a day in the year 2007 (Raniga and Simpson 2011). Joint meetings held with the Bhambayi Reconstruction and Development Forum committee members and the Siyazama support group clarified that the need for a garden project using ABCD an intervention strategy to endeavour to alleviate food insecurity and high levels of poverty in the community was needed. Even though written, signed consent was given by the community members at the onset of August 2009, at the evaluation phase of the project (conducted in 2011) they were given the opportunity to decide whether or not they wanted their verbal input to be used for research purposes. They were also informed that any verbal or written data used for research purposes and publication would be treated anonymously. All participants gave consent to use the data for publication.

Results and significance of findings

Three themes, which could begin to generate an asset-based community development practice culture in community work, distilled from the data: enhancing capacity, building partnerships for change and linking resources from outside the community as strategies to sustain community economic development projects.

Enhancing capacity

During the in-depth interviews held with the community members, it was evident that they perceived the experiences of implementing the community garden project using the ABCD practices in Bhambayi as positive and that it served to enhance their own knowledge about facilitating projects as well as to use the practice tools such as asset-mapping, compiling a resource inventory in the community and relationship building as valuable. Additionally the garden project provided community members with the opportunity to engage in a process of continuous personal reflection. They spoke about acknowledging their own potential to own and contribute meaningfully to the project even though they were faced with challenges of planning the project with minimal resources and infrastructure. Some comments shared by community members were:

> This was a good experience for me because for the first time I got exposed to the positive things in our community.

The project taught me to work with people in the community.

I learnt that we can do things for ourselves and change the community.

I have grown up in Bhambayi and experienced the hardship of living in this community. The training taught me to have hope and to keep an open mind and to deal with poverty problems in Bhambayi.

The garden project helped me understand people and to work in a team. I was very happy and felt like I am changing for the better.

Being part of Siyazama club and starting the garden project in Bhambayi was very exciting. I was looking forward to the training and working with the community on daily basis.

The support I got from the club taught me to believe in myself and accept other people for whom they are.

It was also a positive outcome that the garden project served to increase the daily food security for the 15 families involved in the study. Some comments shared by the community members were:

I don't have to worry about finding enough food for my children everyday.

The gardens give us healthy food as we can plant mealies, herbs and fruit which is what our families like to eat.

I gave up my temporary job to be part of the garden project. I am happy because I feed my children healthy food and sell the extra for money.

For social work and development practitioners, a crucial step to embracing ABCD practices is to acknowledge that this critical organizing framework is a shift from focusing on the deficiencies and needs in communities. It is also a shift from the technocratic problem-solving frame of planning and implementing projects (Pan et al. 2005; Ife and Tesoriero 2006). This study corroborates Pyles' (2009) argument that by focusing on the networks and resources that already exist in the community, local people are able to realize their own potential to contribute valuably to development. It is clear from the community members' comments that reflection on their own potential to feed and sustain their families as well as constantly being aware of their own commitment and participation in the project and how this related to voluntary associations (Siyazama club) was crucial. Pyles (2009: 129) states that the significance of ABCD is community's claiming back power and eloquently reveals that: 'capacity-focused community development provides people with a different kind of opportunity to realize their

FIGURE 6.2 A grandmother cooking a meal on fire

own power'. The asset-mapping exercise provided community members with the opportunity to assess their own knowledge and skills and their valuable contribution to the economic development initiative.

Evidently asset-based community development provides the framework for community members to confidently value local knowledge. Sadly however, an area that has been overlooked and always been given scant attention in the development discourse is valuing indigenous knowledge systems (Ife and Tesoriero 2006). Mtshali et al. (2012) argue that indigenous knowledge systems have the potential to positively contribute to the sustainability of community-based projects. In the focus group sessions, community members also identified the voluntary associations (Siyazama club) to which they belonged and the team approach with the students and academic staff from the university as important assets that empowered them in the implementation of the garden project. This is elaborated in the discussion of the theme on reflections on team meetings.

Building partnerships for change

Building partnerships and the need to constantly nurture relationships in communities is a pivotal part of ABCD (Mathie and Cunninghman 2005; Ledwith 2005). The community members revealed in the focus groups that they learnt to value the existing stakeholders that already provided valuable services in Bhambayi. During the planning phase community members engaged with the councillor and successfully negotiated the use of vacant land as the site for the garden project. Additionally the voluntary associations (such as the Siyathuthuka crèche, Meals On Wheels and Phoenix Settlement Trust) which were manufactured resources existing in Bhambayi were perceived as valuable. Community members were able to co-operate with each other and took responsibility for negotiating with each partner to provide training as well as access to funding sources for the project. Putnam (2000) reminds us that social capital represents a framework for collective action and its starting position is that social networks and relationships are key motivators for taking action proactively. Some comments shared by some of the community members were:

> In team meetings weekly, it was good to talk about people who could help us with the garden project.

> I was excited because I enjoyed the challenge of meeting people who were active in other projects in the community. It gave me a chance to learn and grow from them.

> I liked the idea that we were not told what to do but we were left to do the project ourselves.

> The students and their supervisor were always there with us but we were doing the work like professionals do.

In the training sessions students conducted in phase one, community members were enabled to work independently with minimal interference from the social work students and researcher. This platform served to help community members to reflect more holistically on their community assets and the existing project experiences by active stakeholders in Bhambayi. This critical reflexivity on asset mapping helped the members demonstrate their openness to new ways of accessing support from existing resources in the community. Clearly members' comments reflect that by valuing existing local skills in the community, the quality of interpersonal interactions (existing project leaders, counsellor, social work students and researcher) improved. Another important theme that community members identified as enhancing ABCD practice was linking resources for the project from outside the community. This theme is discussed further below.

Linking resources from outside the community

Writers such as Swanepoel and de Beer (2006), Ife and Tesoriero (2006), Mathie and Cunningham (2005) and Weyers (2011) agree that a vital component of ABCD is networking and working in solidarity with the stakeholders outside of that community. What stood out in the stories shared by community members in the in-depth interviews is the role of particular organizations such as the Department of Agriculture, the Department of Social Development, The Inanda Child Welfare and eThekwini Municipality who played a significant part in investing in the garden project either through training, consultation sessions on Non-Profit Organization (NPO) registration and provision of material resources. Mathie and Cunningham (2005) make the point that in ABCD practice it is important for communities to recognize and make connections with agencies outside of the community and with those who are interested in adding value to the project. An important point to note is that these external agencies were contacted only once the community members had already demonstrated their planning and organizational skills and were able to mobilize capacity based on phase three of the research process. Some comments shared were:

> It was clear that agencies in Inanda understand the problems, issues, strengths and needs in Bhambayi and were able to help us with resources.

> We valued the guidance we got to get on NPO registration. We are so proud that Siayzama is now a recognized organization.

> Planning and working on the project together, I have learnt to be positive about people and, I have gained knowledge and skills that will stay with me forever.

> The social workers in Inanda were very supportive towards us. It felt good to get help because I'm now familiar with most things to manage the project.

Through the facilitation of the garden project using ABCD community members revealed that they were able to gain insight into how a synergy could be created for successful outcomes. At the outset community members were able to see the transparent, empowering and partnership-based approach that is fundamental to participatory action research.

Pyles (2009) makes an important point that since research partnerships are elusive and complex, power imbalances are seldom eradicated. In this study power differentials were neutralized as there was a balance of roles and responsibilities in the facilitation of the community garden project by all stakeholders involved (students, researcher and community members). The benefits of this triadic relationship are manifest in the supportive opportunities to enhance community members' skills, values and knowledge and therefore the potential for them to own and sustain economic development projects in practice (Mathie and Cunningham 2005: 177).

Conclusion

Asset-based community development provides a valuable organizing framework for social workers and development practitioners seeking to increase social capital for economic development projects. This chapter provides insight into community members' community work practice experiences through the implementation of a garden project using ABCD. The central premise of this paper is that ABCD strategies can help community members to engage in a process of continuous capacity development and personal reflection and to effectively process and respond to the challenges of economic development project practice learning. This study highlights that asset-mapping, building on existing relationships within the community and linking with agencies outside of the community were useful ABCD practices for the garden project. It is important for social workers to consider Mathie and Cunningham's (2005) important point that ABCD practices makes power, inequality and transformational possibilities the foci of concern, thus suggesting that priority is placed on collaborative efforts for economic development that makes best use of the community's own resource base. In sum the fundamental principle of ABCD is to mobilize assets in partnership with community members, associations within and outside the community in order to sustain economic development efforts (Pan et al. 2005).

QUESTIONS FOR REFLECTION

- Why is the process of networking and relationship building so important in community organizing?
- Discuss the opportunities and challenges to building social capital in communities.

Note

Figures 6.1 and 6.2 were taken as part of the garden project of which Tanusha Raniga was project leader.

References

Baines, D. (2007) 'Anti-oppressive social work practice: fighting for space, fighting for change', in D. Baines (ed.) *Doing Anti-oppressive Practice: Building Transformative Politicized Social Work,* Halifax: Fernwood Publishing.
Chikadzi, V. and Pretorius, E. (2011) 'Community participation in income-generating projects: an evaluative study', *The Social Work Practitioner-researcher,* 23(1): 39–56.
Department of Welfare and Population Development (1997), *White Paper for Social Welfare,* Pretoria: Government Printers.
Desai, A. (2007) 'Taylorism and Mbekism', *Journal of Development Studies,* 37(2): 272–85.
Fisher, W.F. and Ponniah, T. (2003) *Another World is Possible: Popular Alternatives to Globalisation at the World Social Forum,* London: Zed Books.
Frye, I. (2007) 'The "second economy" as intellectual sleight of hand', *Africanus, Journal of Development Studies* 37(2): 175–90.
Ife, J. and Tesoriero, F. (2006) *Community Development: Community-based Alternatives in an Age of Globalisation,* 3rd edn, Place: Pearson Education Australia.
Kretzmann, J. and McKnight, J. (1993) *Building Communities from the Inside Out: A Path toward Finding and Mobilizing a Community's Assets,* Chicago, IL: ACTA Publications.
Korten, D. C. (1980) 'Community organization and rural development: a learning process approach', *Public Administration Review,* 40(5): 480–511.
Leach, F (1995) 'Development projects and their host institutions: are they compatible?' *International Review of Education,* 41(5): 459–79.
Ledwith, M. (2005) *Community Development: A Critical Approach,* Bristol, UK: Policy Press.
Mathie, A. and Cunningham, G. (2005) 'Who is driving development? Reflections on the transformative potential of asset-based community development', *Canadian Journal of Development Studies,* 26(1): 175–86.
Mtshali, M., Raniga, T. and Khan, S. (2012) 'IKS, poverty alleviation and sustainability of community-based programmes and projects – a case study of Inanda in the urban renewal programme of eThekwini (Durban)', (accepted for publication by *ISA – International Sociological Association* (ISA RC07).
Pan, R.J., Littlefield D., Valladolid, S.G., Tapping, P.J. and West, D.C. (2005) 'Building healthier communities for children and families: applying asset-based community development to commuity pediatrics', *Pediatrics,* 115(4): 1185–87, American Academy of Pediatrics.
Patel, L. (2005) *Social Welfare and Social Development in South Africa,* Cape Town: Oxford University Press.
Putnam, R. (2000) *Bowling Alone: The Collapse and Revival of American Community,* New York: Simon and Schuster.
Pyles, L. (2009) *Progressive Community Organising: A Critical Approach for a Globalising World,* New York: Routledge, Taylor & Francis Group.
Raniga, T. and Simpson, B. (2002) 'Community participation: rhetoric or reality?' *Social Work/Maatskaplike Werk,* 38(2): 182–92.
Raniga, T. and Simpson, B. (2011) 'Poverty, HIV/AIDS and the old age pension: an analysis of older persons in Bhambayi, South Africa', *Development Southern Africa Journal,* 28(1): 75–85.
Raniga, T. 'Book review of Weyers, M.L. (2011) "The Theory and Practice of Community Work: A Southern African Perspective", Keurkopie: Potchefstroom, 2nd edn,' *The Social Work Practitioner-Researcher,* 23(2): 262–3.

Sewpaul, V. (2006) 'The global–local dialectic: challenges for African scholarship and social work in a post-colonial world' *British Journal of Social Work,* 36(3): 419–34.

Sheehan, G. (2003) *Building the Mercado Central: Asset-Based Development and Community Entrepreneurship,* Evanston, IL: Institute for Policy Research, Northwestern University.

Smit, W. (2006) 'Understanding the complexitities of informal settlements: insights from Cape Town', in M. Huchzermeyer, KaramAly, *Informal Settlements: A Perpetual Challenge?* Cape Town: UCT Press.

Stephney, P. and Popple, K. (2008) *Social Work and the Community: A Critical Context for Practice,* Basingstoke: Palgrave Macmillan.

Stringer, E.T. (1999) 'Principles of community-based action research', *Action Research,* Thousand Oaks, CA: Sage Publications.

Swanepoel, H. (2002) *Community Development: Putting Plans into Action,* South Africa, Juta and Co, Ltd.

Swanepoel, H. and de Beer, F. (2006), *Community Development: Breaking the Cycle of Poverty.* 4th edn, Cape Town: Formeset Printers.

United Nations (1981) *Popular Participation as a Strategy for Promoting Communitylevel Action and National Development* New York: United Nations.

Weyers, M. (2011) *The Theory and Practice of Community Work: A South African Perspective,* 2nd edn, Keurkopie Potchefstroom, South Africa.

7

PARTICIPATORY LEARNING OF COMMUNITY WORK IN AN E-LEARNING COURSE

Anne Karin Larsen and Grete Oline Hole

Introduction

Is it possible to construct an online course in community work that manages to give students the experience of being in a community setting? Where the community work method is visible in the construction of the course and through interaction between the participants? Where the core principles and values of community work – participation, democracy and empowerment – are expressed throughout the course, not only through the readings but through participation and co-construction of knowledge in the virtual classroom? These were the questions asked by the partners[1] in the Social Work-Virtual Campus (SW-VirCamp) Consortium of Higher Education Institutions (HEI) when they started to develop the online course in 2008.[2] These questions led to our research question, 'what is the best way to construct a learning arena in community work that demonstrates the use of community work theory and method including participatory, emancipatory and democratic spaces for co-construction of knowledge in an e-learning environment?'

This chapter starts by describing the course, 'community work from an international perspective'. We look at its structure and the philosophy underlying the learning process. Participatory action research/action learning followed two cohorts of students in 2010 and 2011. Results from the students' surveys, reflections and coursework are analysed in the light of the intentions underpinning the course, and the roles, skills and core principles of community work.

Community work from an international perspective

The students who started the course in 2010 came from nine higher education institutions in Europe, representing eight countries. The following year, students came from eleven higher education institutions, representing twelve countries, which this time also included Malawi, Russia, the Komi Republic and Turkey. In both cohorts, two-thirds of the students were female, most of them studying for bachelor degrees, although not all in social work studies. Some were professional social workers with experience of community work. The age span of the students was from 20–39 years. Some students had previous experience of community work but fewer than half the students had participated in e-learning courses before.

Structuring the course

The course of 15 ECTS[3] credits was developed by academic staff from social work educational programmes belonging to 12 institutions in Europe.[4] The course lasted 19 weeks and ran parallel to other courses the students were following. The curriculum plan was competence based (Agten 2010; Kennedy et al. 2007) focusing on three main competences: methods and theories in community work, cooperation and professional development (SW-VirCamp Curriculum plan 2010, 2011).

The course was arranged in the learning management system 'its learning'. From previous online teaching, we knew how to structure courses with students and teachers from different countries to enhance the desired outcomes (Larsen et al. 2007; Hole et al. 2010). A clear structure is important when students with different holidays, exam periods and semester duration are following the same course and are expected to collaborate. An overview of the workload, tasks and readings was given at the course start and the students made a plan for their work on the course. Weekly bulletins gave information about the work to be done and linked up with a detailed programme for the whole course period.

A virtual book with learning material including short screen lectures, audio-visual triggers and a community case contributed to active learning (Larsen et al. 2010). One of the main assignments in the course was group-based and the students engaged in making a project plan after mapping the situation in the community case. The case was constructed in the 'Green Park Community blog', starting with a video of the gardener, introducing some of the people and activities taking place in the Park. Maja, the young girl who started the blog, invites people in the community to present their ideas on 'how to make this a better place'. Some features in the 'local' newspaper address issues in the Green Park Community based on interviews with politicians, public service officers, neighbours and other stakeholders. A map view and text view showing records over a six-month period made the blog navigation easy (see Figures 7.1 and 7.2). The community case helped the students to relate theories to practice. When they mapped the Park, they experienced this as a 'real' community blog presenting true-life issues (Larsen et al. 2011).

To trigger participation and discussion among students and between students and teachers asynchronic discussion forums were used: one for discussions about the content in the course, and another for social 'chat' in an online café. Teacher-led real time group meetings, with seven to nine students, were held in a synchronic chat room every second week, focusing on the tasks and readings the students were

FIGURE 7.1   Green Park Community Blog, text view

FIGURE 7.2   Green Park Community Blog, map view

working on. The synchronic chats were important in giving students a feeling of connection and of being in the same classroom. The students presented their papers in an e-portfolio which was completely transparent for all participants and they used an open blog for reflection on their learning. Teachers' feedback on tasks was open to all course members, allowing sharing of knowledge to be an important part of the classroom. The final assessment consisted of some of the tasks students had been working on during the course. In the last three weeks, they had time to improve their papers before delivering their final assignments, and both individual and group tasks were assessed.

Participatory learning

The pedagogy was based on participatory and student centred learning. The 'Five-Stage Community Organization Model for Health Promotion' (Bracht et al. 1999) triggered the idea of constructing a course that demonstrated community work through participation, action, critical reflection and learning in an online context. The background to the course structure of tasks and supervision was the emancipatory and consciousness-raising pedagogy inspired by Freire (2008), and democracy building through participatory learning-by-doing (Dewey 1966). Critical reflection is seen as a core competence in community work (Ledwith 2005; Payne and Askeland 2008: 31–45) and the students were encouraged to reflect on their own learning process as well as the new knowledge gained during the course.

By raising questions, stimulating discussions, responding to and commenting on tasks in a transparent classroom, both teachers and students gradually participated in creating what Wenger (1998) calls a community of practice (see also chapter four in this book). The tasks students were set to do were meant to trigger both their reading of community work theory and their understanding of methodology through practice. They began to explore the concept 'community', both through the literature and by reflecting on what community meant to them. Inspired by Roehleder et. al. (2008) students made a drawing of their own community and discussed and compared their drawings with a student from another country. The next task was to write an academic paper related to community work and participation or empowerment. The main coursebook was Tesoriero (2010). To learn about community mapping (McKnight and Kretzmann 2005) students were asked to explore the Green Park Community blog and describe and analyze what they noticed. Who used the park, what were their interests and concerns, capability, assets and needs? After this, ideas for community work projects were discussed and the students decided on a plan for further work. Searching for literature and learning from similar projects by studying the methods used was part of the preparation. The project groups arranged at least one meeting with the 'stakeholders' in the Green Park, to hear their concerns and interests and to make sure they developed a plan from a bottom-up perspective. This was arranged as a role-play on Skype. Later project plans were written, using Google.doc as a tool for co-writing. An important skill for community workers is to be able to communicate and address the public. To acquire these skills, students presented their project in the local electronic newspaper, the 'Europe Magazine', constructed for this course as a blog, as shown in Figure 7.3.

Participatory action research/action learning

Led by our research questions and to strengthen participatory learning by involving the participants in course evaluation, participatory action research/action learning (Reason and Bradbury 2008) followed the planning process during the courses in 2010 and 2011. Didactical and reflective methods, focusing on shared knowledge and learning, and the action research spiral (Kemmis and McTaggart 2000: 597) were introduced. The data collection for our research started with e-mailed questions to the teacher group planning the course asking them for a brief response

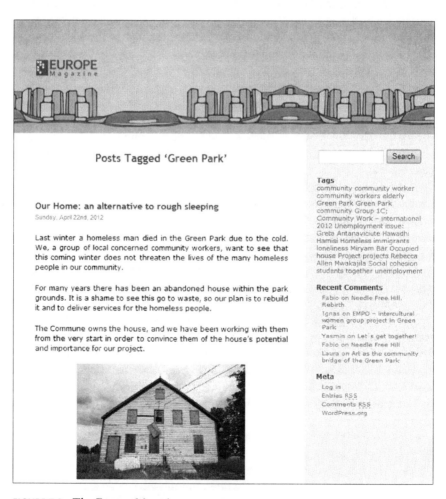

FIGURE 7.3 The Europe Magazine

to our research question (Table 7.1). Their written notes were followed up with a focus group interview exploring these concepts at the beginning of the first teacher meeting. Although teachers found it frustrating to have to respond to the question, the focus group interview turned out to be an inspiration for further work with the curriculum (see chapter four). Three more interviews were arranged later with the teacher group at different stages of the project. As shown in Table 7.1, participants were given transcripts of the interviews to read and comment upon. The development of the course, as well as the first pilot course, was adjusted following the discussion during these sessions.

TABLE 7.1 The action research process with teachers 2009–10 and students 2010–11

Community Work Course Teachers' process 2009–10	Community Work Course Survey with students in the CW 2010 and 2011 course
The working group members' reflection on the research questions presented by email, N/n=10*	
Focus group interview with the course working group before developing the Curriculum Plan, N/n=10	
Transcript sent to teachers for feedback	
Group interview with the teacher group before the course starts N/n=8	Start survey with students 2010: N=37/n=25 2011: N=36/n=33
Transcript sent to teachers for feedback	Results reported to students asking for feedback and suggestions for questions for the next survey
Group interview with the teachers online in the middle of the course N=8/n=6	Midway survey with students 2010: N=24/n=22 2011: N=33/n=25
Transcript sent to teachers for feedback	Results reported to students asking for feedback and suggestions for questions for the next survey
	Final survey with students
Group interview at the end of the pilot course N=8/n=7	2010: N=23/n=19 2011: N=33/n=22
Evaluation report	Evaluation report

*N=total population, n=number of respondents/participants

Throughout the pilot course in 2010, the experiences of the students were followed by action research. Ethical considerations according to the Norwegian Data Protection Authority were adhered to, and only material and survey results from students who gave their written informed consent were used for research. Three surveys were presented to students, in the beginning, midway and at the end of the course (for more details about the questions and focus of the surveys see Larsen et al. 2011: 16). Summaries of the results were given to the students and they were asked for their reactions and to suggest questions for the next survey. The same procedure was followed when 36 students started in 2011, as illustrated in Table 7.1. In the following, data from student surveys, reflection notes and assignments are included in the analysis of results and discussed in the context of learning the community worker's roles and skills.

The essence of being a community worker

Core principles of community work are participation, empowerment, human rights, critical reflection and community building (Hutchinson 2010). The role of community worker is multifaceted and demands complex skills. In a learning situation, the complexity is limited to applying skills and methods to a virtual case in a virtual classroom. Tesoriero (2010) claims that focusing on competences in discussing roles and skills mostly addresses tasks that a worker should be able to perform and does not do justice to the complexity of real community work. He maintains this should be challenged by finding other ways of defining practice and skills. As in Figure 7.4, he suggests clustering what the community worker does into five groups of roles called: 'the facilitative, educational, representational, technical and critical questioning' (Tesoriero 2010: 259-60). In the following section, we analyze praxis in the light of these roles and skills.

Facilitative roles

Included in the 'facilitative roles' are 'social animation, mediation and negotiation, support, building consensus, group facilitation, utilization of skills and resources, and organizing'. The concept 'social animation' includes the ability to inspire others, create enthusiasm for the project, activate and stimulate participation, and create energy and motivation for the work that has to be done (Tesoriero 2010: 260–1). To be a good facilitator demands good communication skills, the ability to deal with and negotiate different interests, understanding different perspectives and relating to different stakeholders and target groups and sometimes being a translator or mediator of different views. As in earlier SW-VirCamp courses, great emphasis was put on promoting this in an online learning environment (Hole et al. 2010).

The students experienced the teachers as facilitators in the way they performed their role as leaders in the classroom. They provided frequent feedback and engaged in initiatives to stimulate activities and enthusiasm among students, and acted as a

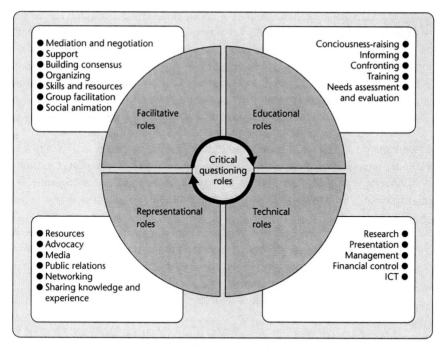

● Mediation and negotiation
● Support
● Building consensus
● Organizing
● Skills and resources
● Group facilitation
● Social animation

Facilitative roles

Educational roles

Conciousness-raising ●
Informing ●
Confronting ●
Training ●
Needs assessment ●
and evaluation

Critical questioning roles

Representational roles

Technical roles

● Resources
● Advocacy
● Media
● Public relations
● Networking
● Sharing knowledge and experience

Research ●
Presentation ●
Management ●
Financial control ●
ICT ●

FIGURE 7.4   Community work practice roles (inspired by Figure 11.2 in Tesoriero 2010: 260)

fellow among the students as exemplified by citations from two students in the 2011 end survey (Q30):

> The teachers were more like fellows and guides and never used their power to force us even when we were missing the deadlines; they were more about motivating us […] and many times empowered me to do good work giving me a lot of support.

> I felt there wasn't really a power relation. It was as if they were equal to us. I also felt I could speak to the teachers. Also the fact that we could call the teachers by their first name gave me that idea. But I must say the teachers kept well to the roles of teacher and coach.

The teachers wanted the students to be empowered through active participation in the learning process and by group collaboration (see chapter four in this book). Group participation in a learning situation is often experienced as a challenging process, especially for students in online courses (McConnell 2005). It demands involvement, negotiation and can be more time-consuming than individual work. The quality of the group processes is often mirrored by the result and product. In the community work course, students were challenged by co-writing in small groups, by having paired dialogue on Skype and by working in project groups with five to six students from different countries. All these activities tested their ability to organize, take initiative and coordinate their work, and were meant to stimulate practical learning in community work as well as awareness of cultural issues. Some students had no experience of participative and collaborative learning when they started the course. When we analyzed the students' reflection notes on their learning from the Green Park project,[1] we noticed how earlier negative experiences of group collaboration were an obstacle for some when they started this task. One of the students admitted to having a negative attitude to working in groups as he thought it was characterized by 'slowness and encourages laziness'. However, when he started to collaborate with the other students, his attitude changed and he recognized the importance of collaboration and saw what they could learn from each other.

> To my surprise, most of the group members were positive about this, and I was forced to like them. After our first Skype meeting, I was completely amazed by the cooperation we had. It was the first of its kind in my life and I enjoyed the chat. I remember being the one who asked for the second meeting [...] If you ask me now what my attitude towards group work is, I will always be positive.
>
> *(M UiN27, 2011)*

Students also managed to link their own working in groups to the community work process. Groups which did not appoint a leader in the beginning struggled with sharing the workload and directing their work. Students who took the lead in a group learned a lot from this and developed personally by doing so. One of the students expressed it in this way:

> Sometimes we need support but other times we really need to wake up and make an effort. [...] Being a chairman of the meeting was challenging and difficult but I liked doing it because I thought that it would make me learn a lot as a CW. I realized the importance of participation and that a project couldn't be done just by the CW, not even the design of the project.[...] Never forget to have structure and pick up people's ideas and discuss them.
>
> *(M UCM10, 2011)*

The experience of the students was that good collaboration is based on respect, trust in each other, stimulating differences of opinion and not only agreement, motivation, setting 'S.M.A.R.T.' outcomes (Specific, Measurable, Attainable, Realistic and Timely, see http://topachievement.com/smart.html). They learned that sharing personal obstacles can obviate misunderstanding and a poor atmosphere in the group, and that it is important to avoid the temptation to do the work yourself when the group does not work properly, because you understand that the group is the most important tool. Some students understood they had to step back to allow others to do their part of the job.

To sum up, students learned: to organize group and stakeholder meetings online; to use each other's skills and knowledge by working together; to inspire each other by creating enthusiasm for the project they were developing; and to find different ways to motivate each other. By working together on the case they became dependent on each other's contributions and activated each other's participation.

The educational roles

A community worker should always have a plan for sustainability before withdrawing from a project and leaving further development to the other participants. During the process the community worker can act as a teacher or coach in project organization. Community work is an ongoing learning process for everyone involved including the community worker. Practical and psychological support is important and is part of the process of empowering the community and the citizens. Educational roles include, 'consciousness-raising, informing, confronting, training, needs assessment and evaluation' (Tesoriero 2010: 268). The educational role can mean being 'a guide on the side' by assisting and accompanying, giving feedback and information needed to help others understand the situation in the community.

The importance of these skills became obvious during the course. When some students did not participate as expected, or had to leave the course for personal reasons, this caused problems for other students. In some cases, the teacher had to confront students having problems about the consequences, reorganize the groups or just be supportive to the students who continued to work. It was, however, best when students managed to handle the situation themselves. One student suggested that a contract should have been drawn up among students at the beginning to clarify things and to prevent problems occurring later on. Contracting skills are important in social work but are not always remembered in a practical situation. Surveys showed that some students would have appreciated more teacher support during this process. Following this feedback, the tutors now recommend that students elect a group leader for a period of time and come to an agreement about a progress plan.

During collaboration, students learned to express conflicting views and to solve these by clarifying their expectations of each other. From their reflection notes it seems that they managed to do this in a critical but respectful way. They expressed it with these words: 'be patient and stay calm; be flexible in coping with challenges, be truthful, active and critical; manage to cope with contradictions'. This also demonstrates the students' understanding of leadership skills. Students gained skills in needs assessment when they mapped the Green Park Community, and when they later had to address stakeholders' concerns in a meeting.

To sum up, by being a 'guide on the side' and by letting the students solve their own problems, the teachers offered students the opportunity for some important learning through collaboration and reflection. This can be a good strategy in many situations and is transferable to the educational role of a community worker.

Representational roles

During the course, students supported each other with 'knowledge sharing' in a transparent classroom and helping each other to obtain the resources needed to solve problems (i.e. the use of doodle.com, to make appointments). These two functions are included in the representational roles together with 'advocacy, using the media, public relations and public presentation, and networking' (Tesoriero 2010: 272). Networking in community work means establishing contact and creating alliances among people with different power, positions, skills and knowledge that can help promote change. A community worker starting to work in a new community needs to find people who can act as 'door-openers' to the different arenas and groups of people. This is part of the networking process. When planning the stakeholder meeting, the students had to search for this kind of people. Making the project known to the public can be a strategy for increasing contacts and involving more people. The students did this when they published in the 'Europe Magazine', and they got training in some of the skills related to representational roles.

Technical roles

Mapping a community includes researching demographic data, carrying out surveys and analyzing findings. The students got some training in this when they entered the Green Park Community blog and formed an overview of who was using the park, the 'inhabitants' contact with others both inside and outside the community and which positive or conflicting issues the 'inhabitants' were raising in the blog. Tesoriero (2010: 275) states that technical roles include 'research, verbal and written presentation, management and financial control.' We see the need for adding ICT competence to the list as community workers will need to promote projects and communicate with participants. Examples from 'the Arab Spring' and the 'Facebook revolution' (Hauslohner 2011), where the Internet played an important part in community changes, show how powerful the Internet can be (for more information about the Arab Spring see chapter 16 in this book).

During the course, students learned to use Internet resources in many different ways and 82 per cent of respondents in the end survey (Q8, 2011) indicated that they had developed ICT skills during the course which would be useful in their future work as social/community workers. Learning to use technology in a professional setting is a bonus of online courses. There is increasing use of ICT in health and social services and learning to handle these tools in an ethical and user-friendly way is important (Ley 2012).

Community work management means mobilizing people to take part in the change process. The students had to mobilize within their own group and plan how they would mobilize people in the Green Park Community. To deliver a common plan for a community work project, they had to address the group process and how each of them contributed to the common product. The question of leadership became important and students chose different models. Some groups had what Ronnby (2009: 126) calls the 'leading light', a person the others had confidence in who took responsibility for leading the group work, but, as we have seen, not all groups decided to have a group leader and these groups struggled with decision making. When working with the project plan the students arranged several meetings, wrote minutes, summarized decisions and presented papers. Part of the project plan was to estimate a budget for the project which is the starting point for financial control. Students found this quite difficult as they had little experience or knowledge about this. All these activities provided them with training in technical roles.

Critical questioning role

The critical questioning role, which imply being a critically reflective practitioner in ongoing practice, influences all the roles already presented. It means raising critical questions without necessarily being negative. 'In a critical reflection approach [...] the specific purpose of the reflective process is to expose or unsettle dominant assumptions with the expressed purpose of challenging and changing dominant power relations' (Fook and Askeland 2006: 47). A community worker has to learn to handle a variety of challenges related to conflict, information, communication, regulations and laws (Tesoriero 2010: 283). These can be conflicts related to different stakeholders and issues that are based on different values and ethics. For most of the students, critical reflection was a new and challenging thing to do but also rewarding when they managed, as one of them expressed 'through reflection and sharing ideas I have learned to critically analyse everything I saw, read and heard. In the end we always come up with new ideas and understanding which I think was good, unlike "spoon feeding" information to students' (from Q11, 2011 midway survey).

Even though the roles undertaken by a community worker are multifaceted, many people have many of the skills needed without being trained community workers. However community work demands the ability to combine many different functions or to establish and coordinate a well-functioning team of people with the necessary skills.

There was an explicit focus in this course on adding a critical view of the teaching and learning process and linking the theory to the practice of the roles.

Participation, democracy and empowerment

As outlined in chapter four the teachers hoped to create an arena for 'co-construction of knowledge' and mutual learning among all the actors. In the final surveys the students were asked how well this had been achieved. The two citations below show that the students experienced a very positive, collaborative learning situation:

Cooperation between teachers and students made this classroom a learning space creating a climate of solidarity and cooperation conducive to developing the skills of each. No word could express better these 19 weeks than 'co-construction of knowledge'.

(From Q36, 2010 end survey)

This course is totally different from the traditional way of learning where the teachers just teach and the students study and have an exam. In this course both students and teachers have an active role and also cooperate, so it becomes an arena for co-construction of knowledge.

(From Q27, 2011 end survey)

What the student is explaining here is how she/he experiences the difference between what Freire (2008: 72) calls the 'banking' concept of education where 'education becomes an act of depositing, in which the students are the depositories and the teacher is the depositor' (ibid), and the emancipatory way of learning in the online course. By the way the teachers acted in this course, they created an open classroom where learning went both ways and among all participants. The teachers' ambitions for the course were to model the democratic, participatory and empowering principles of community work. These principles are all connected to the issues of power. Before the course started the question about how students could influence the content of the course were discussed. The teachers found it difficult to involve the students in every step of the course because of the mixed group of international students belonging to different campuses. To advertise the course, a curriculum plan had to be available for students to know what they were applying for. The way the courses were structured with weekly programmes can in many ways be considered as a 'banking' way of teaching. The weekly programme added suggestions for readings, short screen lectures, and tasks to do. By encouraging students to reflect on their learning, they were inspired to relate what they read and heard to their own context and praxis.

The students evaluated the teachers as facilitators very positively, and felt teachers communicated regularly and gave support to the students. There are visible differences in role performance between teachers and students but, as one student said,

The interaction is democratic in most cases. However, there is a need for all the students to play their role as students who are willing to learn and show submission, as such the teachers sometimes showed that they have the power to make decisions and everybody could follow. This was good and it showed good leadership skills.

(From Q30, 2011 end survey)

This citation probably shows that it is difficult for both teachers and students to get rid of the traditional 'banking' way of education. Higher educational systems are structured systems testing competences and students want to get good marks and to fill the expectations presented in a curriculum plan. In a complex world, it is important to learn how to find the information you need and to strengthen creative power and critical thinking to become a 're-creator', to use the terminology of Freire (2008: 75). This can be encouraged by a dialogic educational praxis and 'learning-by-doing'. Creating good conditions for dialogue to take place needs 'mutual regard and trust, leading to an openness to having one's own ideas examined, as well as examining the ideas of others [...] have to suspend our learning to unlearn and relearn' (Ledwith and Springett 2010: 138).

Participation and empowerment are two closely related concepts which address an anti-oppressive practice (Dominelli 2002; Tesoriero 2010). Empowerment is the process of enhancing individual or community capacity and encouraging participation in groups and society. For some of the students this concept was new. The students were reading and writing about empowerment and participation and from their reflections we learn how they experienced their own empowering process and how some of them tried to empower their peers through active participation. 'The course promoted the empowerment of students, giving a space where we could freely express our opinions and experiences, and was democratic in the sense that all could participate actively and free' (from Q38, 2010 end survey).

Conclusion

Returning to the critical questions presented in the introduction, did we succeed in constructing a community work course that gave the students an experience of being in a community setting? By analysing the students' learning process through the community workers' roles as presented by Tesoriero (2010) we have seen that the course gave the students the opportunity to practise the different roles and to gain skills by working with the case and by participating in collaborative processes. Working with tools and tasks the students used their own imagination, creativity and knowledge, participated in collective action through group work, and developed their professional competences by reflection on their learning. The facilitative roles were modelled by the teachers' being a 'guide on the side', stimulating discussions and creating a rich learning environment which included a variety of theoretical and practical situations related to community work. The students' reflection notes indicate that by participating in this online learning community, the reflective spiral of action learning from teachers and students promoted skills for a community worker.

QUESTIONS FOR REFLECTION

- How can professionalism be contradictory to community work and its core values?
- How does your educational programme stimulate your professional development as a community worker?
- What should the power relation between student and teacher be?

Notes

1. Partners in the project were HEI from: Bergen University College, Norway; Jönköping University, Sweden; Inholland University of Applied Sciences, the Netherlands; K.H.Kempen University College, Belgium, University of Complutense, Spain; Miguel Torga University College, Portugal; Mannheim University of Applied Sciences, Germany; Bodø University College, Norway; University of Liepaja, Latvia; Lusofona University, Portugal; Swansea University, United Kingdom and Mittweida University of Applied Sciences, Germany.
2. Development of the course was one of the aims for the SW-VirCamp project funded by the EACEA Lifelong Learning Programme – Call for Proposals 2008 (EAC/30/07). Reference number: 142767-LLP-1-2008-1-NO-ERASMUS-EVC. This chapter reflects the views only of the author, and the Commission cannot be held responsible for any use which may be made of the information contained therein.
3. ECTS is a standard for comparing the study attainment and performance of students of higher education across the European Union and other collaborating European countries. For successfully completed studies, ECTS credits are awarded. One academic year corresponds to 60 ECTS-credits that are equivalent to 1500–1800 hours of study in all countries irrespective of standard or qualification type and is used to facilitate transfer and progression throughout the Union. Online. Available HTTP: http://ec.europa.eu/education/lifelong-learning-policy/ects_en.htm (accessed 3 September 2012).
4. The same institutions as in Note 1.
5. The students (2011) had a task 10b with the following text: 'Make a reflection in your blog about your experience collaborating with other students. In what way did you contribute to the group work? What did you learn from the others?'

References

Agten, J. (2010) 'Bologna as a frame for Competence Based Learning and Supervision', in O.Chytil, G. J. Friesenhahn, F.W. Seibel and J. Windheuser (eds) (2010) *Social Professions for a Social Europe,* ECSPRESS, Universitas Ostraviensis. Bruno, Czech Republik: ALBERT.

Bracht, N., Kingsbury, L. and Rissel, C. (1999) 'A five-stage community organization model for health promotion', in N. Bracht (ed.) *Health Promotion at the Community Level: New Advances,* 2nd edn, Thousand Oaks, California: SAGE Publications.

Dewey, J. (1966) *Democracy and Education: An Introduction to the Philosophy of Education,* New York: The Macmillan Company/The Free Press.

Dominelli, L. (2002) *Anti-oppressive Social Work Theory and Practice,* Basingstoke, Hampshire, England: Palgrave McMillan.

Fook, J. and Askeland, G.A. (2006) 'The "critical" in critical reflection', in S. White, J. Fook and F. Gardner (eds) *Critical Reflection in Health and Social Care,* Maidenhead, Berkshire: Open University Press.

Freire, P. (2008) *Pedagogy of the Oppressed,* New York: Continuum.

Hauslohner, A (2011) 'Is Egypt about to have a Facebook Revolution?' Cairo: *World Time*, 24 January 2011. Online. Available HTTP: http://www.time.com/time/world/ article/0,8599,2044142,00.html (accessed 10 August 2012).

Hole, G.O., Larsen, A.K. and Hoem, J. (2010) 'Promoting the good e-teacher: didactical choices when developing e-pedagogical competences', *Seminar.net – International Journal of Media, Technology and Lifelong Learning,* 6 (3). Online. Available HTTP: http:// seminar.net/index.php/volume-6-issue-3-2010 (accessed 3 September 2012).

Hutchinson, G.S. (2010) *Samfunnsarbeid. Mobilisering og deltakelse i sosialfaglig arbeid* [Community Work. Mobilisation and Participation in Social Work], Oslo: Gyldendal Norsk Forlag.

Kemmis, S. and McTaggart, R. (2000) 'Participatory action research', in N.K. Denzin and Y.S. Lincoln (eds) *Handbook of Qualitative Research,* Thousand Oaks, Calif.: Sage Publications.

Kennedy, D., Hyland, A. and Ryan, N. (2007) *Writing and Using Learning Outcomes,* Cork: Cork University. Online. Available HTTP: http://sss.dcu.ie/afi/docs/bologna/ writing_and_using_learning_outcomes.pdf (accessed 1 March 2013).

Larsen, A.K., Visser-Rotgans, R. and Hole, G.O. (2011) 'Teaching and learning community work online: can e-learning promote competences for future practice?' *Journal of Technology in Human Services,* 29(1): 13–32.

Larsen, A.K., Olsson, K-G. and Henriksbø, K. (eds) (2010) *Virtual Book Community Work From an International Perspective,* Bergen: SW-VirCamp Production. Online. Available HTTP: http://vircamp.net/cw [password protected] (accessed 19 November 2012).

Larsen, A.K., Hole, G.O. and Fahlvik, M. (2007) 'Developing a Virtual Book – Material for Virtual Learning Environments', *Seminar.net – International journal of Media, Technology and Lifelong Learning,* 3 (3), Online. Available HTTP: http://seminar.net/index.php/ volume-3-issue-3-2007-previousissuesmeny-121 (accessed 3 September 2012).

Ledwith, M. (2005) *Community Development, A Critical Approach,* Bristol, UK: Policy Press.

Ledwith, M. and Springett, J. (2010) *Participatory Practice. Community-based Action for Transformative Change,* Bristol, UK: The Policy Press.

Ley, T. (2012) 'New technologies for practice', in M. Gray, J. Midgley and S.A. Webb (eds) *The SAGE Handbook of Social Work,* London, UK: Sage Publications.

McConnel, D (2005) 'Examining the dynamics of networked e-learning groups and communities', *Studies in Higher Education* 30(1): 25–42.

McKnight, J.L. and Kretzmann, J.P. (2005) 'Mapping community capacity', in M. Minkler (ed.) *Community Organizing and Community Building for Health,* New Brunswick: N.J., Rutgers University Press.

Payne, M. and Askeland, G. A. (2008) *Globalization and International Social Work, Postmodern Change and Challenge,* Aldershot: Ashgate.

Reason, P. and Bradbury, H. (2008) *The Handbook of Action Research, Participative Inquiry and Practice,* London, UK: Sage Publications.

Rohleder, P., Swartz, L., Carolissen, R., Bozalek, V. and Lebowitz, B. (2008) '"Communities isn't just about trees and shops": students from two South African universities engage in dialogue about "community" and "community work" ', *Journal of Community & Applied Social Psychology* 18: 253–67.

Ronnby, A. (2009) 'Empowering people by community building', in G. S. Hutchinson (ed.) *Community Work in the Nordic Countries – New Trends,* Oslo: Universitetsforlaget. Social Work-Virtual Campus (SW-VirCamp). Online. Available HTTP: http://www. vircamp.net (accessed 25 June 2012).

Tesoriero, F. (2010) *Community Development. Community-based Alternatives in an Age of Globalisation,* Frenchs Forest: Pearson Education Australia.

Top Achievement, Creating S.M.A.R.T Goals. Online. Available HTTP: http:// topachievement.com/smart.html (accessed 3 September 2012).

Wenger, E. (1998) *Communities of Practice. Learning, Meaning and Identity. Learning in Doing: Social, Cognitive and Computational Perspectives,* USA: Cambridge University Press.

PART 3

Power and participation in community work

8

POWER AND PARTICIPATION IN COMMUNITY WORK RESEARCH AND PRACTICE

Vishanthie Sewpaul, Ingrid Østhus and Christopher Mhone

Introduction

The community based practice and research[1] with children and youth living on the streets of Durban described in this chapter was informed by critical theory, which concerns itself with social transformation (Dominelli 2002; Mullaly 1998). To be critical does not necessarily mean being negative; it means building insights beyond our taken for granted assumptions to look 'beyond the obvious' (Williamson et al. 1982: 16). The focus is on changing power dynamics that perpetuate powerlessness and helplessness. Leonard (1990. 3) highlights the practical intent and political dimension of critical theory as he asserts that 'a critical theory without a practical dimension would be bankrupt on its own terms.'

The transformative power of critical theory lies in its capacity to interrogate the intersection between individuals and structural dynamics and how this intersection constantly shapes individual and societal consciousness (Babbie and Mouton 2001). It is about allowing people to understand the sources of their oppression and powerlessness (Freire 1970, 1973), and of their privilege (Giroux 1997; Pease 2010) particularly in relation to the intersection of key social criteria such as race, class and gender (Giroux 1997; Purdie-Vaughn and Eibach 2008; Mullaly 2010). Our objectives must thus be simultaneously directed at helping people to be emancipated from the structural constraints on their lives and from the constraints of their own thinking and taken for granted assumptions (Althusser 1971; Gramsci 1971).

Adopting a Participatory Action Research (PAR) approach (Reason and Bradbury 2008), this research sought to give participants voice and to engage them as mutual partners in taking action on the issues that impact their lives. This is consistent with Article 12 of the United Nations Convention on the Rights of the Child (1989) and regional (see Article 7 of the African Charter on the Rights and Welfare of the Child (Organisation of African Unity 1990)) and national instruments (see e.g. Section 10 of the Children's Act No 38 of 2005) which indicate that children and young people have the right to be involved in decisions that are about them. The research was conducted over a period of four years, with current work in progress, with intensive and sustained engagement with children and youth on the streets.

On critical social research, power and participation

Critical social research and participatory action research are shaped by two basic principles: 1) improving a social situation and 2) involving those most affected (Humphries 2008). Guided by these, we appreciated that: participation of the children and the youth would bring to life their creative potential and experiences; that real change starts from within people themselves through the use of their knowledge about their problems; and that this might allow them to take up advocacy initiatives on their own behalf. Critical theory seeks to understand the political nature of social phenomena (Alvesson and Sköldberg 2009) and it endorses research as a political activity (Miller and Brewer 2003). It is not enough to only understand the socio-political and cultural dynamics that impact the consciousness of people.

Critical social research and theory assert that people are not merely passive victims, and that given the right circumstances they are capable of developing strategies of resistance when faced with exploitative circumstances. It is about enabling people to realize their own power through reflection and action, to challenge structural injustices and to be agents of change (Sewpaul 2003). This is cogently enunciated by Miller and Brewer:

> Critical theory, which allows for the uncovering of power at the point at which it is exercised, has the benefit of bringing critical theory down from a rarefied atmosphere of high theory to a point where it can help the dynamics of day to day life.
>
> *(Miller and Brewer 2003: 60)*

Critical theory and critical social research are consistent with the service user movement with its emphasis on people getting to support each other, working towards change, having one's voice heard, and engaging in self-advocacy efforts (Beresford and Branfield 2006). These authors go on to argue that service users are best placed to understand themselves, their situations and how they need to be treated. However, for the most part the voices of service users have been ignored, despite them being experts of their own experiences. One of the reasons for this is the acceptance of the positivist paradigm in social work practice that emphasizes distance in professional relationships. Beresford (2003) writes about the limits of such an approach claiming that it contributes to knowledge that is likely to be distorted and unreliable. Our research and community practice approaches were designed to obtain rich and meaningful data with maximum levels of participation with children and youth living on the streets.

From the onset, even before we began the community work we recognized that meeting the requisites of authentic participation was not easy. We were aware of our dominant socialized 'expert' and power positions, that participation might be used to reflect mere tokenism to lend credibility to projects, and that participants might be co-opted into systems that de-politicize development (Williams 2004). We did not want to fall into the same traps. While we had a vision of genuine participatory encounters, the problem was how do we *do* participation and how do we make it a reality? We learnt of a project in India called Butterflies that was reported to have developed expertise in working with children in participatory ways (see http://butterflieschildrights.org). A study tour by Ingrid and Chris (co-authors on this paper) provided us with inspiration and helped us with pragmatic strategies to turn our vision of participation based on dialogue, negotiation and shared decision-making with participants into a reality (Sewpaul and Østhus 2009). But this was not without its difficulties.

Power is an extremely difficult issue to deal with in practice and all too often our identities as experts betray us. While we were aware about the importance of egalitarian relationships, we acknowledged the existence of skewed power relationships, especially when working with marginalized groups of people (Sewpaul and Østhus 2009). Foucault (1978) argued that power is complex and multifaceted; it is dynamic, fluid and exercised from multiple perspectives. Power can be used constructively and positively – not only negatively. There were times when we consciously used our power in the interests of the children and youth – for example advocating for them to have access to health care, including anti-retroviral treatment. Critically reflecting on power makes it possible to challenge and deconstruct assumptions about everyday practice. Although as social workers, we would like to believe that we work in empowering ways, there is often a lack of reflexivity that prevents us from undergoing the painful process of confronting the paternalism that frequently exists in our identities and our practices. Social workers are generally socialized into the dominant positivist paradigm, with rarefied notions of the social worker as the detached, neutral expert who knows best (Sewpaul and Østhus 2009). Such a paradigm is inconsistent with principles of critical and radical social work. The more aware we are of the complex dynamics of power, the more conscious can our efforts be to engender authentic participation and to work against the negative influences of our power. Bearing this in mind we made concerted efforts in supervision, and in process recording and journal entries to reflect on how power played out in the practice context.

It is not only our complicity in asserting power that might negate genuine participation. Service users who are socialized into dominant top-down approaches might often push us into traditional ways of working. On the challenges of promoting true participation, characterized by Arnstein's (1969) conceptions of partnership and delegated power, Chris wrote:

> Often times as a practitioner you are faced with longstanding established traditions that cripple the efforts to effectively engage with the people that

you are working with. In the case of the children and youth living on the streets, this was a challenge. Emancipatory education and practice [...] is an initiative that demands working with service users. Allowing them to be directors of the process [...]. The children and youth living on the streets are among some of the lowest ranked. The use of participatory approach with the aim of achieving real empowerment [...] was really a difficult task [...] it was even surprising to them that we wanted them to participate in every stage of the processes that we were engaging in.

It was reflexive exercises such as these, weekly group supervision and student team meetings that facilitated processes of cooperative enquiry (Reason and Bradbury 2008) that helped us to be constantly aware of our participatory aims and objectives vis-à-vis the strategies that we were adopting. This is also reflected in one of Ingrid's journal entries:

> As part of the field practice education experience Vishanthie asked that we keep journals. Constantly writing reflections on the processes and events I experienced has helped me in several ways. Firstly, it has helped me to incorporate critical thinking [...] journaling helps me to take a step back and look at situations from different perspectives. It has thus helped me to look beyond the personal problem. Secondly, it is a practical tool for self-reflection. It has helped me to constantly be aware of power dynamics, both among my colleagues and myself and the people I/we work with. It has furthermore helped me to always align what I am doing with my intentions; to scrutinize what is happening and compare with critical theories or the goal of social justice.

The research methods and sampling strategies that we adopted were consistent with those of critical social research, as reflected below.

Research methods and sampling

The study targeted children and youth living on the streets of Durban Central Business District. The key research questions were:

1. How does gender influence survival strategies of the children and youth living on the streets of Durban?
2. How are resources mobilized on the streets on a daily basis?
3. What roles do subgroups play in street life?
4. What are the experiences of violence among children and youth living on the streets?

Critical to the success of the PAR was the democratic election of a Young Leaders Development Committee (Sewpaul and Østhus 2009) that facilitated the

FIGURE 8.1 The core group of young street children that actively participated in World Social Work day

involvement of the children and youth in every step of both the quantitative and qualitative research processes. Their active participation and capacity to reflect on their life experiences contributed to their understanding of themselves, and on structures that influenced their lives, consistent with the emancipatory calls of Freire (1970, 1973); Gramsci (1971); Giroux (1997) and Mullaly (1998, 2010).

We used several methods of data collection, one of which was a social survey. The participants collaborated with us in designing the social survey; they negotiated entry into the broader networks of youth living on the streets and worked with the researchers in collecting the data. The data, which was analyzed by us, was fed back to them and they made decisions about what to do with it. We used availability and snowball sampling as children and youth that we had established regular contact with helped us to access others to participate. A total of 101 children were engaged in the survey; there were 12 spoilt questionnaires so 89 constituted the final sample.

We also used a series of weekly focus group sessions via convenience and snowball sampling; one series of groups was female only over a period of two years. Several of the Participatory Learning in Action techniques discussed by Bozalek in chapter five were used with the participants in the group sessions. The sessions were audio recorded and transcribed. On average there were eight males and five females per group in the mixed group. In addition, we used in-depth interviews, home visits where feasible and observations of street life. It is important to indicate

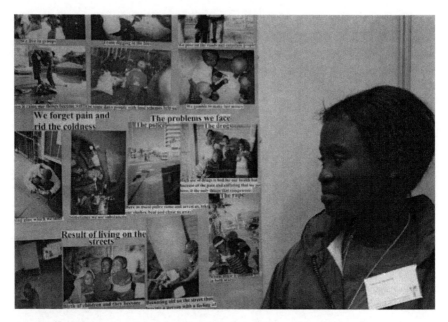

FIGURE 8.2   Children and youth presenting their life situation with a poster at the
Global Social Work Congress

that we had prolonged community engagement with the children and youth from
the beginning in 2008 when they were trained to and participated in the 34th
Global Social Work Congress that was held in Durban. They participated as on-site
ushers, street helpers for the congress delegates, workshop participants and plenary
speakers (Sewpaul and Østhus 2009), and reported that it was one of the most
validating experiences of their lives.

Our humanizing encounters over a prolonged period of engagement, the use of
triangulation with both qualitative and quantitative approaches and multiple
strategies of data collection increased the validity and reliability of the study.
Triangulation is important in social research, as Humphries (2008: 98) indicates, 'it
offers a range of perspectives on what the reality or the "truth" of a situation is'.
Although surveys do not provide in-depth information, they can be useful because
they produce 'statistics [that] are powerful in part because they are concise. Their
brevity makes them easily communicated to reporters and lawmakers who seek
information' (Reinharz cited in Humphries 2008: 151).

Although we had volumes of qualitative data we had difficulty in getting the
authorities to hear our concerns. The main reason for doing the survey was to have
information that would be easily communicated to the local authorities and the
press that we hoped would be a powerful tool in social action, one of the ethical
imperatives of critical social research. Policy makers and planners often deem
statistics to be powerful, convincing and reliable and the stories and direct reports
of children and youth to be anecdotal. Our experience showed quite the contrary

FIGURE 8.3 Drawing reflecting the experience of police round-ups and violence, by children and youth living on the streets

– those that we had sustained relationships with through qualitative research were more honest and open than those who responded to the questionnaire only. The results of the survey corroborated our qualitative findings with regard to the high levels of violence and sexual abuse inflicted on them by the Metro Police, and the high levels of violence and sexual abuse from within their own groups on the streets. It is not within the scope of this paper to provide details of the research results. See Sewpaul et al. (2012) for research results.

Ethical considerations

As this study involved dealing with sensitive information of children's and youth's life accounts, there was a constant endeavour to work within ethically required principles. Informed consent that was verbally recorded was sought from the participants and confidentiality was maintained. We used pseudonyms in all our research reporting. Consistent with the requisites of critical social research, this study combined social work practice and research. We were not outsiders to the research process. The relationship was infused with empathy, support and care and all participants were helped to deal with emotional and sensitive issues. Doing no harm was always an over-arching ethic. Ryen (2007) wrote about the limitations of an approach where we allocate fixed roles to researchers and research subjects that widen the gulf between the private and the professional in research studies. Writing on the impossibility of the separation between the personal and the professional, Bauman (1993: 19) powerfully asserts that 'away from mere "role playing", we are indeed "ourselves", and thus we and we alone are responsible for our deeds' (Bauman 1993: 19). Being a supportive human being, a professional and a researcher at the same time were integral to the research process.

An ethical challenge with focus groups is related to confidentiality. Researchers cannot guarantee confidentiality since they cannot control what group participants will say and do outside the group (Humphries 2008). Because of this, the participants in the girls-only group were given the power to decide on new participants, so that they could to some extent control the level of trust. In both groups facilitation was done carefully and sensitively, to ensure that participants did not feel compelled by others to disclose issues if they were not ready to. Solidarity, group cohesion and commonality were emphasized in both groups, to encourage the principle of *Ubuntu* (the African idea that one's humanity is recognized through one's relationship with fellow human beings) and to promote ethical handling of the issues outside of the group setting.

It was our acute understanding of the inherent power differentials amongst us, as university staff and students, and the population that we were working with that enabled us to work against an approach that might reduce participation to mere tokenism or co-option into processes that subjugates participants. We were also deeply aware of our privileged positions relative to theirs. Given our understanding of the impact of structural factors on their lives and guided by critical social research our aim was to move beyond using participation as a research technique to using it as a means of empowerment (Williams 2004), as reflected in the discussion below.

Research, community based social work and participatory social action

The focus of critical social research and critical theory is on power dynamics that reproduce oppression and privilege in an effort to disrupt such dynamics. Harkavy (2008: 89) makes reference to the work of William Harper who shared the 'conviction that collaborative, action-oriented, real world problem-solving, was by far the best strategy to advance knowledge and learning.' Although it is true that 'when it comes to civic engagement, higher education's rhetoric far exceeds its performance' (Gibson cited in Harkavy 2008: 93) and that 'universities are generally detached from the "real world"' (Novek 2009: 179), social work education has, as its core mandate, preparing students for responsible and democratic citizenship; for engaging with and helping individuals, families, groups and communities and for working toward organizational and societal transformational and change.

It is important that we understand the importance of addressing locally specific issues against broader contextual realities, including those at the global level. Harkavy (2008: 101) argues that, 'universal problems (such as poverty, unequal health care, substandard housing, hunger, and inadequate, unequal education) [...] manifest themselves locally'. Structural unemployment, social exclusion, poverty and inequality have a way of seeping into the lives of individuals and families to manifest in a range of self-defeating and destructive behaviours such as substance abuse, domestic violence, child neglect and abuse that social workers deal with on a daily basis. It is therefore important that we simultaneously aim toward both structural changes and direct intervention with individuals, families and communities. The aim is to 'empower individuals by linking their personal predicament to structural inequalities and seeking to rectify both of these' (Dominelli 2002: 61).

Understanding that the dichotomy between individual and society is an erroneous one, we hoped to engender structural changes by actively engaging the children and youth on the streets. While the research itself reflected democracy enlivened in localized contexts, we involved the children and youth in decided ways with regard to how the research results were to be utilized.

To this end we discussed the results of the research with them and asked them to come up with a plan/s of action. They wanted to pursue the issue of violence inflicted upon them by the Metro Police and were left alone to discuss what could possibly be done. This initially caused some anxiety, as they believed that they could not make a difference without the direct involvement of the project facilitators. However, we did not relent and insisted that they meet on their own, make decisions and then inform us about what course of action they thought would be feasible. With regard to the outcome of this the journal entry of one of the students (Emma) read as follows:

> After some time we were called in and I was so amazed with what they managed to come up with. Firstly they allowed everyone to have a say in what they had agreed upon [...] that letters should be created [...] to invite the young people living on the streets as well as the organizations' leaders (to discuss the issue of violence on the streets). I was impressed with the way they put everything in a sequential manner.

The group agreed that they were going to have a meeting with the Metro Police but only after they had the chance to discuss the issues among the broader network of children and youth living on the streets and with the leaders of the various service organizations. They decided that they would take responsibility to deliver the letters to each of the organizations.

On another day, Emma's journal entry read as:

> Today the letters were ready to be delivered. The group was eager to do that. We finished the meeting early so that they could start delivering the letters [...] I loved their spirit of togetherness and commitment as it showed that with unity everything is possible. They asked us to wait by the park when they were taking the letter to Scopes [name of service organization]. When they came back they were so happy saying that Mr. X [name withheld] [...] was really impressed with them [...]. Their self-esteem was so high that they were looking forward to delivering the rest of the letters [...]. The little worry I had, that the people in power would intimidate them, vanished.

On the day of the meeting it was heartening to note the leadership roles that the children and youth undertook. One of them served as the Programme Director and others as facilitators and presenters. Drawing on their lived experiences they focused on their exposure to violence and discussed strategies for the way forward in collaboration with the service organizations. We sat back and listened. They called upon the students to present the quantitative data on violence, which was in the form of graphs and they facilitated a discussion on this. We had the media present and in the media write-up the children and youth were reframed as ambassadors for change, rather than the usual stereotypical views of them as problems and perpetrators of crime (Mbonambi 2009). We always strove to engage them in humanizing encounters but events such as these provided them with public affirmation. The gift of validation is one of the most important empowerment strategies that social workers have to offer people. It validates people's inherent dignity and humaneness, strengthens self-esteem, allows people to believe in themselves and releases their creative potential to engage in change efforts, all of which are aligned with the emancipatory strategies and ideals of Freire (1970, 1973), Gramsci (1971) and Giroux (1997).

One of the discourses that evolved as we met in focus groups, was how can those socialized into street life be of help to others. One of the youth living on the street said: 'It might be too late for us but what can we do to help other children. What can we do to stop younger children from coming onto the streets' – a sentiment shared by some of the others. The desire to give of oneself, to be of service to others and to be committed to a common good despite one's own extremely vulnerable and disadvantaged position, is a reflection of interdependence, reciprocity, solidarity and altruism (Dominelli 2002), which are defining principles of citizenship. We tapped into their desire to make a difference, as we understood the power and credibility of peer influence and education. Several group discussions ensued about how we transform their idea into reality and how their own narratives on street life could be used in the service of children at risk. The idea that evolved was to produce a video that could be screened in schools. We thus developed a partnership with the School of Drama at University of KwaZulu Natal for the production of a video, based on the narratives of the youth who live on the streets, that has been screened in schools (the video is available on: http://www.youtube.com/channel/UCqKxyPlevVIGA23lo-iLVUA, you can also Google Vishanthie YouTube for easy access).

The youth, who acted in the video, are present during the screenings. We explain the purpose of the video and the youth answer questions that children might have about street life. The video is a powerful depiction of what happens to a young person on the street – showing how a boy moves from being naive and innocent to a life of crime and violence who is killed by his own mates on the streets. During the school visits, children in small group contexts discuss: 1) what they saw in the video; 2) their thoughts about what they saw in the video; 3) the major problems experienced in their communities that might contribute to children leaving home to go to the streets; 4) the resources that they can reach out to should they experience difficulties; 5) whether the screening of the video and the discussion might help prevent children from leaving home to go and live on the streets. The idea is to help them deal with some of the push factors that predispose children to street life and to de-romanticise the pull of street life. The message, portrayed in the video and through the testimonies of the youth who are present at the schools, is clearly that: *It is not worth it; street life is dangerous and difficult; it hurts and it kills.* This is work in progress and the direct feedback from the school children and the teachers is overwhelmingly positive. However, given structural determinants, linked primarily to poverty and inequality that serve to push children onto the streets (Sewpaul et al. 2012), we acknowledge that in the absence of strong political intervention to engender structural changes, no matter how well intentioned social workers might be, our efforts might produce small gains. This is a constant struggle and social workers need to agitate for such structural changes.

The youth who helped to produce the video co-presented with us, at a national teaching and learning social work conference in 2010, demonstrating the power of service user inclusion. Of particular importance to emancipatory education and anti-oppressive practice is not only who speaks; who gets to listen is equally important. Representatives from both national and provincial government were present and got to listen to the youths' narratives of structural injustices on their lives, their exposure to violence on the streets and their efforts, as engaged citizens, to make a difference. We also petitioned in support of a Basic Income Grant, which research has shown can drastically reduce poverty levels in South Africa (Samson et al. 2004).

Conclusion

Adopting a multi-systemic approach to understanding privilege and oppression, including both structural macro level and micro-interpersonal level factors, this chapter describes the application of critical social research with children and youth living on the streets of Durban. One of the main objectives of critical theory is to enhance our understanding of the political nature of social phenomena. As reflected in this chapter, critical theory is not satisfied with merely describing or understanding power relationships or the social realities of the researched. Its greater emphasis is on challenging social issues and shifting the balance of power to address some of the most pressing problems faced in contemporary society. The taken for granted assumptions held by researchers, practitioners and service users, in large measure, support the status quo of social inequalities and might mitigate authentic participatory initiatives. There is thus a need for critical interrogation of these assumptions and the need to use reflexive strategies to ensure that participation is used for the emancipation and empowerment of people whom we work with.

QUESTIONS FOR REFLECTION

- What do you understand by the concepts 'critical social research' and 'critical theory'?
- What does the phrase 'our identity as experts betray us' mean to you?
- What social work/community work skills and strategies can you identify to ensure authentic participation in community base research and community development initiatives?

Notes

Figures 8.1 – 8.3 were taken as part of the community project of which Vishanthie Sewpaul was project leader.

1. This study was made possible through funding from the National Lotteries Board. We are also indebted to the South African Netherlands Partnership for Alternatives in Research and Development (SANPAD) that funded an earlier phase. The policy and practice implications of the early research served as precursors to this current research and work with children and youth living on the streets of Durban. We also acknowledge the contribution of Emma Sibilo and Sithembele Mbhele to the project.

References

Organisation of African Unity (1990) *African Charter on the Rights and Welfare of the Child*. Online. Available HTTP: http://www1.umn.edu/humanrts/africa/afchild.htm (accessed 23 February 2013).

Althusser, L. (1971) *Ideology and Ideological State Apparatuses, Lenin and Philosophy, and Other Essays,* trans. Ben Brewster, London: New Left Books.

Alvesson, M. and Sköldberg, K. (2009) *Reflexive Methodology: New Vistas for Qualitative Research,* London, United Kingdom: Sage.

Arnstein, S.R. (1969) 'A ladder of citizen participation', *Journal of American Institute of City Planners* 35(4): 216–24.

Babbie, E. and Mouton, J. (2001) *The Practice of Social Research,* Cape Town: Oxford University Press.

Bauman, Z. (1993) *Postmodern Ethics,* Oxford: Blackwell Publishing Ltd.

Beresford, P. (2003) *It's Our Lives: A Short Theory of Knowledge, Distance And Experience,* London: Citizen Press.

Beresford, P. and Branfield, F. (2006) 'Developing inclusive partnerships: user-defined outcomes, networking and knowledge – a case study', *Health and Social Care in the Community* 14(5): 436–44.

Butterflies Programme. Online. Available HTTP: http://butterflieschildrights.org (accessed 16 August 2012).

Department of Social Development (2005) *Children's Act 38 of 2005,* Republic of South Africa. Online. Available HTTP: www.justice.gov.za/legislation/acts/2005-038%20 childrensact.pdf (accessed 24 February 2013).

Dominelli, L. (2002) *Anti Oppressive Social Work Theory and Practice,* London: Palgrave Macmillan.

Foucault, M. (1978) *The History of Sexuality*, translated by Robert Hurley, New York: Pantheon.

Freire, P. (1970) *The Pedagogy of the Oppressed*, Harmondsworth: Penguin Books.

——(1973) *Education for Critical Consciousness*, New York: The Seabury Press.

Giroux, H. A. (1997) *Pedagogy and the Politics of Hope: Theory, Culture and Schooling*, Colorado: Westview Press.

Gramsci, A. (1971) *Selections from the Prison Notebooks*, trans. A. Hoare and G.N Smith (eds), London: Lawrence and Wishart.

Harkavy, I. (2008) 'The role of universities in advancing citizenship and social justice in the 21st century', *Citizenship Education* 4: 87–118.

Humphries, B. (2008) *Social Work Research and Social Justice*, Hampshire: Palgrave Macmillan.

Leonard, S. T. (1990) *Critical Theory in Political Practice*, Princeton: Princeton University Press.

Mbonambi, G. (2009) 'Street children can be city envoys', *The Mercury* 21 August 2009. Online. Available HTTP: http://www.highbeam.com/doc/1G1-206996801.html (accessed 24 February 2013).

Miller, R. L and Brewer, J. D. (2003) *The A–Z of Social Research*, London: Sage Publication.

Mullaly, B. (2010) *Challenging Oppression and Confronting Privilege*, Ontario: Oxford University Press.

Mullaly, R. (1998) *Structural Social Work: Ideology, Theory and Practice*, North Carolina: Oxford University Press.

Novek, E. (2009) 'Service-learning in communication education: a case study investigation in support of prisoners' human rights organization', *Education, Citizenship and Social Justice* 4(3): 179–94. Online. Available HTTP: http://esj.sagepub.com/content/4/3/179 (accessed 9 January 2013).

Pease, B. (2010) *Undoing Privilege: Unearned Advantage in a Divided World*, London: Zed Books.

Purdie-Vaughn, V. and Eiback, R.P. (2008) 'Intersecting invisibility: the distinctive advantages and disadvantages of multiple subordinate group identities', *Sex Roles*, 59: 377–91.

Reason, P. and Bradbury, H. (eds) (2008) *Sage Handbook of Action Research: Participative Inquiry and Practice*, 2nd edn, London: Sage Publications.

Ryen, A. (2007) '*Exporting ethics: the West and the rest?*' in P. Leer-Salvesen and I. Furseth (eds) *Religion in Late Modernity*, London: Sage Publication.

Samson, M., Lee, U. and Ndlebe, A. (2004) *The Social and Economic Impact of South Africa's Social Security System, Final Report*, Claremont: Economic Policy Research Institute.

Sewpaul, V., Østhus, I., Mhone, C., Sibilo, E. and Mbhlele, S. (2012) 'Life on the streets of Durban: no millionaire ending', *Social Work/Maatskaplike Werk* 48(3): 241–54.

Sewpaul, V. and Østhus I. (2009) 'Critical action research: transferring lessons from the streets of New Delhi, India to the streets of Durban, South Africa', in D. Zavirsek and S. Ramon (eds), *Critical Edge Issues in Social Work and Social Policy*, Ljubljana: Faculty of Social Work, University of Ljubljana.

Sewpaul, V. (2003) 'Reframing epistemologies and practice through international exchanges: global and local discourses in the development of critical consciousness', in L. Dominelli and W.T. Bernard, *Broadening the Horizon: International Exchange in Social Work*, Hampshire: Ashgate Publishing Limited.

United Nations Convention on the Rights of the Child (1989). Online. Available HTTP: http://www.regjeringen.no/nb/dep/bld/dok/veiledninger_brosjyrer/2006/Barnekonvensjonen-engelsk.html?id=601078 (accessed 2 March 2013).

Williams, G. (2004) 'Evaluating participatory development: tyranny, power and (re) politicization', *Third World Quarterly* 25(3): 557–78.

Williamson, J.B, Karp, D.A., Dalphin, J.R. and Gray, P.S. (1982) *The Research Craft: An Introduction to Social Research Methods*, Boston/Toronto: Little Brown and Company.

9

HOW DO WE MAKE ROOM FOR ALL? THE POWER OF CONTEXT IN SHAPING ACTION

Bliss Browne and Caroline B. Adelman

Introduction

Imagine a community in which nothing and no one is wasted, in which everyone's contribution matters to the way forward. This chapter is the story of one attempt to bring this vision to life in a large and divided American city, beginning in 1992, by a small, non-profit organization called Imagine Chicago. Over the last twenty years this organization has inspired a self-organizing global Imagine movement which has included universities in Nepal, health workers in London, UNICEF in India, churches in Australia, municipal planners in central Singapore, community activists in Cape Town, journalists in Argentina, policy makers in Scotland, and native youth in Montana, to name a few. This chapter will share some of what we have learned about the power of context in shaping action and how to cultivate hope, build community capacity and unleash collective imagination to bring about positive change.

The role of context in shaping behaviour

The social sciences have long recognized the vital role of social context in shaping human behaviour and identity. As far back as the 1930s, Kurt Lewin (the 'father' of social psychology) and his colleagues demonstrated that changes in the social environment led to subsequent changes in the behaviours and beliefs of individuals within those environments (Lewin et al. 1939). By the late 1970s, developmental psychologists had delineated the reciprocal effects between various social and cultural systems and individual development (e.g. Bronfenbrenner 1979). The notion that people are largely defined by (and reciprocally influence) the systems and social contexts in which they develop – family systems, educational settings, neighbourhoods, work settings, and cultures, among others – has been established and revalidated numerous times in the social sciences.

Research has also demonstrated that context is a more accurate determinant of individual behaviour than any individual characteristic (Kunda 1999). Traits that we perceive to be relatively stable within a given individual (e.g., honesty, reliability, confidence, etc.) do not appear to be stable when measured across different contexts; rather, individuals are far more consistent in their behaviour when the contexts themselves are consistent (i.e., honesty in a business transaction predicts similar behaviour in the next business transaction, but does not predict honesty in one's marriage (Ross and Nisbett 1991). How, then, do we create social contexts that mobilize hope and help individuals and communities work together productively?

Hope as a context for action

Hope is generative. Where hope is alive and connections abound, possibilities expand. New buildings are developed, new businesses and projects started. Hope is a vital energy that focuses motivation and encourages investment.

In Chicago, in 1992, hope was under siege. Public cynicism, which erodes hope and creativity, passed for sophistication. Increasing use of terms like 'underclass' and 'lost generation' served as evidence that despair and injustice were becoming established in the collective imagination as social inevitabilities. Citizens were dying young and youth were killing each other. Apathy, addiction, and violence were symptomatic of the loss of hope. Chronic social exclusion and isolation, internalized images of inadequacy, and poor education were leading whole communities of people to lose confidence in their future. Negative images in the mass media played an influential role in the cancerous internalization of disorder and decay. Discrimination by race, economic status, and ethnicity had become institutionalized in housing patterns, neighbourhoods of concentrated poverty, and partisan political boundaries. Many people isolated with segregated communities and mind-sets could not imagine themselves as meaningfully connected to others who were different. Without confidence in a viable future, personal investment made no sense.

An animating vision

Dissonance awakens imagination and I (BWB) began to wonder what might inspire commitment to a future in Chicago where young people could live into the full promise of their lives. What might encourage local citizens to see themselves as co-creators of Chicago's future and to work together across traditional divides? How could those who had been segregated discover a unifying purpose that could help Chicago become a place where life flourished for everyone?

My first step was to organize a conference in which participants described images of Chicago's future worthy of our life-long commitment. The image that came to me was of the recycling symbol as representing an economy in which nothing and no one was wasted, in which everyone's participation counts. I began to imagine a city …

- where everyone is valued
- where every citizen, young and old, applies their talents to create a positive future for themselves and their community
- where hope comes alive in the flourishing and connecting of human lives, and
- where young people and others whose visions have been discounted develop and contribute their ideas and energy.

Within three days, I had set aside a sixteen-year corporate banking career to discover what it would take to bring this vision to life.

My first organizing action was to convene a 'design team' of interdisciplinary thinkers and activists. This group observed that the problem- and deficit-oriented public discourse undermined hope for change. Public policies and funding applications that treated families, neighbourhoods, and other groups as problems to be solved had the unintended consequence of disempowering local action. We wondered how to instead create a public discourse that helped groups discover, gather, and connect their strengths. We decided positive communication frameworks were essential to nurturing hope and civic imagination. Since Imagine Chicago wanted to open up possibilities and energy for community renewal, we needed to shift from deficit-based to vision-oriented language, and from answers to inquiry. Perhaps we could thereby jog individuals out of traditional problem-oriented mind-sets, reawaken their belief that positive change could happen, and create structures within which unlikely, reliably constructive partnerships developed. If public conversations built new relationships and helped to identify community strengths, skills, hopes, resources, and visions, maybe a positive community image and identity could develop. This, in turn, might inspire higher participation and attract investment.

The power of the question

We recognized how consequential the questions we chose would be. Questions lead somewhere based on their often hidden assumptions. For example, 'Why can't you ever do anything right?' presumes and creates an identity of incompetence. 'How do we get even?' rallies support for retaliation. 'Why bother to invest in a "lost generation"?' reinforces despair about the future. Asking communities to compete for funding by portraying themselves as having the greatest deficits, the highest crime, and the most intractable problems leads to service programs that foster dependencies and perpetuate negative identities.

Conversely, constructive questions can be used to inspire, clarify, invite, and build community, create pathways to positive experiences and affections, and to invite reflection on issues of importance. For example questions like, 'How did you learn to do your job so effectively?' honours an individual's skill and generates useful information about creating a path to work for others. 'How can we support and learn from your community?' assumes there is much to be learned and invites relationship and trust. 'How can we get this done now and how can I help?' infer confidence in an idea and a readiness to act on it, building solidarity and momentum to move forward. A positive community image is reinforced by asking 'What makes you glad to live in this neighbourhood?' instead of 'What are the biggest problems here?' Shifting ownership of the future to citizens is activated by asking, 'What's a small change that could make a big difference, that you are committed to working for?'

The design team wanted a citizen interview process that encouraged community visioning and strengthened community connections. Months were spent designing what we hoped were a few 'right questions' to get people 'thinking from the whole' and seeing Chicago's future as one they could create. We ultimately designed an intergenerational interview process focused on affirmative topics, using appreciative questions, and involving dedicated citizens. Each design team member made a list of ten such 'glue people' (i.e. community leaders with a reputation for holding the city together) to be interviewed. We asked traditionally marginalized young people to conduct the interviews, in hopes of sparking their imagination, connecting them to opportunities for leadership, and inspiring a commitment to a future that included them.

An inspiring future

The interview questions were field-tested and greatly improved by the teenage interviewers. This process built trust that we took their leadership seriously. In 1993, 50 young volunteer interviewers asked 150+ adult community leaders the following questions:

1. How long have you lived in Chicago? In this community?
    a. What first brought your family here?
    b. What is it like for you to live in this community?
2. When you think about the whole city of Chicago, what particular places, people or images represent the city to you?
3. Thinking back over your Chicago memories, what have been real high points for you as a citizen of this city?
4. Why did these experiences mean so much to you?
5. How would you describe the quality of life in Chicago today?
6. What changes in the city would you most like to see? What do you imagine your own role might be in helping to make this happen? Who could work with you?
7. Close your eyes and imagine Chicago as you most want it to be a generation from now. What is it like? What do you see and hear? What are you proudest of having accomplished?
8. As you think back over this conversation, what images stand out for you as capturing your hopes for this city's future?
9. What do you think would be an effective process for getting people across the city talking and working together on behalf of Chicago's future? Whom would you want to draw into a Chicago conversation?

The first question established a context within which to understand the interviewee's history and to get comfortable speaking with them; it assumed relationship to Chicago as a matter of choice. The next invited the interviewee to reflect on the city as a whole by asking for images that held that understanding. Our research indicated that few people thought about the city that way, so the question prompted them to do so. The heart of the interview was the high point citizen story, which evoked an operating definition of citizenship and established the interview as a citizen-to-citizen interaction. As the interviewee interpreted their story, their values came more clearly into view and the community connection was reinforced as meaningful. The next question offered space to express current positive perceptions of the city and any lingering frustrations that might otherwise block an authentic conversation. The next two questions queried desired changes in the city from two perspectives: standing in the present looking forward, and standing in the future looking back; both linked hope for changes to active engagement on behalf of the changes. The desired future was conjured imaginatively with all the senses. From that enchanted place, one could look back on the path to community change without the weight of present obstacles as a mental impediment. The penultimate question invited a summary reflection on the conversation in an integrating image of hope (often, the interviewee would point to the young person and answer 'YOU!'). The interview concluded by asking for suggestions of how to expand the public conversation, beginning with the person interviewed as the agent of change. The interview was followed up by a 'thank you' letter from the young interviewer, summarizing the person's vision and the learning it prompted.

A design team member mentioned that the protocol we used reminded him of 'Appreciative Inquiry' (AI), a then emerging research methodology at Case Western Reserve University that encouraged people to envision positive future images based on inquiry about the best of the past (Cooperrider and Whitney 2005). Unlike the traditional problem-based tools and models that focus on what is not working well, AI focuses on what is working well (Appreciative) by engaging people in asking questions (Inquiry) and telling stories. Through constructive dialogue, new possibilities are then imagined and new partnerships created to bring the desired future into being. Early AI research suggested a strong link between positive image and positive action and that problem solving as a process for inspiring and sustaining human systems change was limited. The research also showed that deficit-based analysis, while powerful in diagnosis, often undermines human organizing, because it creates a sense of threat, separation, and defensiveness. By contrast, innovation methods that evoke stories, and encourage groups of people to envision positive images of the future grounded in the best of the past, have greater potential to produce deep and sustaining change and inspire collective action. Imagine Chicago intuited its way to such an appreciative approach, using young people as change agents and applying AI practices to larger public spaces, including neighbourhoods and cities.

What worked? The intergenerational interviews created the very thing they investigated: more focus on a promising future. Hearing inspiring stories shaped positive identities and connections; respectful listening built trust. Adult commitments were refreshed. New possibilities for engagement were imagined and shared. Asking constructive open-ended questions established a shared civic identity and expanded the sense among the young people that they could make a difference; the experience and wisdom of seasoned community builders invigorated the energy and commitment of youth searching for purpose, yielding deep insights into the collective possibilities for Chicago's future. Young people previously written off as 'lost' came to see themselves as agents of change and became the symbol of the transformation that was possible. One young interviewer referred to having previously had a case of the 'uns': unneeded, unwanted and unloved. In the Imagine Chicago process, she gained new perspectives:

> The environments I lived and worked in were completely contrasting. I would go to the lofty office of a multi-millionaire and have a conversation that would open up the possibilities. Then I would go home to a flat with a 'For Sale' sign in the front. My family was struggling and I could see drug dealers all around my neighbourhood. It was hard.

She subsequently finished college and worked with city leaders to develop policies incorporating youth into leadership roles in the city.

Many suggested that the positive results of the intergenerational interviews were propelled by the contagious mind-set of positive question/positive image/positive action imbedded in the process. It brought to the surface deeply held hopes and values, and created trustworthy connections between people who could band together to bring the hopes to fruition. An adult participant summarized the power of the process thus:

> People who have never been together have come together to do something positive ... to bridge a gap between young people and adults. It has sparked energy ... It has sparked hope ... We have worked together; we have collaborated, young and old. It took all of us. We know it's going to happen, because we've become one family, everyone encouraging one another. Now it's going to become a reality. This has formed respect for our young people, that they can get an idea and bring it to life.

The limits of the process also became evident over time. The interviews were only a first step of understanding what was possible, and imagining where that could lead. There was no structure within which to create that future. Imagine Chicago learned that the appreciative intergenerational interview process needed to be imbedded within structures that could move more readily to action.

Language as a socially constructed context

The interview process demonstrated vividly that words and images create worlds; in this process, images of possibility gained new authority. Social constructionist theory helps us to understand why. According to social constructionist theory (e.g. Gergen and Gergen 2004; for further reading, see Taos Institute website), we make sense of things, not according to a single inherent way of perceiving, but according to shared understandings. Language gains its meaning and life its order within relationships and broad patterns of practice.

Each person develops a unique worldview as a result of the particular relationships and contexts in which they have participated. Language, stories, and expectations surrounding a given child shape how that child begins to see life, to name it and to manage it. According to what a person is told, and what stories the person creates, he or she learns to notice some things and not others, to understand the world in a certain way. He or she internalizes ways of seeing and knowing, of speaking and interacting, and these become self-reinforcing. These might include seeing oneself within an exalted sense of life's promise and opportunities or within limiting stereotypes, labels, and socially prescribed beliefs and norms. As a person grows, and interacts with others, more ways of seeing become available.

Many ways of seeing are implicit, buried within language, prevailing worldviews, and common social practice. Commonly agreed patterns of meaning get institutionalized in social roles, language, norms, rituals, and culture and may come to be seen as fixed, unable to be challenged or changed. Over time, ways of seeing develop authority, becoming traditions in which many people become invested. The multiplicity of cultures, languages, discourses, and ways of naming things differently demonstrate this. In one culture, a tree might be seen as a nurturing, 'mother of life' deserving sacred protection; in another, as an insensible object cut for lumber. Each view has consequences. A public standoff between indigenous tree guardians and loggers is not only about economics but about the authority and validity of cultural traditions.

Descriptors are consequential and summarize a distinct relationship context and set of cultural sensibilities. Think of the power of the following words which can describe the same person: 'mother', 'daughter', 'customer', 'friend', 'voter', 'lover', 'activist', 'American'. Different norms, practices, and understandings govern the roles to which these words refer and make those descriptors intelligible; certain learned actions are 'appropriate' to each.

Now imagine the different treatment a child receives if they are labelled a 'bully' or a 'gifted child' when they arrive in a new school, or the ongoing negative impact of describing certain communities as 'poor' or certain countries as 'developing' which tends to privilege market-driven understandings of what constitutes 'development'. Shifting our language about community regeneration to speak about and recognize all communities as places of strength and resourcefulness increases the probability of identifying, leveraging, and connecting those strengths in productive ways.

The good news, toward which social construction theory points, is that if patterns of meaning and their related social systems are invented and agreed, they can also be shifted and reconstructed. We experience this when we learn from or interact with people whose different worldviews change our fundamental beliefs and understandings. The adaptive challenge for all human systems is to create contexts within which better worlds get co-created, in which discourse and action mobilize resources, enable learning, and help people act on their innate capacity to recreate systems in more life-giving directions. Understanding life as socially constructed challenges us to bring to consciousness the beliefs and patterns that govern our lives, to examine if they serve life and us well, and to be intentional about the values, language, and practices out of which we speak and live. The stories we tell and language we use constitute a moral choice with impacts. As creators of meaning, we bear responsibility for the worlds we create (Browne 2008).

Social construction theory also helps us understand why it is important to create public contexts within which people's orienting hopes, values, beliefs, language, and stories are shared and their meanings unpacked, rather than assuming people start from commonly held assumptions and understandings. A common Imagine Chicago practice is to open a community forum by inviting participants to do the following activity and to share the results with their table group:

> Reflect for a moment about 'the shape of the future', a deep hope you carry within you as you think about the future of your life or community. Please draw that image.

Next, please share:

1. Something you have discovered makes constructive change possible ...
2. One way you are working on the change you want to see in your community ...
3. One question (or hope) that has drawn you here today that you would appreciate the chance to discuss with others here ...

Such a context makes meaning making visible and creates respect for particular orienting ways of seeing. As strangers express and explain their dreams, experience and questions, they unpack their mental maps and meanings. They also develop a *shared* identity as people who hope, who act, whose experience matters, and who want to learn from each other. Their questions invite and encourage connection. Listening to each another's hopes, stories, and commitments, confidence deepens that change is happening and more is possible. People rediscover the energy and desire to move forward. Public accountability increases the likelihood of action and the possibility of new partnerships to work on behalf of the dreams. As their visions get connected to the resources of others, their capacity to make a meaningful difference increases.

A shared framework for moving from idea to action

Since 1992, Imagine Chicago has developed partnerships involving a wide range of individuals and institutions: grassroots leaders who want to improve their neighbourhoods and learn from other committed citizens; public schools who want to forge deeper community connections; immigrant and faith communities seeking to understand democracy and American pluralism; school children and parents trying to impact the systems and communities of which they are a part. Rather than proposing a 'top-down' change process with Imagine Chicago in the 'expert' role, we have created learning frameworks and then listened for what is practical and possible.

Central to all of the initiatives has been an iterative applied learning and action cycle:

- *Understand* what is
- *Imagine* what could be
- *Create* what will be

UNDERSTAND: As in the initial interviews, all projects begin with and are grounded in asking and teaching others to ask open-ended, value-oriented questions about what is working, meaningful and important. The focus is on asking questions that encourage sharing of best practices, and articulation of strengths, values and mental maps upon which new possibilities can be built. In a school program, a parent might be asked, 'What is something your child has accomplished of which you are very proud? What connections with the school would best support your child's learning this year?'

IMAGINE: Imagination is a core adaptive capacity, a truly democratic realm of the future, not bound by current arrangements. New possibilities are inspired by telling and hearing stories of what has been lived and what matters. Human beings use stories to accelerate learning and inspire creative thinking. As we listen and share, new ideas are generated in us and in others. Grassroots leaders discussing what they have accomplished encourage others to imagine how they can make a difference. Young parents sharing how they are caring for their children helps others consider new parenting practices and to see them as possible. Moving from understanding to action *through imagination* redefines the present as being shaped in service of the valued future, a possibility not yet created but which could be. It is a realm of freedom and choice.

CREATE: For imagination to become change, it has to be embodied in something concrete and practical, a visible outcome. In Imagine Chicago's Citizen Leaders program, for example, grassroots leaders articulate their visions for community change and then design and create high impact, low cost community development projects. In interactive forums, they learn to recruit volunteers, design and organize a project, prepare a proposal, and implement, evaluate, and sustain their efforts. Learning occurs principally through sharing experiences within a common framework of organizing questions. Inevitable differences in learning styles and skills get managed. For example, when literacy skills are uneven, the workshops encourage different forms of expression. People are given the chance to meet in pairs before sharing an idea with the larger group and to express their ideas creatively through drawings or role-playing; partners more comfortable with writing record the ideas.

In 1996, a group of committed citizens involving six leaders and twenty-five team members, from the same low-income Chicago neighbourhood, participated together in this program. Their projects included block clubs, community gardens, intergenerational sports programs, and a youth club. With support from a local community organization, these citizen leaders launched a neighbourhood-wide program to bring residents together to address important issues. The Every Block is a Village program they started expanded to 60 block clubs, each with resident 'citizen leaders', and organized around issues like community cleanliness, economic development, and youth opportunities. The process was strengthened by sharing stories weekly about what had happened and how, and lessons learned. As successes grew, so did their confidence and skill level. The outcomes and growing volunteer effort inspired more people to make a difference.

Developing identity as citizens

Imagine Chicago helps individuals and institutions see themselves as ones who create the future of the community – and think of cities as a constructive context within which meaning is created through connections (Browne and Jain 2002). Many initiatives have focused on developing civic identity and citizenship skills giving organizations as well as individuals the experience of being part of a WE who act to create a positive future that otherwise would not exist. Imagine Chicago has brought uncommon partners together to listen for what is practical and possible and to help each partner achieve their mission in a way better than they could accomplish working alone.

Imagine Chicago's Urban Imagination Network (UIN), for example, was designed to improve reading comprehension in schools, strengthen museum education, and develop family citizenship skills. Seven struggling Chicago public schools were paired with six museums. Museums co-developed programs consistent with school curriculum priorities. Schools reordered themselves as centres of hands-on community education. Students created exhibits showcasing what they learned and incorporated museum content into their lessons.

Of course, not all schools were equally successful in implementation. The sheer weight of bureaucratic requirements in a large standardized system dragged down people's energy and availability to participate in developing a creative learning community. Over time, we found that it was more productive to focus on areas where voluntary (rather than mandatory) commitment could be leveraged, namely engaging families in creating a culture of learning in their homes and personal renewal of teachers.

The parent connection was an obvious one, though UIN schools were initially pessimistic about the possibility of engaging parents in low-income neighbourhoods in personal development. 'Reading Chicago and Bringing It Home' was designed to develop 'civic literacy' skills necessary to connect families to their city as a learning context. Monthly 'Reading Chicago' workshops, held at museums, engaged parents in researching and discussing content at the heart of a family and city – like food, housing, energy, communication, transportation, water, education, recreation, and health. Through reading, reflection on experience, museum visits, presentations, and discussions with parents from other cultures, participants thought through what makes a family and city work. The content of daily life became interesting as a set of ideas, values, and choices. Parents developed life skills like budgeting, saving, and reading and learned to make sense of information from any source. They developed an identity as family educators and of Chicago as 'home'.

'Bringing It Home' workshops were held monthly at each school to apply what parents had learned in the workshops to facilitating their children's learning at home. Each month focused on a core competency essential to city living (like map skills, budgeting, reading a bill, computer literacy). Parents skilled in a given competency served as mentors to others. Parents designed activities that reinforced the key ideas and learning.

The program's different components helped develop systems thinking. Parents learned about city systems in a location outside their own neighbourhood; they learned core competencies at their local school; they taught creative activities to their children at home. They became aware of the city as a complex system, with key vocabulary and choices. They reflected on how systems change over time. For example, parents studied transportation at the Chicago Historical Society. They heard narratives of a pioneer journey to help them connect to the artefacts in the Pioneer exhibit, and thought through items they might have put in their own pioneer wagons (an exercise in setting personal priorities). They discussed the invention of refrigerated railroad cars and its impact on the development of Chicago as a stockyard centre. They examined the citizen action transportation plan being voted on in the state legislature. They learned that individuals and communities both create and are shaped by the systems of which they are a part (Browne n.d.).

Imagine Chicago emphasized the interrelatedness of systems as well as each individual's importance as a change agent. We affirmed their intelligence and commitment as involved parents and citizens. Parents shifted from seeing themselves as 'objects' in a city ('IT'), to 'subjects' that decide, create, connect, and think within a city ('WE'). They re-envisioned themselves as educators and community leaders within their families, schools and city, which in turn reshaped their self-understanding as citizens. It shifted their perception of who had power from unresponsive bureaucratic structures to parents who could act on behalf of what they valued.

A generative framework for collective action

Imagine Chicago has challenged people and institutions to understand, imagine, and create the future they value, and to move from understanding and dreaming community to building it. We have helped communities articulate and stay focused on their strategic intentions and opened up a path to participation through meaningful questions.

What has been the result? It is difficult to attribute specific changes in Chicago or elsewhere to Imagine Chicago's work. We have also not wanted to claim credit for outcomes but for participants to deserve the credit themselves, with our helping facilitate the changes and documenting lessons learned. That said, the attractiveness and power of the approach has been validated in many cultural contexts by the growing global Imagine movement. And, over the last two decades, the power of positive imaging and conversation has gained widespread acceptability in other community practice groups like AI, Asset Based Community Development, and positive youth development which began around the same time as Imagine Chicago.

What have we learned works best? To create contexts in which people are seen as capable and competent citizens and their capacities for participation activated in meaningful ways, our most trusted 'Frameworks for Inspiring Change' include:

1. Opening public space for hope and acceptance where everyone has a voice and seat at the table and their hopes and ideas are creatively expressed and validated
2. Understanding social construction, including working from end-goals to designing processes that reflect the change people want to see (e.g. involving marginalized young people to bring a more promising future into focus) and understanding language as a moral choice
3. Inspiring a sense of possibility through questions and shared storytelling
4. Constructive communication, including appreciative questions and effective group decision making which builds trust
5. Understanding the impact of deficit vs. strength-based communications
6. Helping people shift to more effective communications practices
7. Creating uncommon collaborations around a collective strategic goal, where innovation results from differences in views and experience
8. Aligning actions and accountability around shared goals.

We hope that this chapter and the practices illustrated by Imagine Chicago's story provide a creative context for activating your own imagination and hope.

QUESTIONS FOR REFLECTION

- How would you describe the 'mental maps' out of which you now do your community work? What words and questions do you use to evaluate communities? What questions do you tend to ask?
- How does focusing on hope fundamentally redefine community work?
- What kinds of contexts and people tend to bring out your best ideas? Why?

Suggestions for further reading

Imagine Chicago. Online. Available HTTP: http:// www.imaginechicago.org (accessed 2 March 2013) for detailed case studies and evaluations of all projects discussed in this chapter.

The Taos Institute. Online. Available HTTP: http://www.taosinstitute.net (accessed 2 March 2013) for resources on social constructionist ideas.

Appreciative Inquiry (AI) Commons. Online. Available HTTP: http://appreciativeinquiry.case.edu (accessed 2 March 2013) for resources and case studies on Appreciative Inquiry.

References

Bronfenbrenner, V. (1979) *The Ecology of Human Development: Experiments by Nature and Design,* Cambridge: Harvard University Press.

Browne, B. (n.d.) *Renewing Public Education.* Online. Available HTTP: http://www.imaginechicago.org/renewing_public_education.html (accessed 27 February 2013).

Browne, B. (2008) *Frameworks for Inspiring Change,* Guest Lecture at Governor's School of North Carolina, Raleigh, NC, (August 2008).

Browne, B. and Jain, S. (2002) *Imagine Chicago: Ten Years of Imagination in Action,* Chicago: Self-Published by Imagine Chicago.

Cooperrider, D.L. and Whitney, D. (2005) *Appreciative Inquiry: A Positive Revolution in Change,* San Francisco: Berrett-Koehler Publishers.

Gergen, K.J. and Gergen, M. (2004) *Social Construction: Entering the Dialogue,* Taos, New Mexico: Taos Institute Publications.

Kunda, Z. (1999) 'Knowledge about others' attitudes, behavior, and personality', in *Social Cognition: Making Sense of People,* Cambridge, MA: MIT Press.

Lewin, K., Lippit, R. and White, R.K. (1939) 'Patterns of aggressive behaviour in experimentally created "social climates"', *Journal of Social Psychology,* 10(2): 269–99.

Ross, L. and Nisbett, R.E. (1991) *The Person and the Situation: Perspectives of Social Psychology,* New York: McGraw Hill.

Taos Institute (n.d.) Online. Available HTTP: www.taosinstitute.net (accessed 2 March 2013).

10

COMMUNITY WORK WITHIN THE NORWEGIAN WELFARE STATE

Barriers and possibilities for work with particularly vulnerable groups

Gunn Strand Hutchinson

Introduction

The Norwegian welfare state is built on the values of democracy and stresses the need for active participation of citizens and equality in living conditions. The mandate given by the lawmakers to the welfare institutions that employ social workers is to keep themselves informed of, and to act to prevent and resolve adverse welfare conditions and social problems. The law also embodies the Norwegian welfare state's commitment to active citizen participation. Community work is a method in social work that can be used to increase participation. It involves a range of strategies supporting bottom-up actions which enable citizens to participate in the development of the community, the development of services in welfare institutions and in changing conditions in their society. It has to do with capacity building, empowerment and active engagement in democratic processes. Community work is about involving groups who experience marginalization, social exclusion and discrimination.

Community work in Norway in which publicly employed social workers have been involved has mainly focused on neighbourhood projects. In a study of community work in the Nordic countries, Turunen (2009) characterizes Norway as 'the land of co-ordinated projects'. She describes community work in Norway since the 1980s as environmental neighbourhood work, local development and social housing estate work.

Community work with underprivileged and vulnerable groups is often undertaken by voluntary and civic organizations rather than publicly employed social workers. Such organizations have played, and still play, an important role in the Nordic welfare model (Matthies 2006).

One may ask why publicly employed social workers should engage in community work. Why not leave this kind of work to voluntary and charitable organizations? The answer is that social workers, in their role as public employees and in their position within public service institutions, are provided with instruments of power influence both individual lives and the conditions of life that contribute to deprivation and dependency. The mandate given through the Social Services Act (Lov om sosiale tjenester i arbeids- og velferdsforvaltningen 2009) and the Health and Care Act (Lov om kommunale helse- og omsorgstjenester m.m. 2011)[1] gives social workers the possibility to focus on living conditions in general, not only specific problems, and to interact outside the office with people who experience problems and are users of individual services. The law also gives them the possibility to focus on problems created and maintained by the system itself.

The welfare laws repeatedly state that one of the purposes is to ensure active participation in society. This is visible in the first sub-paragraph of the statement of purpose of the Social Services Act (§1) (translated by the author):

> The purpose is to improve the living conditions of disadvantaged persons, to contribute to social and economic security, including allowing the individual to live independently, and promoting the transition to employment, social inclusion and active participation in society.

The Norwegian authorities emphasize the participation of welfare services users, both in their individual cases and at a collective level when it comes to services, and their active participation in the society. Involving service users and ensuring their active participation is a clearly stated part of the mandate given to social workers by the politicians.

Despite the generally good living conditions in Norway, there are groups who, for different reasons, have challenging life situations. I will focus here on two such groups, people with multiple problems linked to drug abuse and paperless migrants. Individuals in the first group often experience difficulties accessing help from the welfare institutions and the second group does not have the same rights as people living in the country legally. These are two groups who experience disadvantage and have difficulty with making their voices heard. Social workers have resources to assist them and a mandate to do so. I will discuss the barriers and opportunities for social workers to use community work with these two groups, within the remit of implementing the Social Service Act and the Health Care Acts. First, I will describe the living conditions and the challenges these groups face.

Living conditions

Norway is a country with a high standard of living. Life expectancy as a general indicator of living conditions is among the highest in the world, and is still increasing. A high percentage of the population is employed. In the age group 15–74 years of age the employment rate in the third quarter of 2012 was 68.7 per cent for women and 74.4 per cent for men. Thirty years ago, less than half of all Norwegian women were employed or actively seeking work (Statistisk sentralbyrå

2012a). At the end of 2011, nearly 90 per cent of all children aged 1–5 years attended municipal and state supported kindergartens (Statistisk sentralbyrå 20012b). Parents have 12 months paid leave when a child is born, and this is financed by the state.

The majority of individuals and households have experienced a substantial rise in real income in recent years. Statistics Norway reports that the median income increased by 34 per cent from 2000 to 2010. Though less than in many countries, there are still differences of income in Norway. The 10 per cent of the population with the highest income had 20.6 per cent of the total income in Norway while the 10 per cent with the lowest income had 4 per cent. The groups strongly represented among those with low incomes are recipients of the basic pension and supplementary benefit, immigrants, and individuals with long-term illness, the long-term unemployed and young single people (Statistisk Sentralbyrå 2012c). I will now focus on two of these groups with challenging living conditions.

Living conditions for drug abusers

Many individuals in this group have other problems in addition to their substance abuse. A study from 2004 concluded that the heavier the abuse, the more problems the individual will have (Friestad and Hansen 2004). These include extensive health problems (chronic diseases, mental disorders, infections, hepatitis, HIV, dental health and nutrition problems, etc.) and social problems (problems related to housing, income, education and social networks) (Arbeids- og inkluderings-departementet 2006). Many individuals will therefore require considerable support from welfare institutions. Specialized multidisciplinary treatment for substance abuse has, since 2004, been a state responsibility, delegated to the health authorities. Nevertheless, most people in this situation are not receiving treatment in institutions, but at home. The local social services, under the requirements of the Social Service Act and the Health and Care Act, are responsible for housing for those who cannot manage themselves, for social benefit for those that have no other income and for help in daily life.

In 2003 it was estimated that about 4000 people in Norway suffer from both mental health and substance abuse related problems (Sosialdepartementet 2003). There is uncertainty about the number and many argue that there is considerable underdiagnosis of mental disorders among those who also have problems related to substance abuse (Evjen et al. 2007; Gråwe and Ruud 2006). Even if we do not know the exact number of drug addicts, we know something about the relationship between substance abuse and other serious problems, for example that 60 per cent of both prison inmates and the homeless have a drug problem (Friestad and Hansen 2004). The Directorate of Health estimated in 2000 that 19 per cent of the estimated 4000 people with a dual diagnosis lacked housing or lived in temporary accommodation (Statens Helsetilsyn 2000). These people are among society's poorest (Helsedirektoratet 2012). They need support from the welfare institutions, but the way services are organized and function often results in their falling out of the system. There is a need both to change the services and to make the social problems visible, for instance when it comes to problems with getting a place to live. The ways that community work is implemented can help to make the situation visible and effect institutional changes.

Living conditions for paperless migrants

Paperless migrants are people who, for different reasons, do not have permission to stay in the country. These might be people who have been issued a visa or residence permit under false pretences, people whose visas have run out, or whose residence permit has expired. They might be asylum seekers who have received a final rejection of their application or people who have come to Norway without permission and without registering with the authorities. They can include people who cannot be returned to their home country.

There is considerable uncertainty about how many paperless migrants are living in Norway. Statistics Norway has estimated that in 2006 there were about 18000, 12000 of whom were former asylum seekers (Zhang 2008). The Norwegian state office for handling asylum applications (UDI) processed about 13,000 asylum applications in 2010, of these 5290 people were granted residence, 7673 people were refused, while about 2400 people will have the matter dealt with in another European country in keeping with the Dublin accords as they have made an application there first.

There has been, and still is, a discussion about whether people in this situation should, after some time, be given permission to stay and work or, alternatively, that the authorities should speed up the process of returning them. The situation for children in these families has received particular focus as many of them have been born in Norway and grow up here with the family living under very difficult conditions and never knowing when they might be sent out of the country.

Paperless migrants are not allowed to take a job, and are therefore not able to have a legal income. However, as long as there is a need for labour, this leads to undeclared work and potential abuse in the labour market with under-pay, lack of employment rights and no employment contract. Paperless migrants usually work in cleaning, fast food, restaurants, shops, construction or in various artisan trades (Ottesen 2008). There are many problems with not having legal residence status in addition to the uncertainty. Some paperless people choose to live in hiding, which leads to challenges in daily life and in relation to the community.

People who stay illegally in Norway have limited rights to services from the welfare institutions. The only rights to income assistance are covered by the Social Services Act that is administered by social workers employed in the municipalities and these rights are limited to pure 'relief'. This was made clear in a letter to the municipalities from the government (Arbeids- og inkluderingsdepartementet 2004). For the local social workers who meet these people while giving them the only legal assistance they have a right to, it is obvious that there is a need to make their desperate situation visible. Community work strategies could be useful in this respect.

Examples from practice

I will now present three examples which will form the basis for discussing barriers and possibilities for social workers to use community work.

In the welfare institutions, users are invited to participate both in their individual cases and at a collective level in the development of services. This developmental work is often organized as a project, as in the following example with the project TIUR (Tiltak for unge rusmisbrukere/Initiatives for young drug abusers). The background was that 33 young people between 17–25 years old had lost their work training centre (Tronvoll and Pedersen 2009). Six of them had died and this led to questions about whether the services were able to reach out to these young people in the way they were working. In the project, they tried a new way of working, which was developing the services in close collaboration with the young people involved. Social workers started a dialogue with each young person about what could be done to make his life situation better and tried to support the individual to make changes in his life. The project recommended that certain features were included in the ordinary services if they wanted to reach this group successfully. These features were:

- good accessibility and a flexible organization with room for outreach work
- individually tailored services developed in collaboration with the individual, family, community and societal institutions
- being able to build close relationships that last over time (Tronvoll and Pedersen 2009: 73).

The aim was to change services and the people in focus played an important role in the process. The project was successful. The social workers changed their way of working in the project but this was not followed up in continuing practice. Both lack of time and a bureaucratic organization were seen as barriers by the participating social workers. The researchers say they doubt it is possible to continue working this way without structural changes. This is an experience shared with many projects which aim to make changes in the welfare institutions. The discussion here will be how community work can be accommodated in general social work practice.

The organization, Albatross, was started as a self-help group by former drug users because they were not satisfied with existing services. Albatross provides drug-free after-care for addicts in the city of Bergen (Albatrossen 2012). The aim is to improve the individual's quality of life by providing courses, recreational activities, a social meeting place and work with the aim of returning to society and working life. In the steering committee, and among the people employed, there are former drug users. Albatross also provides after-care for drug addicts on disability benefits to help improve their quality of life. The organization is financially supported by different welfare services including the social services in the municipality and different NGOs. In order to help users return to society and working life, cooperation with publicly employed social workers using community work strategies could be useful. The possibilities will be discussed.

A third example is of a grassroots action using media and Facebook to address the problems of young asylum seekers trying to make their case to the politicians. An Ethiopian family with a seven-year-old boy, Nathan Eshete, born in Norway, was the focus. He is one of the 450 undocumented children in Norway who have lived in asylum seeker reception centres for several years. Although he was born and raised in Norway, he and his family had their application for a residence permit rejected. The focus was set through grassroots action using media and the cases of two nine-year-old children have been taken to court to determine whether the practices of the Norwegian Immigration Appeals Board are in accordance with the law (Norwegian Organisation for Asylum Seekers 2012). The discussion here will be how a social worker employed in the social services can collaborate with paperless migrants and grassroots movements using community work approaches to highlight their living conditions with the aim of changing them.

Barriers faced by social workers in public service employment

In the first case above, successful use of community work in a project was not instituted in continuing practice. I will first focus on the barriers confronted.

To understand the barriers faced by social workers, whether they have to do with exposing living conditions for groups or with working for changes in welfare institutions or in the society, one has to look at the relationship between the state and the municipalities, at institutional factors, disciplinary processes and the loyalty expected from employees.

The state determines the laws and goals for welfare and local government and the people working in the welfare services are supposed to implement the goals. Vike (2004) points out that ambitions and tasks grow side by side but there is an economic ceiling for municipal services. The state guarantees better welfare, while the institutions and services at municipality level experience poorer and poorer conditions for implementing this. This means that services are slowly becoming less accessible. The widening gap between the ideals set by the state and the reality for the implementing services has not been raised and described. New forms of organization of social services, such as New Public Management, have led to more distance between management and the executors. The political and administrative leadership has little involvement with concrete services, while service providers who meet citizens must cope with capacity problems.

Social workers' ethical obligations and professional training to see the individual in his unique context come up against the institutional framework for professional practice. When these employees attempt to report their experience through the system, they are perceived as disloyal. Kroken (2006) argues that the professional's responsibility is gradually being turned away from ethical demands towards the system's requirements for financial accountability. The system's institutional norms are internalized and the social workers are disciplined. Mathiesen (1978) has written about processes that bring professionals to silence and to slowly accept situations they do not at first agree with. You may be isolated or in a minority when decisions are taken even if you feel support outside the organization. If you choose not to take part in decision making because you fundamentally disagree, you might be punished later by not being invited when decisions are made. If you take part and keep quiet in 'small' decisions in order to avoid being labelled as 'in opposition' you may wait too long to be able to influence the 'big' decisions that you have become party to. Through the relationship to the people you collaborate with, you get involved in secrets necessary to take the right decisions and you become responsible for the decisions and start to defend them. In other words, social workers are disciplined. Loyalty is expected even if this means ignoring parts of the mandate and professional judgement of the situation and the necessary action.

Possibilities for using community work strategies

The cases mentioned all need to be put on the political agenda in such a way that decision makers have to relate to the phenomena if there is to be a possibility of effecting change. Social workers are in positions where they may see that this is needed. The barriers for doing it have been discussed. How can social workers employed in the social services approach the need to gather information, gain the insight and the strength to decide to work with the people in focus and then actually take action? How can they handle expectations of loyalty, disciplinary processes and the institutional factors that may silence them?

To decide to act

First of all it is necessary for the social worker to believe that changes are possible. Thomas and Thomas (1928: 571–2) remind us how important the definition of the situation is, why and how one acts: 'If men define situations as real, they are real in their consequences'. If you see something as impossible, you do not try to find solutions. As a gate keeper, a social worker is required to ensure that actions are in accordance with the law and this puts a lot of pressure on acting correctly. But in addition to acting in accordance with the law, a social worker also has to act in accordance with the values social work is based on, their professional knowledge and the duties that these impose on them.

When confronted with debasing life situations, social problems, or practices in their own or other institutions which may be exacerbating problems, social workers have a duty to act in accordance with their mandate. Recalling this duty is essential for providing an impetus to look for and find strategies to use within the broad definition of the mandate for the institution.

The codes of ethics and the global agenda of international social work organizations make it a duty for social workers also to focus on the collective level in order to prevent social problems and exclusion. In the statement of ethical principles in social work, it says as regards to unjust policies:

Social workers have a duty to bring to the attention of their employers, policy makers, politicians and the general public situations where resources are inadequate or where distribution of resources, policies and practices are oppressive, unfair or harmful. Social workers have an obligation to challenge social conditions that contribute to social exclusion, stigmatization or subjugation and to work towards an inclusive society.

(Fellesorganisasjonen 2002)

The Global Agenda agreed in March 2012 by social workers organizations says:

We commit ourselves to supporting, influencing and enabling structures and systems that positively address the root causes of oppression and inequality. We commit ourselves wholeheartedly and urgently to work together with people who use services and with others who share our objectives and aspirations, to create a more socially just and fair world that we will be proud to leave to future generations.

(International Association of Schools of Social Work, International Council of Social Welfare and International Federation of Social Workers 2012)

This obligation comes with being a professional social worker and to make it clear to the public and leaders is essential, in addition to emphasizing the purpose of the Social Service Act and the Health and Care Act which gives the mandate for the institutions.

Cooperation with people concerned and others in empowering processes

The key to overcoming the disciplinary processes is to be conscious of them and to cooperate with others to overcome them. Mathiesen (1978) highlights the importance of taking an active role and making oneself aware of what is happening, creating a mental space where you have room to act, deconstructing the situation and deciding that alternative actions are possible and collaborating with others.

In community work, participation of the people concerned is a core requirement. This means being in dialogue with the people concerned throughout the whole process. Working with other partners is very often necessary. In all three examples given, social workers need to make aspects of the group's living situations apparent to decision makers. Through contact in individual cases, the social worker will be in a dialogue with the people concerned. Quite often an organization that works for the rights of the group will also exist. In the case of improving ways of working with young drug abusers, social workers found that their report with suggestions for change, based on their experience of the project, led nowhere. In the report social workers could have given their organization more specific recommendations for responsibility and action. They could have pursued the matter further through official channels, using formal opportunities and their professional organization and union. They could also have given information to the service users about the decision makers and the structure of decision making and offered them assistance in making use of the democratic possibilities to make their voices heard.

In the case of Albatross, social workers have the opportunity to work with a resourceful organization to develop strategies of change. Such organizations have an interest in making services more attuned to individual needs and have their own channels of influence in the administrative and political system.

If we turn back to paperless migrants, many would argue that any assistance to them other than emergency assistance would be in conflict with the mandate. But street level bureaucrats also have a mandate and a responsibility to inform decision makers about living conditions. A European network has prepared guidelines/ recommendations for working with undocumented migrants (PICUM 2002) and they also underline the importance of providing information about living conditions. The guidelines say that in addition to individual follow up work, social workers should also work to inform the public and politicians about the situation undocumented migrants live in. So what can a social worker do apart from giving individual relief help? What can social workers employed in public institutions do to cooperate with these people and help make their life situation more visible and debated?

One strategy is to work together with grassroots movements in the process of describing the situation paperless migrants find themselves in. Social workers can help grassroots movements in making contacts with the media and discuss how vulnerable and marginalized groups are represented to promote human rights and social justice.

Another strategy is to work through the social workers' union, which in Norway also is the professional organization. Social workers in contact with paperless migrants can make connections with the unions so they can cooperate. The union has the opportunity to raise debate and can play a different role from an employee. The union can cooperate with the people concerned to focus attention on the situation of paperless asylum seekers including using the media. The union can also pass information to politicians directly when in contact both on national and local levels. The leader of the Social Workers' Union (FO), Rigmor Hogstad, calls for a Norwegian debate on the right to stay on humanitarian grounds (Viggen 2011). She highlights the situation of children.

Conclusion

The Norwegian welfare state gives social workers in local social services a mandate to use community work in cooperation with vulnerable groups. The relationship between the state and the municipalities, the institutional culture, disciplinary processes and the loyalty expected of employees creates barriers to the use of community work. This is particularly visible when social workers are dealing with groups who are marginalized in society, such as the two groups in focus here. It is possible for social workers to overcome these barriers by being aware of disciplinary processes and choosing to work to overcome them, being aware of the whole mandate and the ethical and professional obligations social workers have and cooperating with the people involved, interest groups and the social workers' union. This needs courage in addition to professional knowledge.

QUESTIONS FOR REFLECTION

- What does courage mean to you?
- If you were employed in a welfare office in Norway and met paperless migrants who had very poor living conditions, how do you think your courage could be challenged?
- If you have been working in a social work organization, how might you react if you were to be exposed to disciplinary processes?

Note

1.   Further in the text I will refer to those two laws by using the English translation only.

Suggestions for further reading

Grigorieva, I., Kildal, N., Kuhnle, S. and Minina, V. (eds) (2004) *Welfare State Development: Nordic and Russian Perspectives*, St. Petersburg: State University of St. Petersburg.

Kildal, N. and Kuhnle, S. (eds) (2005) *Normative Foundations of the Welfare State: The Nordic Experience*, London/New York: Routledge.

Kuhnle, S., Yinzhang, C., Petersen, K., and Kettunen, P. (eds) (2010) *The Nordic Welfare State*, Shanghai: Fudan University Press. Published in Chinese.

References

Albatrossen (2012) Online. Available HTTP: http://www.albatrossen.no/ (accessed 11 September 2012).

Arbeids- og inkluderingsdepartementet [Labour and Social Inclusion Ministry] (2004) *Nødhjelp til personer uten lovlig opphold*. Brev til landets kommuner datert 4. oktober 2004. [*Relief support for people without legal residence status*. Letter to the Norwegian municipalities dated 4 October 2004].

Arbeids- og inkluderingsdepartementet [Labour and Social Inclusion Ministry] (2006) St. meld.nr. 9 [White Paper nr. 9] (2006–2007) *Arbeid, velferd og inkludering* [Work, Welfare and Inclusion], Oslo: Arbeids- og inkluderingsdepartementet. Online. Available HTTP: http://www.regjeringen.no/nb/dep/ad/dok/regpubl/stmeld/20062007/stmeld-nr-9-2006-2007-.html?id=432894 (accessed 16 November 2012).

Evjen, R., Kielland, K.B. and Øiern, T.(2007) *Dobbelt opp* [Double up], 2nd edn, Oslo: Universitetsforlaget.

Fellesorganisasjonen (FO) (2002) *Yrkesetisk grunnlagsdokument* [Professional Ethical Code document].

Friestad, C. and Hansen, I.L.S. (2004) *Levekår blant* innsatte [Living conditions among inmates], Fafo-report 429.

Gråwe, R. and Ruud T. (2006) *Rus og psykiske lidelser i psykisk helsevern for voksne* [Substance abuse and mental disorders in mental health care for adults], Report SINTEF Helse.

Helsedirektoratet (Directorate of Health) (2012) *Nasjonale retningslinjer for utredning, behandling og oppfølging av personer med samtidig ruslidelse og psykisk lidelse ROP lidelser* [National Guidelines for diagnosis, treatment and follow-up of persons with substance abuse and mental disorders ROP disorders], IS 1948, Helsedirektoratet 03/2012.

International Association of Schools of Social Work (IASSW), International Council of Social Welfare (ICSW) and International Federation of Social Workers (IFSW) (2012) *The Global Agenda for Social Work and Social Development, Commitment to Action.*

Kroken, R. (2006) 'Nye perspektiver på sosialarbeideres samfunnsoppdrag' [New perspectives on the role of social workers], *Nordisk Sosialt Arbeid* [Nordic Social Work], 26(4): 319–29.

Lov om sosiale tjenester i arbeids- og velferdsforvaltningen [The Social Service Act in Labour and Welfare Administration](2009), Arbeidsdepartementet [Ministry of Labour]. Online. Available HTTP: http://lovdata.no (accessed 16 November 2012).

Lov om kommunale helse- og omsorgstjenester m. m. [Health and Care Act] (2011) Helse- og omsorgsdepartementet [Ministry of Health and Care]. Online. Available HTTP: http://lovdata.no (accessed 16 November 2012).

Matthies, A-L. (ed.) (2006) *Nordic Civic Society Organzations and the Future of Welfare. A Model for Europe?* Copenhagen: Nordic Council of Ministers, Tema Nord 2006: 517.

Mathiesen, T. (1978): *Den skjulte disiplinering: artikler om politisk kontroll* [The hidden discipline: Articles on political control], Oslo: Pax.

Norwegian Organisation of Asylum Seekers (2012) *Barn på flukt får bred støtte.* [Children on the run receive wide support]. Online. Available HTTP: http://www.noas.no/barn-pa-flukt-far-bred-stotte/ (accessed 16 November 2012).

Ottesen, S. H. (2008) *Papirløse migranter. En undersøkelse av situasjonen for mennesker uten lovlig opphold i Norge og humanitære tiltak for denne gruppen i andre europeiske land* [Undocumented migrants. A survey of the situation of people without legal residence in Norway and humanitarian measures for this group in other European countries], Rapport fra Kirkens Bymisjon, Oslo, Mangfold og Oppvekst [Report from the Church City Mission, Oslo, Diversity and Childhood].

PICUM (Platform for International Cooperation on Undocumented Migrants) (2002) *Some Guidelines for Assisting Undocumented Migrants.* Online. Available HTTP: http://picum.org/en/resources/ethical-guidelines/ (accessed 11 September 2012).

Sosialdepartementet (Ministry of Social Affairs) (2003) *NOU 2003:4: Forskning på rusmiddelfeltet. En oppsummering av kunnskap om effekt av tiltak* [Research in the field of substance abuse. A summary of knowledge and the effects of interventions]. Oslo: Sosialdepartmentet, Online. Available HTTP: http://www.regjeringen.no/nb/dep/hod/dok/nouer/2003/nou-2003-4.html?id=583942 (accessed 16 November 2012).

Statistisk sentralbyrå (SSB) (2012a) *Labour Force Survey.* Statistics Norway. Online. Available HTTP: http://www.ssb.no/english/subjects/06/arbeid_en/ (accessed 16 November 2012).

Statistisk sentralbyrå (SSB) (2012b) *Children in Kindergarten by Age and County 2011.* Statistics Norway. Online. Available HTTP: http://www.ssb.no/english/subjects/04/02/10/barnehager_en/ (accessed16 November 2012).

Statistisk sentralbyrå (SSB) (2012c) *Income Statistics for Households.* Statistics Norway. Online. Available HTTP: http://www.ssb.no/english/subjects/05/01/10/inntekt_en/ (accessed 16 November 2012).

Statens Helsetilsyn (State Board of Health) (2000) *Personer med samtidig alvorlig psykisk lidelse og omfattende rusmisbruk* [People with severe mental illness and extensive substance abuse], Oslo: IK-2727.

Thomas, W.I. and Thomas, D.S. (1928) *Child in America,* New York: Knopf.

Tronvoll, M. and Pedersen, H. (2009) *Tilgjengelig, tålmodig og kreativ: sosialfaglig arbeid i tiltak for unge misbrukere (TIUR)* [Available, patient and creative:social work with young drug abusers], Rapportserie for sosialt arbeid og helsevitenskap [Report series for social work and health science], Trondheim: NTNU, Institutt for sosialt arbeid og helsevitenskap.

Turunen, P. (2009) 'Nordic community work in transition', in G.S. Hutchinson (ed.) *Community Work in the Nordic Countries, New Trends,* Oslo: Universitetsforlaget.

Viggen, E.D. (2011) Palestinsk teltleir utfordrer Norge. Asylsøkere med avslag flykter fra ørkesløse asylmottak. FO leder Rigmor Hogstad etterlyser debatt om tomrommene i velferdsstaten [Palestinian tent camp challenges Norway. Failed asylum seekers flee from idle asylum. FO leader Rigmor Hogstad calls for debate on gaps in the welfare state]. Online. Available HTTP: http://www.fontene.no/nyheter/article5817800.ece (accessed 16 September 2012).

Vike, H. (2004) *Velferd uten grenser. Den norske velferdsstaten ved veiskillet* [Prosperity without limits. The Norwegian welfare state at a crossroads], Oslo: Akribe.

Zhang, L.C. (2008) *Developing Methods for Determining the Number of Unauthorized Foreigners in Norway,* Oslo: Statistisk sentralbyrå [Statistics Norway].

11

COMMUNITY WORK AS PART OF NEIGHBOURHOOD RENEWAL

A case study

Kjell Henriksbø and Anne Line Grimen

Community work in Norway

A lot of work has been done in Norway to improve neighbourhoods and the welfare of different population groups and geographical areas. Much of this will be recognized as community work despite being presented under other headings (Kaasa 1989; Hutchinson 2009, 2010; Turunen 2004; Thyness 2006). Most often central or municipal authorities have taken initiative as a top-down approach. However, Norway also has a long tradition for 'bottom-up' approaches, with different groups trying to promote their interests and improve their living conditions. Examples are movements with a specific social, cultural or religious character or with a more mixed background as in the new social movements (Wollebæk and Selle 2002). It is an interesting comment on welfare policy in Norway that initiators from below often want the state or municipality to be a partner in, or take responsibility for, the changes (see chapter 10 by Hutchinson).

When looking at how community work has been carried out in Norway, it is important to understand the central role the state and the municipalities have had and still have in the welfare system of Norway. Today we see a 'mixed economy of welfare' gradually developing (Halvorsen 2005). For Norwegian community work, welfare policy signals about area based community development, participation and capacity building are important. Area based community development can be defined as

> cooperation with local actors to promote sustainable physical, social and environmental changes over a period of time. Local actors can be from the civil society, voluntary or market based organisations. Cooperation and coordination between different public actors are important in this approach.
> *(Husbanken 2011)*

The government underlines the importance of participation by voluntary organizations and groups who represent socially and economically disadvantaged people, in the development of good local communities (Ministry of Labour 2008). The government also considers different forms of citizen participation to be useful supplements to representative democracy (Ministry of local government and regional development 2007).

A neighbourhood project in Bergen

Background

The project area of Slettebakken has 500 publicly owned flats built in the 1950s. About one-third of the Slettebakken population of 7180 people live in these flats (Bergen Municipality 2012). Eight out of ten Norwegian households own their own dwelling (Ministry of Local Government and Regional Development 2011). People on low income or with various social problems can for a period rent flats owned by the local municipality. The living conditions in Slettebakken are ranked among the lowest in the municipality of Bergen. On average, 5.6 per cent of children in Bergen live in a household with an income below 50 per cent of the national median income. In Slettebakken, we find 23 per cent of children in this category (Bergen Municipality 2012).

Over the last ten years, the inhabitants in the public flats in Slettebakken have changed from mostly elderly people to immigrant families. About 45 per cent of the public tenants are non-western immigrants. There are around 450 children in the public flats and 124 of the households live with a single parent (mostly ethnic Norwegians). Because of national housing reforms and general de-institutionalization, people with problems such as drug abuse and mental illnesses have also been given flats in the area.

A community mapping was carried out by a research company (Asplan Viak 2009) before the project started. The mapping process aimed to involve tenants, voluntary organizations and municipal departments in the planning process through open discussions and group interviews. A survey among the public housing tenants focused on their views about resources and challenges in their living environment. Twenty-five per cent of the tenants responded to the survey, about 30 per cent of these were immigrant households.

In cooperation with three primary schools, a 'child paths mapping' was organized. The children walked through their residential area with cameras to document positive and negative aspects of their surroundings (Photo Voice 2012).

According to the mapping report (Asplan Viak 2009), 70 per cent of the informants were willing to take part in voluntary work to improve their neighbourhood, and about as many regarded it as positive to have neighbours with a different ethnic background.

The mapping report pointed out the following main challenges for the residential area:

- stigmatizing and insecure surroundings for children and young people
- cultural and social barriers between different groups of inhabitants
- lack of communication between public services and local inhabitants.

The following improvements were suggested by the informants:

- meeting-places and social activities in the neighbourhood
- leisure activities for children and young people
- tidy, safe and secure surroundings
- renovated buildings and outdoor facilities.

Project description

The Slettebakken Neighbourhood Renewal Project (2010–2013) was initiated by the municipal landlord, Bergen Housing and Urban Renewal Company and organized in cooperation with other public services, voluntary organizations and representatives of the public housing tenants (Bergen Municipality 2010).

A project team was engaged by the Bergen Housing and Urban Renewal Company in February 2010 and included a community worker, one coordinator for the housing renewal process, one coordinator for the cross-sector collaboration programme and a project leader. About 60 public and private participants took part in an opening seminar in October 2010. NGOs like the Red Cross and the Church City Mission joined in as partners together with a range of municipal departments. In January 2011 the project established a local information office in Slettebakken.

The project's aim was to improve the living environment in the residential area of Slettebakken, with particular focus on children and young people, and on social and cultural inclusion. The objectives and expected outcomes were set by Bergen Housing and Urban Renewal Company and reflected the results of the mapping process. Annual funding was given by the Norwegian State Housing Bank.

Project objectives were to create:

- a well-functioning and attractive residential area with good housing and outdoor areas
- better dialogue, cooperation and competence in community development among inhabitants, landlord, public servants and local community organizations
- better public services that served the needs of the inhabitants.

The expected outcomes included:

- establishment of a community centre, outdoor meeting-places and social activities
- promoting the feeling of security and well-being for everybody
- stimulating voluntary organizations to establish leisure activities for all ages
- promoting tenant engagement and involvement in the development process
- upgrading the buildings, flats and outdoor areas.

Reflections in the project team

As part of a qualitative research project which focused on the knowledge base of community work (by KH), a focus group interview was held early in the Slettebakken project between the members of the project team. The interview was recorded, transcribed and analysed, and below some of the team's reflections are presented.

The interview started with the group reflecting on the situation in the Slettebakken area, a situation which the project team saw as posing a lot of challenges due to the living conditions. Key words, which arose early in the reflection, were security and well-being. One of the team members had been told that many tenants felt insecure and experienced some people as frightening (such as drug abusers). The team made this a serious concern for their future cooperation with the inhabitants. The project team did not see the community as homogenous – rather the opposite – and certainly not as static. They experienced little contact between the different ethnic and social groups, and many of the inhabitants seemed not to know each other. But within some of the groups project team members referred to close relationships, with rather clear external boundaries. With reference to the mapping, the team pointed out that many of the inhabitants had a wish to come together, and a willingness to take part in a process for improving their community. The existing cooperation between different actors needed to be built on, and extended to include representatives of all the tenants, and closer contact with the public tenants and other inhabitants in Slettebakken. The team saw that initiatives which would promote well-being were important for general community building.

The team also thought it was very important to get to know the inhabitants and to stimulate some contact between them. They presented a process-oriented approach, using dialogue and involvement with the inhabitants where listening, trying to understand, giving information, clarifying and showing respect were central ideas for making connections. Team members expressed the view that participation was the key word for dealing with the situation. However, it was considered equally important that people should not feel forced to have contact with the team or others in the area.

By focusing on the women's role in a process of making the community a better place to live the team saw mothers as key people in the participation process, who could establish cooperation and create activities for the children as well as promoting general well-being. As one of the team members said, 'we have to reach the mothers, especially the immigrant mothers, but not forget to respect the fathers. We must also remember there are many single mothers among the tenants'.

Being aware of the situation, encouraging activities which would gradually build a sense of community (Bracht et al. 1999) and strengthening the community's capacity were seen as important. The team was well aware of concepts like empowerment and social capital. However, in their reflection, they used terms like strengthening the individual as well as groups or the wider community, and talked about how the inhabitants could act in a collective way for the better of the community. Trust, as a central concept in social capital, was mentioned several times: trust between the tenants as well as trust in the municipality, the house owner, and the project workers.

Initiatives taken by the tenants, if they wanted to improve the paths between the houses, create meeting places or social gatherings for instance, would be supported by the team. The team felt that getting some visible results, even small, was necessary for a good process. They felt it was vital to open up possibilities for change, and give some kind of hope. Supporting tenant representatives, on the basis of their own motivation and reasons for engagement, was seen as important for participation. Building on the self-interest and concern for others and encouraging local engagement was considered to be a good platform for developing the project. The team considered it important to work with both the physical upgrading of the houses, common area and meeting places, and with the social and cultural aspects of the residential environment.

The team ended their reflection by saying they were building on experiences from earlier projects they had taken part in, and reports from similar projects in Norway. Important guidelines for this project were seen as:

- working closely with the tenant representatives to enable mutual competence and capacity building
- discovering and supporting local resources and initiatives
- building trust and a sense of community between the different inhabitants, finding their common interests and ways of promoting these together
- acting in predictable and reliable ways to ensure visible results from the project activities as well as from the inhabitants' efforts.

Participation and project activities

The following project information is based mainly on political documents from Bergen Housing and Urban Renewal Company (Bergen Municipality 2010), and project plans and reports sent from the project leader to the Norwegian State Housing Bank, which is proving funding.

The tenant representatives

Bergen Housing and Urban Renewal Company has established an informal system of tenant representatives. Most of them are elected by people living in the same neighbourhood, while some have been recruited by the community worker, with acceptance from their neighbours (they are all called tenant representatives). The intention is to create better information and lines of cooperation to facilitate a good living environment in the residential areas. The representation system includes basic training and social gatherings for the representatives.

The residential area of Slettebakken has about 20 tenant representatives. They represent their different local neighbourhoods, and have been partners in the project both together and in smaller geographical and thematic groups. They have taken an active part in the planning of the project objectives and activities through meetings and discussions with the different project actors.

Interviews with seven of the female tenant representatives in Slettebakken (Grimen 2011) show that they know their local environment well and have extended social networks among the inhabitants. Between them, the representatives have broad experience of different social problems, and are capable of playing an active part as network agents in this socially challenging area. They share their own experiences on how to get established in the residential area. They also demand that everybody takes their turn to keep the common areas in order, and follow the house rules. In this way, they make it easier for new members of the neighbourhood to be accepted and contribute to increased levels of reciprocity and trust among the neighbours.

Gradually, the individual representatives started meeting together on their own initiative at the café in the new community house, where they discussed issues in their neighbourhood, and organized local social events and activities.

Meeting places and activities

As a first visible step responding to the tenants' requests, one of the local common areas was upgraded with a playground for children of different ages (see Figure 11.1). Later it was supplied with benches and a barbeque grill for the adults. The location was chosen between some blocks of flats where the tenant representatives had already taken the initiative to improve their outdoor area. The representatives joined the planning committee and when the playground was established, they organized an opening event for the large, multicultural group of children from the blocks.

FIGURE 11.1 A new playground is taking shape among the houses

One of the small residential blocks has been rebuilt as a community house (see Figure 11.2). The interior was planned with the representatives, some of whom who had experience of running a small neighbourhood café previously. This house has become the central meeting point of the neighbourhood and the centre of the project activities. At weekends the house is used by the local families to celebrate birthdays and similar family events. Otherwise it has been filled with intercultural community activities organized by local NGOs and by the tenant representatives. There is an open family day care centre, a neighbourhood café and meeting point, a youth club, home-work assistance, empowerment-groups for women and different activity rooms for music recording, sewing, photography classes etc.

The project has established groups for young people who do not take part in organized sports or leisure activities, many of them from immigrant families or children of single parents. The groups visit different sport clubs and cultural activities and are introduced to local organizations. Different toddler groups have been initiated and run by the parents to activate their youngest children. This has helped the parents become better acquainted and solve other daily life challenges together. This has led to some more informal discussion groups for women.

In the summertime, many of the representatives and the other inhabitants keep up the tradition of this neighbourhood of initiating informal outdoor gatherings among the houses. They take their cup of coffee outdoors, sit down to watch the children play or make a small barbeque. Newcomers are invited to join in, and in this way get a chance to observe the local habits and ways of living together.

FIGURE 11.2 The community house in the centre of the Neighbours' Day festivities

In the spring of 2012, the group of tenant representatives played a vital role in organizing the International Neighbours' Day festivities. The representatives recruited new helpers to assist them with the arrangement, as did the project team. For a couple of weeks many private, public and NGO representatives worked side by side. The inhabitants brought food from their own culture to share with the others. This event has become the social happening of the year, gathering nearly 500 of the inhabitants to celebrate solidarity and neighbourliness.

Anchoring the project activities

In February 2012, the project team invited cooperation partners and other local stakeholders in the Slettebakken area to establish a local community committee. Many local actors were enthusiastic about taking part in further development of the area, particularly to improve conditions for the children and young people growing up in Slettebakken. A committee was established, with representatives from the parent organizations of the local schools, a sports club, a private housing welfare group, two of the tenant representatives from the municipally owned flats and one representative from the project team. A local inhabitant with experience from public services and the local political administration was elected leader of the committee.

In Norway, there is a governmental support system for establishing and running local centres for voluntary work (Norges Frivilligsentraler 2012). The project is preparing an application to establish a voluntary centre at Slettebakken, to run the Community House and coordinate the activities there, starting during the last year of the project in 2013.

As we have seen, the tenants are involved in different ways and there are a number of new meeting places.

Issues to consider

Knowledge base – a trust in people and participation for change

Community workers are sometimes accused of just doing things without reflecting on the ideas and theories behind their work. An integration of theories and practice, what Freire called praxis, is often missing (Freire 1996; Ledwith 2005). The planning documents of the project did not say much about a theoretical platform, but gave a description of the situation, the project organization and expected outcomes, and the importance of dialogue was mentioned several times. In the project team, two of the members had written Masters' theses, one in community work and one in social geography using key words like social capital, empowerment and capacity building (Grimen 2011; Mjeldstad 2004). Their references include central scholars in community work, and this indicates a firm theoretical platform. The other team members did not have any theoretical education related to community work, but instead had considerable experience from working with community projects. It is interesting that during the team interview theoretical concepts (like the key words mentioned) were nearly absent, but a strong concern for the inhabitants and the community was highlighted. The team reflected a shared understanding of the situation and the way to improve it. Concepts like security, safety, trust, well-being and potential for participation and change were expressed. The project team considered the ideas about participation to be especially important. There is a clear understanding of the value of a bottom-up approach, even though this project started as a top-down initiative and the funding and management were influenced by top-down decisions. It seems the team was aware of a combination of both approaches, where participation is vital for practice.

The reflection in the team reminds us of the words of Twelvetrees (2008: 11) and the values behind community work, 'justice, respect, democracy, love and empowerment'. These values seem to be central for the team, and how they built their working ideas. We think this corresponds with their women centred approach, especially involving the mothers. By her question, 'whose voice, whose choice?' Cornwall (2011: 203) reminds us that there will be different opinions and not all will be present. These thoughts were clearly represented in the team's reflections.

In line with Ledwith (2005), the Slettebakken Project emphasizes the importance of starting with people's everyday life. We see this in the way attention has been paid to the mothers' concern for children, physical upgrading of the houses, meeting places and different activities.

Activities – participation and 'bottom-up' approaches

The Slettebakken Project is in line with the new governmental approach, which is area-based. This is also a wider European approach (Matthies et al. 2011). In the project we see different forms of participation, which are an important strength of the project (Tesoriero 2010). By establishing and taking part in different activities together, people get to know each other and they gradually create a sense of community (Bracht et al. 1999). They learn about diversity as well as equality, building trust and reducing fear. From the community mapping, the team knew this was something important to work with. The tenant representatives have been an active part of the development process from the beginning of the planning period.

Gradually, as the new community house has started functioning as a local base for all the actors in the project area, this has become a catalysing forum for social activities in the neighbourhood. The many activities organized by NGOs have drawn many different inhabitants to this community centre, and introduced them to each other and to what is going on in the neighbourhood. People discover that they can have more in common than what separates them. The community is becoming more open and able to include the social and cultural diversity of the area.

The different forms of participation can have different potentials. The forum of the tenant representatives gives opportunities for more direct forms of participation, and voices from individuals and informal groups can present needs, experiences and alternative ways of doing things in the community. This can be new activities, or new ways of coordinating or using existing resources. Local partnership, like the community café, has got a broader base. All this opens for more informal contact not only by representatives.

Ledwith and Springett (2010: 15) refer to the importance of participatory democracy and voices to marginalized people, but also power to local governance, as we can see in the Slettebakken project. The municipality, tenant representatives, public tenants and NGO representatives are gradually developing and running the activities in the Community House together, drawing on their newly established communication lines. The different actors negotiate and establish partnerships. The tenants have more influence, and some of the activities are delegated to voluntary organizations in cooperation with tenants.

For different reasons, many of the inhabitants in the project area are in a difficult life situation. The effect this might have on their participation in the project activities is illustrated by Dominelli (2002: 109), 'Oppression individualizes people in ways that isolate them and fragment their experience, leaving an individual feeling uncertain, without alternatives or incapable of taking action to change his or her situation.' Dominelli continues by pointing at collective action like we have seen in the Community House, as a way of enabling the inhabitants in this deprived area to influence their living conditions more.

> Coming together in groups is a major way of reversing this fragmentation. Realising their power within a group setting engaging in collective action can be a response that empower an individual and enable him or her to work with others to redefine their state of being and develop a greater range of options within which to live.
>
> *(Dominelli 2002: 109)*

We have already referred to women-centred ideas where women with children or grandchildren growing up in the local community have involved themselves in their children's activities and thereby also with each other. The way these women participated can relate to what Ledwith and Springett (2010: 18–19) call 'participation as critical education' and 'participation as empowerment'. The women try to develop an understanding of their situation and collectively act to improve the conditions. They found opportunities for new activities, recruited participants and discovered how they could act to change their situation.

In some of the activities related to children, we can see a mix of bonding and bridging strategies (Putnam 2000; Burnett 2006). Some of the immigrant women gathered and started to do things together, talked about their situation and their children. So did some of the ethnic Norwegian single mothers. As group members they strengthened each other, and wanted to do something for their children. Stimulated by themselves and the community workers they saw the possibilities and strengths of bridging strategies, joining their efforts as mothers to do something for the children. This also led to new bonding strategies, between the women themselves, learning language from each other and discussing what to do.

What happened in this 'sub-community' captures what Wenger (1998) called 'a community of practice'. The community of women was founded on a 'joint enterprise' – doing something about the situation for children and young people. There was a 'mutual engagement' including negotiation and shared meaning and dual development of a shared repertoire (Wenger 1998: 72–85; Anyidoho 2010).

The new 'community committee' is an example of establishing contact and communication lines between the tenants and other inhabitants in the area of Slettebakken, and with other actors like different departments in the municipality. This can help influence the structural frames of this residential area, and is an opportunity for the tenant representatives, in cooperation with other local actors, to pass messages on to the administrative and political level. Participating in this way is a form of bridging strategies as well as linking strategies concerning social capital (Burnett 2006: 289) connecting to resources outside the community.

Capacity building and sustainability

In Slettebakken the challenges that the tenants, the tenant representatives and other actors confront are quite demanding. They need both support and guidance in their work for capacity building. Tesoriero (2010: 263) points to the importance of providing support for people involved in community structures, processes and activities. According to him this involves recognizing and acknowledging the value of their contribution, giving them encouragement and being available for them.

As individuals and as a group the tenant representatives need to gain experience in organized voluntary work. The project has shown that it takes time and effort to maintain the group, to recruit new members, and to facilitate a long-term, constructive dialogue between them and the different project partners. It has also been necessary during the project to protect the representatives from getting exhausted in their roles in this demanding neighbourhood. But interviews with the representatives (Grimen 2011) show that they are building action competence, social skills and supportive networks both on their own behalf and on behalf of the neighbourhood.

Another important role and approach in community work is to identify and use the skills and resources that exist within the local community (Tesoriero 2010: 265). This approach is illustrated by the central role of the tenant representatives in the development activities in Slettebakken. It is reflected in the way the team emphasized the importance of building upon the established cooperation with the tenants and supporting their initiatives.

The tenants' knowledge and understanding of the local community are particularly important, to be able to find suitable and sustainable solutions for development. In this community, the marginalized groups in particular seem to have strengthened their voices. The tenants have seen that they are capable of changing parts of their situation.

Structural factors with great influence on the local community might be the tenants' lack of access to and possibilities to improve their positions in the labour market, the impact of housing policy and rapidly increasing social and cultural diversity. Perhaps these are the most important factors for people's living conditions. It might be naive to give the impression that this can be significantly influenced by this project. Still a project like this might strengthen the inhabitant's capacity to deal with different aspects of their life, and this can hopefully become a long-term effect of the project activities

By taking part in social activities, people experience that cooperation can improve the well-being of themselves and their children. This is a way of building psychological as well as community empowerment (Bracht et.al. 1999). Getting 'power from' by taking part in groups can lead to 'power to' (Dominelli 2002: 17). An example is the group of mothers creating activities for their children. By getting new experience, this led to new ways of acting. We can link what happened to what Freire called 'praxis', 'Human activity consists of action and reflection' (Freire 1996: 106) and also his work related to dialogue. People gradually get a voice in the community, and can take part as citizens in shaping what they want their community to be. In this way the project is contributing to capacity building.

The project is, in our opinion, in line with the Budapest declaration of community development (2004): 'it strengthens the capacity of people as active citizens to their community groups, organizations and networks, and the capacity of institutions and agencies to work in dialogue with citizens to shape and determine change in their communities.' The combination of empowering people, strengthening the institutions and the cooperation in the community can lead to community empowerment and hopefully a more sustainable development. Establishing a voluntary centre can be seen as a step in this direction.

Ledwith (2005: 86) describes the following functions of community forums developing in the 1980s:

- To bring people from the community together
- To provide an umbrella organization for community activism
- To provide a platform for debate and action
- To act as a pressure group for improved service delivery
- To organize leisure and cultural activities
- To manage the community centre
- To provide a collective voice for the community.

The Slettebakken Project with its development through the Tenant Representative Forum, the Community House and the Community Committee can be seen to have a similar function and similar intentions in its local community. We believe the Slettebakken Project has covered these functions.

At the end of the project the survey among the tenants will be repeated, using the same questionnaire as in the first mapping. In this way it will be possible to measure the effect of the development project on the inhabitants' views about the quality of their residential environment. The group interview with the tenant representatives regarding their living environment will also be repeated, supplemented by questions about their experiences as participants in the community development project.

QUESTIONS FOR REFLECTION

- Reflect on the impact of different forms of participation in a neighbourhood project from the perspective of different actors. (Make a list of possible actors.)
- How can the community worker(s) mobilize participation in a neighbourhood project?
- What challenges do you see in the mobilization/participation processes?

Notes

Figure 11.1 Playground, photo by Kjell Søderstrøm.
Figure 11.2 Community House, photo by Anne Line Grimen.

References

Anyidoho, N.A. (2010) '"Communities of practice": prospects for theory and action in participatory development', *Development in Practice*, 20(3) 318–28.

Asplan Viak (2009) *Kartlegging av bomiljøet tilknyttet kommunens boliger på Landås/Slettebakken* [Mapping of the living environment in the public housing area at Landås/Slettebakken] Bergen, Norway: Asplan Viak Research Company.

Bracht, N., Kingsbury, L. and Rissel, C. (1999) 'A five-stage community organization model for health promotion', in N. Bracht (ed.) (1999) *Health Promotion at the Community Level*, Thousand Oaks, Calif.: SAGE Publications.

Bergen Municipality (2010) *Board of Bergen Housing and Urban Renewal, Case 14/2010*, Bergen: Bergen Municipality.

Bergen Municipality (2012) *Levekår og helse i Bergen* [Living conditions and health in Bergen Municipality] Bergen: Bergen Municipality.

Budapest Declaration (2004) Online. Available HTTP: http://www.iacdglobal. org/publications-and-resources/conference-reports/budapest-declaration (accessed 13 November 2012).

Burnett, C. (2006) 'Building social capital through an active community club. University of Johannesburg, South Africa', *International Review for the Sociology of Sport* 41(3–4) 283–94, SAGE Publications. Online. Available HTTP: http://irs.sagepub.com/content/41/ 3-4/283.refs (accessed 13 November 2012).

Cornwall, A. (2011) 'Whose voices? Whose choices? Reflections on gender and participatory development' in A. Cornwall (ed.) (2011) *The Participation Reader*, London: Zed Books.

Dominelli, L. (2002) *Anti-Oppressive Social Work. Theory and Practice*, Basingstoke, Hampshire: Palgrave Macmillan.

Freire, P. (1996) *Pedagogy of the Oppressed*, 3rd edn, New York: The Continuum Publishing Company/Penguin Books.

Grimen, A. L. (2011) *Naboskap i utsatte boområder* [Neighbourliness in marginalizedresidential areas] MA thesis. Online. Available HTTP: https://bora.hib.no/handle/10049/296 (accessed 21 January 2013), Bergen: Høgskolen i Bergen.

Halvorsen, K. (2005) *Grunnbok i helse og sosialpolitikk* [Introduction to health and social policy], Oslo: Universitetsforlaget.

Husbanken (The Norwegian State Housing Bank) (2011) *Områdesatsing* [Area based approaches]. Online. Available HTTP: http://www.husbanken.no/english/other-areas-of-responsibility/area-boost/ (accessed 13 November 2012).

Hutchinson, G. S. (2010) *Samfunnsarbeid i sosialt arbeid* [Community work in social work] 3rd edn, Oslo: Gyldendal akademisk.

——(ed.) (2009) *Community Work in the Nordic Countries – New Trends,* Oslo: Universitetsforlaget.

Kaasa, A. (1989) *Samfunnsarbeid: om lokal oppgaveløsning* [Community work: local solutions], Oslo: TANO.

Ledwith, M. (2005) *Community development. A Critical Approach,* Bristol: Policy Press.

Ledwith M. and Springett, J. (2010) *Participatory Practice,* Bristol: The Policy Press.

Matthies, A.L., Kattilakoski, K. and Rantamäki, N. (2011) 'Citizens' participation and community orientation – indicators of social sustainability of rural welfare services', *Nordic Social Work Research,* 1(2) 125–39. Online. Available HTTP: http://www.tandfonline.com/doi/pdf/10.1080/2156857X.2011.613575 (accessed 13 November 2012).

Ministry of Labour (2008) *Frivillige organisasjoner og integrering og inkludering av Innvandrerbefolkningen* [Voluntary organizations and the integration and inclusion of the immigrant population] Report, Oslo: Ministry of Labour. Online. Available HTTP: http://www.regjeringen.no/nb/dep/ad/dok/rapporter_planer/rapporter/2008/frivillige-organisasjoner-og-integrering.html?id=526634 (accessed 13 November 2012).

Ministry of Local Government and Regional Development (2007) St.meld.nr. 33 (2007 2008) *Eit sterkt lokaldemokrati,* [A strong local democracy], Oslo: Ministry of Local Government and Regional Development. Online. Available HTTP: http://www.regjeringen.no/nb/dep/krd/dok/regpubl/stmeld/2007-2008/stmeld-nr-33-2007-2008-.html?id=517539 (accessed 13 November 2012).

Ministry of Local Government and Regional Development (2011) NOU 2011:5 *Rom for alle* [Room for everyone] Oslo: Ministry of Local Government and Regional Development. Online. Available HTTP: http://www.regjeringen.no/nb/dep/krd/dok/nouer/2011/nou-2011-15.html?id=650426 (accessed 13 November 2012).

Mjeldstad, K. (2004) *Integrering av innvandrere i boligområder* [Integration of immigrants in residential areas] MA thesis, Bergen: Universitetet i Bergen.

Norges Frivilligsentraler (2012) [Norwegian volunteer centres]. Online. Available HTTP: http://frivilligsentral.no (accessed 13 November 2012).

Photo Voice (2012) Online. Available HTTP: http://www.photovoice.org/ (accessed 13 November 2012).

Putnam, R.D. (2000) *Bowling Alone: The Collapse and Revival of American Community,* New York: Simon & Schuster.

Tesoriero, F. (2010) *Community Development. Community-based Alternatives in an Age of Globalization,* 4th edn, Frenchs Forest: Pearson Education Australia.

Thyness, P.A. (2006) *Sosialt arbeid, lokal organisering og selvhjelp: en innføring for helse- og sosialarbeidere* [Social work, local organization and self-help: an introduction for health and social workers], Oslo: Universitetsforlaget.

Turunen, P. (2004) *Samhällsarbete i Norden: diskurser och praktiker i omvandling* [Community work in the Nordic countries, changing discourses and practices] Växsjö: Växsjö University Press.

Twelvetrees, A. (2008) *Community Work,* 4th edn, Basingstoke: Palgrave Macmillan.

Wenger, E. (1998) *Communities of Practice,* Cambridge: Cambridge University Press.

Wollebæk, D. and Selle, P. (2002) *Det nye organisasjonssamfunnet* [The new organization society] Oslo: Fagbokforlaget.

12

PARTNERSHIP AND PARTICIPATION

Art in community work

Rina Visser-Rotgans and Eduardo Marques

Introduction

This chapter focuses on the use of art in urban communities and public spaces as social arena for artists and social workers. Social work and art might seem an illogical combination. However, if we look at projects in different countries, it does seem to work as a way of activating partnership and participation. The focus is on art and what makes it so special that it can be used in community work to support people achieve participation and partnership in and with their own environment and community. We investigate the social aspects of art, in particular those situations and places in which it can be used, with and by whom. We explain why art can be an effective tool to help people deconstruct oppressive cultural discourse and reinterpret their experience from an alternative perspective. In this way we want to contribute to a critical understanding of the relation between art practice and social work and how a creative solution can be found to old social problems. We will discuss the difficulties, related to the many different groups of actors involved in the process and product development. In the final section, we will present and analyze examples of different social art projects in the Netherlands and Portugal.

The social aspects of art and its importance to social work

As far back as human memory stretches, art has been an influential part of our lives. The 'evidence' can be seen throughout history: from pre-historic caves and Greek drama to famous painters like Rembrandt in the seventeenth century or the twentieth-century land art artist, Richard Long. The relations between art and society are clearly illustrated in certain art movements such as: Dadaisme, Land Art, Arte Povera and Spencer Tunick, who transformed hundreds of gold and red body painted naked people into art by making them part of the performance of the opera Ring der Nibelungen in Munich 2012.[1]

Traditionally the role of the audience is to see, hear or to listen to art, to enjoy it and to reflect critically on what the artist wants to show us about societal or political issues. These are the usual examples given, and they suggest that art is something for the 'happy few' who are able to go to museums, theatres or music halls. Art is made for 'all of us' but is often only accessible to the so called 'elite', of highly educated and socially integrated people. Yet, we have observed a change in thinking over recent decades in the Western world and, more recently, in Asia or Africa. Art is seen increasingly as important in the everyday life of people. It is in your own neighbourhood, on streets, in schools, and even on the World Wide Web! As citizens, we are becoming more and more involved in art as an integral part of public space which has a positive influence on different aspects of our society. Art is part of our culture. According to Hawkes:

> The arts are the paramount symbolic language through which shifting social meanings are presented. In the context of working towards a more inclusive and engaged democracy, it is active community participation and practice in the arts (rather than the consolidation of professional elites, 'audience development', economic development or cultural tourism) that should be the primary focus here.
>
> *(Hawkes 2001: 30)*

Article 27 of the Universal Declaration of Human Rights (United Nation 1948) says, 'Everyone has the right freely to participate in the cultural life of the community, to enjoy the arts and to share in scientific advancement and its benefits'. For social work, art and culture are seen as important aspects in the development of people's lives, and this can mean enjoyment of art in a 'passive' way, or creation and participation in art making in an 'active' way.

The welfare state in Western societies has not been able to deliver the promised social justice and a fairer society. Instead, we have experienced a growth of inequality with the gap between rich and poor becoming increasingly larger (EUROPA bericht 325 2008: 27). In this fragmented world, art and culture play a central role. Imagination and interpretation are needed to integrate different ideas. This is exactly what art and culture can do. Recent research has shown art to be an effective promotional tool. According to Cuylenburg (2004) and Matarasso (1997) art projects might encourage social inclusion; they can improve the self-confidence and well-being of participants, and work against stereotyping and discrimination. Public performance also brings the struggles of those suffering into a public forum, and acts as an advocate for their concerns and experiences.

The terms 'art' and 'culture' need clarification. The broad meaning of culture is 'values, attitudes, beliefs, orientations and underlying assumption' that exist between people (Huntington cited in Borrup 2006: 4). According to Borrup (2006: 5) art is part of culture and refers to the results of one's labour or the outward expressions of people from one of the many cultures on the planet. Art can be both object and act, precious and routine. It is practised individually and collectively. Borrup says, 'Culture describes the human ability to communicate and to navigate the natural and social environment together. Culture functions as a kind of operating system: culture provides people and organizations with the capacity to communicate and function' (2006: 5). That is why it is vital that the arts are equally accessible to everyone. Every human being needs to communicate and wants to express him or herself. Every human being is essentially creative and has something valuable to contribute to society through their creativity.

Art enables people to express themselves in many ways – more than just talking or writing. One of the most important characteristics of art is that it shows the individual feelings and ideas of the person who expresses them. By portraying their own ideas and expressions through images, music, dance, poetry, painting etc. people show their feelings in a very personal and individual way, in relation to their culture.

Community art and activism

'Community art' is a human manifestation of creating art works held in a participatory manner by a community in which the involvement in the creative process is more important than the final art work. The context in which this art is presented is also important because it appears more in public or symbolic places, which are more accessible. It faces the public and is often permanently on display. 'Community art' is often linked to activism and may be based on cooperation between artists and the community, giving a voice to different groups and cultures in order to maximize their involvement and social participation.

> Community-oriented public art is art that includes people from the lower classes in its creation, consumption, or both. This does not mean that the upper classes are excluded from participation, only that they are not the exclusive audience. Art created for insiders in the art world is never referred to as community art.
>
> *(Finkelpearl 2001: xj)* AQ:?

Community arts projects focus on getting people, who are excluded from society, to participate and to take control of their own situation. In his presentation on the Festival 'Art in my Neighbourhood' ('Kunst in mijn buurt') 2006 in Utrecht Francois Matarasso, a British community artist and researcher states,

> Community arts practice sets out to ensure that people have access not to the arts but to their rights. That requires a process of empowerment, helping people acquire skills, confidence and means of artistic participation. Community arts projects empower people. It helps them build the skills, confidence and knowledge to become autonomous and self-determinant actors in their own stories.
>
> *(Matarasso 2006)*

Community art is important for social work as it relates to our collective sense, but also to our multiple identities, opening up spaces for critical thinking constructed from the questioning of reality. It contributes to social change, to the extent that it makes us think and feel, making us more accountable to each other, because we feel we are part of a network of meaningful relationships. It is a work that is constructed through metaphor and imagination, giving us a body of ideas, relationships and symbols that can catalyze social change. 'Community art' is based on a 'bottom-up', strategy, valuing the needs and desires of the community. This strategy is the opposite of prescriptive classic social intervention or 'top-down' approaches more related to political intervention.

In historical terms, 'community art' appeared in the mid 1970s in the United States (Cohen-Cruz 2002) as results from a set of works and projects at the intersection of art and activism.[2] According to the author (ibid), it is the collective nature of this work which makes it so powerful for the individual. This kind of art gives people the capacity to question the status quo and break the usual visions of life and, therefore, acts as a prerequisite for activism and social transformation. The intersection and complementarities between art and activism are, according to Cohen-Cruz (2002), reflected in the thinking of the philosopher Herbert Marcuse who argued that art is what best serves as an imaginative space for freedom to regenerate the hidden capabilities, creative, spiritual and the intuitive human life. The concept of Marcuse's aesthetic dimension has two points that are transferable to community work: 1) the art has a responsibility to help society deal with its conflicts and hidden contradictions; 2) the artistic work must embody hope, human capacity to imagine what doesn't exist and give it shape (Cohen-Cruz 2002: 6). For these reasons, we advocate 'Community Art' as a participative, creative and innovative method of community intervention, which is based in the community, in the co-existence of citizens with the focus on the artistic tasks and not on the individual problems. It is also more effective in helping relationships than traditional approaches because a dialogue is established with the citizens using a new language, and in the end it is the heart that decides. Art is, by definition, the language of the heart, affections and feelings.

The role of culture and art in capacity building and participation

Charles Landry (2006), economist and authority on the culture of cities and how it can revitalise economies, analyzed a large project (period 1990–2005) from SCP (Swiss Cultural Program) that consists of about 15 projects in Eastern Europe. Landry (2006: 14–20) 'believes the arts can help create an open minded culture that is more resilient and adaptable to the changes brought about by political ructions and globalization. Think of any problem or opportunity and the arts can help.' According to Landry, art seems to be the best activity to use in all kinds of situations where change is necessary: in conflict situations, to gain confidence, to change the mindset or to involve citizens in a community. Engagement with arts means using the language of the senses. By singing, acting, dancing, painting or sculpting, one can express things in another, more powerful way. It can help people to look at society in different ways, for example by making us look at our prejudices. Art enables us to think 'out of the box', to use our imagination in other disciplines, and arts projects can also provide a lot of enjoyment.

Important and interesting lessons can be learned from Landry: art should be part of the community, part of the culture and be carried out by the people of the community. But what is also important is the involvement of partners in this process, and especially the role of the artist involved in community arts. Looking at the importance of cooperation, we can say that because of the intended effects of community arts, co-creation – a form of cooperation involving joint ownership of the process and the product by all the participants – can be seen as one of the crucial aspects of being successful for proposed changes regarding complex societal problems.

Community work and participation: from citizens to stakeholders

Community work is understood as practice by professional social workers or volunteer services which consist of helping people in a community and activating citizen participation in a locality (Smith et al. 2006). This often involves collaborative work in a non-profit coalition between public institutions and grassroots associations. Community work is associated with community development when it involves development of human, social, physical, financial and environmental capital to create community sustainability (ibid). Participation is a key word in community development and it means actual involvement of the people affected by the planned changes. Nowadays, with the impact of online social networks, it can realize a new citizenship, new citizen empowerment, and the rebirth of urban democracy in the world (Smith et al. 2006: 41). Participation in the arts can widen the range of people who engage with, question, challenge, re-imagine and revive our cultural, social and political life.

Matarasso's research from Australia (2005: 18), demonstrates that, although society as a whole is more materially prosperous than ever before, many of its members feel excluded, powerless and unhappy. What is good for the economy is not necessarily good for society. As stated before, community art is an important tool in community development, to develop social and cultural capital, empowering citizens and encouraging them to participate. The inclusion of dissonant, contradictory, excluded voices will change our culture, but will change it for the better.

The community art project, the artist and creation management

Who starts community art projects, why and with what intended outcome? What are possible barriers to developing successful projects?

In community art projects, there are many different actors:

- The community and the societal circumstances/societal deficiency
- The target group
- The artist
- Local partners (stakeholders).

The first condition is that there has to be a deficiency, certain circumstances in a society, or a question from a number of citizens of that community, often a deprived area. In most cases, the deficiency will have to do with lack of empowerment or lack of social cohesion or exclusion and the people themselves are aware of or arguing for change in their community. Community members need to be involved in the process of regeneration of their community as well as other stakeholders/partners in their community. The cooperation and co-creation between the partners is crucial. This starts with researching the 'question' in cooperation with the target group. After this, there needs to be a bonding with the artistic and creative strength of the artist. The artist needs the social skills to bring together the experiences of the citizens with his own artistic abilities in co-creation with the target group and other stakeholders. The artist and the community worker should be able to help focus the group's view on reality and life, deconstruct oppressive cultural discourses and reinterpret experiences from alternative perspectives to motivate them to get involved in changing or improving their situation.

Sikko Cleveringa (2012: 25) introduces 'creation management' as a tool for process and project management.[3] He transformed the concept to make it usable for community arts. The core of creation management is to distinguish the four different powers that have to be approached in the right sequence. It is important to keep these four powers activated and in balance. The four steps of creation management coincide with the most important elements we often see in the definitions of community art:

- An artistic project (*creative power*)
- That reacts to social deficit (*power of maintenance*)
- With the efforts of concerned citizens as well as professionals (*power of co-creation*)
- Delivers a rise in value with imaginative power (*power of imagination*).

These terms ask for an explanation. To manage a project like this, it is important to start with the 'grassroots'. First, the community worker needs to be in contact with members of the community to clarify what it is they want to change or improve. This is focusing on the deficit and addressing the power of maintenance. The artist needs to get involved in the community and with the inhabitants. He is working as an artist but also has a role as co-worker, listener, navigator and democratic activist. When the artist is sufficiently involved in the community and its social deficit, he suggests an artistic intervention which allows the community to interpret the deficit in a different way and to find solutions in ways that promote empowerment and participation. The artist, the community and other stakeholders mobilize the power of co-creation throughout the creation process, to come to the final artistic result showing their power of imagination.

The artistic project manager (the artist) has to supervise this process of co-creation, although often with the help of the community worker or others. This is a difficult process where the participants are working towards a common understanding of what the product is going to be. The process itself and its effects are as important as the end result. This is always one of the challenges for the artist. Nevertheless, art seems to be the perfect tool with which to develop citizenship, participation, criticism, social inclusion and social cohesion. The goal is to help people communicate with others, to feel better about themselves and to take charge of their lives. People need to know that there is no 'right way' or 'wrong' way to create art and that experimenting is good.

Community art outcomes: reflection on results and the use of research methods

The development of strategies based on art projects and programmes is becoming more common in community work. Because of that, it is important to understand the impacts on a community. Delgado wrote:

> Numerous measures can be used in determine the extent of success achieved by a project. However, the process of systematizing the methods for measuring the success falls within the realm of evaluation. The evaluation phase of community capacity enhancement is just as important as the initial assessment phase. In fact, the success of a mural, for example, must be evaluated using methods and tools that can help generate lessons for a community.
>
> *(Delgado 2000: 206)*

Because of the world economic crises, all societies face a reduction in, and in some cases, the destruction of welfare services. The focus on cost to governments of community art projects and programmes has become more important. Community workers cannot avoid issues like cost-effectiveness and prevention. It is very important to find the right evaluation model for this kind of intervention; one that allows us to get a clear idea of the results and savings achieved by community art projects. Individualism fragments societies and community arts projects can help develop a more inclusive society and more participatory democracy. The effects of this kind of project can outweigh the costs of social disaffiliation. It is always cheaper to use preventive social work through art in communities than cover the costs related with social disaffiliation. According to Zaretzky, Flatau and Brady,

> The net cost of providing support with clients of a social program is the gross cost net of any savings achieved elsewhere resulting from program participation. Savings, or cost offsets, occur when social programs lower outlays in non-program related areas and/or increase revenues.
>
> *(Zaretzky et al. 2008: 232)*

Projects are expected to have positive and measurable impacts on communities and evaluation of projects have become a condition of investment. Everybody understands and agrees with the need for an evaluation process and is aware of the difficulties quantifying the impact of the arts in terms of social gain. The methodological challenges are arguably greater than in any other field of evaluation. Merli finds that most research in community arts is based on a weak theoretical grounding that makes it difficult to evaluate the social impact of participation in arts activities. 'It is not tenable that any kind of participatory arts activity in any kind of community and culture would have identical social impacts.' She argues the need 'to know the real, specific effects of the arts, and in which circumstances they occur' (Merli 2002: 107–18). Despite scientific debate about the evaluation of the social impact of community arts programmes, community workers and other practitioners believe that community art programmes can produce positive social effects which outweigh their cost. A range of theoretical frameworks, like community arts, experiential learning and action research can be brought together and reconstructed in ways that bring about an increase in personal and professional knowledge. The arts do not fit neatly into conventional quantitative assessment frameworks. A qualitative research method, such as in-depth interviews, seems to be preferable for research in subjects like community arts.

Different research results have shown that:

1. The arts enhance the awareness as well as the understanding of other cultures and enable better understanding and communication. They contribute to social cohesion (Brouwer 2008).
2. Participants learn different skills: thinking skills like decision making, creative thinking, problem solving and social skills, like speaking, listening, cooperative work and tolerance of differences ('Ik-Vrouw', Delft 2009).[4]
3. Participants report that they have improved personal skills: such as confidence, increased levels of self esteem, individual responsibility, improved communication skills and improvement in their quality of life (Cultural Ministers Council Statistics Working Group 2004).

According to McIntosh (2010: 178) research is needed because, 'this type of work has value precisely because it is not mainstream. If it were, it would have been reduced to a table or a chart, worked through by an application of a methodology deemed satisfactory by the mainstream gatekeepers.' For McIntosh, critical creativity is an antidote to positivism and a welcome addition to interpretivism, which enables a challenge to the status quo and supports the development of practice and qualitative research in the real world. Community workers should feel confident with their involvement in research and evaluation that provide them with new possibilities for action. It is an opportunity to become more reflective and creative in their practice, and action research can help a lot.

Whatever the method chosen for evaluation or research, community workers must be aware that creativity underlies all human endeavours and can be used to frame significant themes, juxtapose interpretations, launch new directions and propel people to pursue innovative directions in community arts.

Examples of community art projects in Netherlands and Portugal

There are many good international community art projects. In the following we present two projects and relate these to the four steps of creation management.

IkVrouw (I Woman)

The population of the Netherlands includes many people with different cultural background and for several of them it is a huge problem that they do not speak Dutch. Especially for the women it is important that they can share their feelings with others and become aware of opportunities and possibilities in which changes can improve their lives and the well-being of their families.

A good example is a community art project in Delft (a multicultural city) called 'Ik-Vrouw', which means 'I-Woman'.[5] It is the story of seven women with different cultural backgrounds, from Surinam, Iran, Turkey, Poland and the Netherlands (see Figure 12.1). The specific theme of this performance was to show that all women were able to find their own way in life, unless they had to face different problems and cultural differences. They were recruited by a social worker in a Mother-Child community centre in the city. This is a centre for vulnerable women with children where they can build a social network, share knowledge and take specific courses. A theatre professional and a social worker discussed the women's situation with them, their feelings and their questions. The women shared their individual problems, for instance their fear for the unknown, their hope for a better life and encouragement to go on with their lives. This is what Cleveringa (2012) calls 'addressing their power of maintenance'. How can these women be given a different view of their situation and their qualities? Together with a theatre professional, the women created an impressive theatre and music production about their individual cultural differences, experiences and problems which showed they have a lot in common (activating their creative power). They learned to act, to sing, to play and discovered unknown talents, and together they developed their power of co-creation. It became their common story and they performed it in several locations in the town in front of large audiences. All seven women were proud of themselves. Not only did they learn about the commonalities and differences in their stories, but most importantly, they learned a lot from working together and they experienced an increase in self esteem. All of these women gained a positive view of their future and activated their power of imagination (Mittertreiner 2009: 32–3). This is a good example of how theatre can help people make fundamental changes in their lives. This way of working is similar to the 'Theatre of the Oppressed', funded by Augusto Boal in Brazil in the early 1970s. His hypothesis is, 'If the oppressed person himself (and not a surrogate artist) performs an action, this action, performed in a theatrical fiction, will allow

FIGURE 12.1 'IkVrouw' theatre group 2009 Delft (The Netherlands)

him to change things in his real life' (Boal, 1990: 35). It is about the concept of learning-by-doing: learning by acting yourself, by playing, by talking, by watching. Theatre is instrumentalized to help people express and control emotions, to develop reflective and social competencies. In the case of 'Ik-Vrouw', we have been able to see the results described above.

Risen from the Ground (Levantados do chão)

In Portugal, poverty and social exclusion still are key social problems. In 2010, a Portuguese NGO called Associação Hemisférios Solidários started developing several community art projects to give a voice to and empower disadvantaged groups, mainly homeless people. The projects were designed by Eduardo Marques as Executive Director of the NGO, with social workers from third sector organizations, local artists, homeless people and volunteers. They developed a creative platform to involve disenfranchised people in social and individual change processes through community art work ('creative power').

The Project 'Risen from the Ground' started in 2011 and is still ongoing. It allows disadvantaged groups along with other citizens and volunteers to create art installations in public spaces. It was seen as a way to tackle social deficit caused by poverty or social disaffiliation. This can be seen as implying the power of maintenance. Street workers identified loneliness and individualism as major problems for homeless people that made it more difficult for them to be/feel included socially in these groups. In response to this, in 2011, an important participatory art project was started, called 'Labyrinth: Checkmate Poverty'. This project was started to deconstruct oppressive social and cultural discourse and to empower excluded groups. The project was carried out in a creative partnership, mobilizing the power of co-creation, with many different actors and organizations from the town of Coimbra. The aim was to raise awareness of poverty in Portugal as an issue of structural violence that undermines the democratic state, human rights and social peace. More than 200 individuals were involved and the outcome was a square labyrinth made with black dishes (see Figure 12.2). These were painted or written on by homeless citizens, to narrate their stories about poverty, loneliness, discrimination and fear. This local community art installation was replicated on the web through a 3D virtual platform InWorldz and is global allowing people all over the world to visit our community art work through 'Inworldz Dreamz and Visionz Art Fest'.[6] By these community art projects, televisions and newspapers were the witness of the need of a community capacity enhancement to deal with poverty.

From the start, this project has had an integrated research dimension based on visual methodologies. In line with the work of Tolia-Kelly:

> The politics of using participatory art enable the research to be engaged ethically, plurally, creatively and inclusively towards the development of theory, policy and practice. The use of participatory art has two critical aims; firstly as researchers we engage with textual communication that offers 'voices' and perspectives of participants in a visual process. Secondly, the process of engaging with 'visual' communication goes beyond that which written questionnaires and oral interviews can engage.
>
> (Tolia-Kelly 2007: 132)

FIGURE 12.2   In one of Coimbra's main squares, the voices of people could be seen. From the project 'Risen from the Ground' – 'Labyrinth: Checkmate Poverty', Portugal

The project shows its potential to promote social inclusion with a low cost budget, and encourages the community and social actors to keep cooperation with citizens going in other projects that arise from this one. This is a good example of the power of imagination. Community arts is a powerful process that enriches what already exists in a community and complements social work strategies which focus on wellbeing and the right of all citizens to participate. It is also an opportunity to increase evidence-based knowledge based on an objective and a subjective dimension.

Our participatory action research with this project was based on multi-focus evaluation with interviews, participation observation and visual meaning-making. The findings show the multi-factorial dimensions of poverty and also show that, sometimes, loneliness can be more painful than having no money. More information about these community arts projects can be seen on the website of Associação Hemisférios Solidários. As a result of this project, some individuals who had lost hope a long time ago began to feel like part of society again, with a voice and a wish to be part of the solution.

Conclusion

Art is an important dimension of culture and everyday life, but there are still many challenges. How can the artistic, the social and the economic aspects be connected? How can the outcomes of community art projects be evaluated and researched, particularly in terms of sustainable participation, empowerment, liveability and citizenship? In the coming years, this will require a lot of commitment from researchers and community workers and, above all, co-operation between social actors and artistic and economic professionals to co-create innovative and sustainable solutions.

QUESTIONS FOR REFLECTION

- Do you know any projects in your community like murals, gardens, playgrounds, sculptures that were built to undertake community capacity enhancement and development?
- Why are the arts generally not considered to be of relevance to community social workers?
- What are the potential benefits of art in community work?

Notes

Figure 12.1 'Ik-Vrouw', photo by Herman Zonderland, Delft 2009.
Figure 12.2 Project 'Risen from the Ground' – 'Labyrinth: Checkmate Poverty'. Portugal, photo by Eduardo Marques.

1. On the webpage 'Contemporary Art', information about the artists and their projects can be found. Online. Available HTTP: http://en.wikipedia.org/wiki/Contemporary_art (accessed 7 March 2013).
2. A good example of this kind of project is AIDS Memorial Quilt. Online. Available HTTP: http://en.wikipedia.org/wiki/NAMES_Project_AIDS_Memorial_Quilt (accessed 21 March 2012).
3. Creation management (Creatieregie) is a concept from Robert Coppenhagen for project creation. It is a concept for a process-oriented approach in project and organization development with a strong focus on the human factor. See R. Coppenhagen (2002) *Creatieregie: Visie en verbinding bij verandering* [Creation Director: Vision and connection with change], Schiedam: Scritpum Uitgeverij.
4. For example, statements from the women in discussion with the audience after the last play in De Hofstee Delft, 20 March 2009 (Rina Visser).
5. See Kunstindewijken. Online. Available HTTP: http://www.kunstindewijken.nl/ (accessed 29 November 2012).
6. Inworldz Dreamz & Visionz Art Festival 2011. Online. Available HTTP: http://www.youtube.com/watch?v=cNt9crWMTug (accessed 14 December 2012).

References

Associação Hemisférios Solidários. Online. Available HTTP: http://hemisferiosolidarios.pt.vu (accessed 20 June 2012), http://www.facebook.com/hemisferios.solidarios (accessed 20 June 2012).

Boal, A. (1990) 'The cop in the head: three hypotheses' in *Drama Review,* Fall 1990, 35–42.

Borrup, T. (2006) *The Creative Community Builder's Handbook: How to Transform Communities Using Local Assets, Arts and Culture,* Minnesota: Fieldstone Alliance Publishing Centre.

Brouwer, P. (2008) 'TNO-rapport Kwaliteit van leven', *Effectenmeting Jalan Jalan* [Quality of *Life Effect Measurement of the Jalan Jalan Festival*] Research Report, TNO: Kunstenaars & Co.

Cleveringa, S. (2012) *Cultuur Nieuwe Stijl, praktijkboek Community Arts en nieuwe cultuurfuncties* [Culture New Style, Practical Guide to Community Arts and New Cultural Positions], Amsterdam: PCK Publishing.

Cultural Ministers Council Statistics Working Group (2004) *Social Impacts of Participation in the Arts and Cultural Activities: Evidence, Issues and Recommendations,* Canberra, Autralia. Online. Available HTTP: http://culturaldata.gov.au/publications/statistics_working_group/cultural_participation (accessed 3 December 2012).

Cuylenburg, G. (2004) 'What is the role of public relations (PR) within an arts organization when attempting to create beneficial social change in specific relation to the mental health sector?' *High Octane Arts Marketing Tools and Ideas.* Online. Available HTTP: http://www.australiacouncil.gov.au/_data/assets/pdf_file/0017/40904/PRPaper_Cuylenburg_1901051.pdf (accessed 28 September 2012).

Cohen-Cruz, J. (2002) *An Introduction to Community Art and Activism.* Online. Available HTTP: http://www.artdesigncommunity.com/uploads/6/2/1/2/6212450/an_introduction_to_community_art_and_activism_cohen_cruz-2.pdf (accessed 21 March 2012).

Delgado, M. (2000) *Community Social Work Practice in an Urban Context – The Potential of a Capacity-enhancement Perspective,* New York: Oxford University Press.

EUROPA bericht nr. 325, May 2008: 2/Dossier: Europa groeit, de armoede blijft ... [Dossier: Europe is growing, poverty is staying ...]. Online. Available HTTP: http:// ec.europa.eu/belgium/information/.../nl/eurinfnl325_nl.pdf (accessed 28 September 2012).

Finkelpearl, T. (2001) *Dialogues in Public Art,* Massaechusetts: The MIT Press.

Hawkes, J. (2001) *The Fourth Pillar of Sustainability. Culture's Essential Role in Public Planning.* Online. Available HTTP: http://www.culturaldevelopment.net.au/ community/Downloads/HawkesJon(2001)TheFourthPillarOfSustainability.pdf (accessed 14 December 2012).

'Ik-Vrouw' (2009) *Kunst in de Wijken,* Delft.

Landry, C. (2006) *Culture at the Heart of Transformation: The Role of Culture in Social and Economic Development: Lessons Learnt from the Swiss Cultural Programme* Schweiz: Direktion für Entwicklung und Zusammenarbeit, Pro Helvetia DEZA.

Matarasso, F. (1997) *Use Or Ornament? The Social Impact of Participation in the Arts,* London: Comedia.

Matarasso, F. (2005) 'Art for our sake: the artistic importance of community arts', paper given at *The Sorcerer's Apprentice,* community arts conference in Whitby, Yorkshire, 28 April 2005.

Matarasso, F. (2006) *Presentation on festival 'Kunst in mijn buurt' [Art in my neighbourhood],* Commmunity Art Festival: Utrecht.

McIntosh, P. (2010) *Action Research and Reflective Practice. Creative and Visual Methods to Facilitate Reflection and Learning,* New York: Routledge.

Merli, P. (2002) 'Evaluating the social impact of participation in arts activities. A critical review of François Matarasso's *Use or Ornament?' International Journal of Cultural Policy,* 8(1): 107–18.

Mittertreiner, M. (2009) *Wijktheater en actief burgerschap,* Bachelorproef, Haagsche, Hogeschool, Den Haag, [Community theatre and active citizenship, Bachelor thesis, the Hague University of Applied Sciences].

Smith, D.H., Stebbins, R.A. and Dover, M.A. (2006) *A Dictionary of Nonprofit Terms and Concepts,* Bloomington and Indianapolis: Indiana University Press.

Tolia-Kelly, D.P. (2007) 'Participatory art; capturing special vocabularies in a collaborative visual methodology with Melanie Carvalho and South Asian women in London, UK', in S. Kindon, R. Pain and K. Mike (eds), *Participatory Action Research Approaches and Methods Connecting People, Participation and Place,* New York: Routledge.

United Nations (1948) *Universal Declaration of Human Rights.* Online. Available http:// www.un.org/en/documents/udhr/index.shtml (accessed 22 June 2012).

Zaretzky, K., Flatau, P. and Brady, M. (2008) 'What is the cost to government of homelessness programs?' *Australian Journal of Social Issues,* 43(2): 231–54.

PART 4

Addressing new global challenges

13

(RE)IMAGINING COMMUNITIES IN THE CONTEXT OF CLIMATE CHANGE

A saving grace or the evasion of state responsibilities during (hu)man-made disasters?

Lena Dominelli

Introduction

Community has been a contested term which has been used for decades as a 'portmanteau word'[1] (Wilson 1990; Dominelli 2006) in which to contain peoples' sense of connectivity and aspirations for support from others in their endeavours to secure a better life. The notion of community as a form of social capital has traditionally been conceptualized as bringing people in a particular locality together for the common good (Putnam 2000). More recently, as natural and (hu)man-made disasters, especially those linked to climate change and the extreme weather events (that are associated with it) are increasing in frequency, there is a growing recognition of the interdependencies that exist between different parts of the globe. 'Interdependency' as a concept and the basis of connectivity within and between communities has been rethought in terms of social problems crossing transnational borders and includes a critique of the degradation of the environment perpetrated under capitalist globalization, in its neoliberal forms (Dominelli 2012a). 'Interdependencies' expose the links or connections that exist in and between communities and are particularly evident when communities interact with each other.

In this chapter, I examine the concept of community from an international, enviro-developmental or 'green' perspective. This highlights the links between people and their environments. I go on to argue that social connectivity has to: become intergenerational and borderless; engage with the physical, socio-economic, cultural, political and physical environments if the earth's well-being is to be maintained for future generations as well as current populations; distribute resources globally equitably within and between generations. An international enviro-developmental or 'green' perspective acknowledges interdependencies between peoples and countries and how action in one can impact upon another.

In making this case, I refer to examples of community action that: call for environmental justice; question the roles that the state plays in both undermining and supporting local and global connectivities; and enable communities to affirm their demands for social progress that does not destroy the environment in the process (Dominelli 2012a). I conclude that social workers and community workers can facilitate the processes of (re)imagining communities as interdependent entities that cross borders (real and virtual), e.g., through projects that aim to reduce greenhouse gas emissions. These affect poor and marginalized communities more than others. Poor people suffer disproportionately from disasters and take longer to recover because their communities lack the resources and funding necessary to re-establish themselves (Pyles 2007; Dominelli 2012a; Islamic Relief 2012). In making my case, I also draw upon research that I have undertaken through three different projects. 'Internationalising Institutional and Professional Practices', 'Climate Change', 'the Built Environment and Older People' (BIOPICCC); and support offered by the International Association of Schools of Social Work (IASSW) to people suffering from disaster.[2]

Communities: contested entities that affirm collective values and action

Communities are variously defined, according to the aims and objectives of those determining the definitions. Newby and Bell (1971) collected 98 different versions several decades ago, and thereby indicated its contested base. Tönnies (1957) drew a distinction between the connections that existed between people at the local level (gemeinschaft) and those at the societal level (geselschaft). His analysis is often picked up by politicians who attempt to enforce notions of community as 'warm, friendly' places in which people support each other because they share values and identity linked to location. This defines communities as geographically based, usually associated with small neighbourhoods, and unitary identities that hold people together. Politicians on all sides of the political spectrum have utilized the concept to promote communitarian impulses (Blair 1998), and lately with more conservative variants (Cameron and Clegg 2010).

Currently in the UK, these conservative tendencies are specifically linked to David Cameron's 'Big Society'. This exploitation of the term community displays Delanty's (2003: 187) contention that 'communities are formed 'through communicative practices and normative concepts'. Cameron utilizes social norms and values to impose particular structures and expectations on communities. In the context of the 'Big Society', this draws heavily on notions that communities are homogeneous entities where peace and harmony reign, thus ignoring potential sources of conflict, structural inequalities and endemic forms of social exclusion. It also requires communities to expand their own resources to make good the loss of state-provided goods and services, and do so with minimal state intervention or publicly funded resources. Consequently, the 'Big Society' becomes a fig leaf covering the barrenness of the neoliberal ideology that underpins it conceptually and practically.

The withdrawal of the state from its responsibilities to care for its people as required under the Universal Declaration of Human Rights (UDHR) of 1948, particularly Articles 22 to 27 (George 2003), undermines social solidarity and assumes that communities can manage without external resources (Dominelli 2012b). The lack of external resources inhibits community development and resilience regardless of the issue. Yet, public policy in the West has been devised with the explicit aim of forcing communities to become self-sufficient regardless of their capacity to rise to the occasion. This is particularly true for poor communities that need external resources to develop beyond the limitations of self-help. Carol Stack (1983) reveals how poor African-American communities utilize bonding social capital to survive poverty, but they cannot escape it without external assets coming into their localities. The same difficulty has been exposed by recent natural disasters, whether occurring in rich countries like the United States during Hurricane Katrina, for example, or in industrializing countries like Pakistan during the 2010 floods or Sri Lanka during the 2004 Indian Ocean Tsunami (Pyles 2007; Dominelli 2012a).

A common thread between these diverse views of community is its importance in promoting collective action and achieving goals that community groups have articulated together. Collective action draws upon notions of connectivity, solidarity and trust, building on the idea that by sticking with each other, people can achieve more by acting as a group than as individuals. Building ties of solidarity is difficult and social workers can mobilize communities to work for its achievement. Various authors, e.g., Putnam (2000), have argued that social capital, as the encapsulation of community ties locally, has been lost as communities have become more fragmented, diverse and dispersed. This view is challenged daily in communities across the world as people organize to help each other. In disaster situations, when formal providers fail to arrive during extreme weather events, for example, people on the spot provide the care needed, as BIOPICCC indicated (Dominelli 2012b).

Shocks, initiated through disasters in general and climate change in particular, are more likely than ordinary everyday events to stress the availability of local internal resources. Shocks are by definition extraordinary happenings that stretch local communities' capacity to deal with them and require external intervention to return to their normal state (Perez and Thompson 1994). Disasters can be natural or (hu)man-made, although the distinction between them is often challenged as their boundaries become increasingly blurred (Dominelli 2012a). Even climate change is believed to lead to an increase in the frequency of their occurrence, especially those linked to extreme weather events including flooding, tsunamis, landslides, hurricanes, earthquakes, volcanic eruptions and drought. (Hu)man disasters, especially those normally linked with industrial pollution like that which occurred in Bhopal, India in 1984, or environmental degradation resulting from armed conflict associated with the exploitation of natural resources, for example, those that arose in Rwanda, the Democratic Republic of the Congo, Iraq, Afghanistan and other war zones, contribute to climate change as tonnes of carbon emitted through military ordinance exploded during ensuing battles (O'Carroll 2008).

Mitigating vulnerabilities and growing resilience in communities

The UN, UNDP, OECD, the World Bank and other agencies have attempted to develop indicators that will enable practitioners to formulate and assess both vulnerability and resilience (Burton 2007). These seek to encompass both processes and outcomes, and have done so with varying degrees of success. Social workers can assist local communities in formulating more holistic and empowering initiatives by engaging residents in the processes of co-producing the solutions that are most appropriate to resolving their problems.

Vulnerability refers to 'the susceptibility of a community to the impact of hazards' (UN 2006: 11). It is not a property of a system, but a product of social processes which create vulnerability as an outcome of social relations with particular spatial and organizational characteristics (Bankoff et al. 2004). By understanding human vulnerabilities or community susceptibilities, social workers can help lay the foundations for addressing unexpected hazards and other stresses. Tackling vulnerabilities is linked to development processes that enable people to reduce risk as part of a sustainable approach to hazards (Lewis 1999). Developing and enhancing community resilience becomes one way of mitigating vulnerabilities. Human agency is an ingredient in initiating reductions in vulnerabilities and enhancing resilience (Bankoff et al. 2004). Social workers can facilitate the processes for developing capacity to withstand and/or adapt to the impact of disaster and retain functionality in systems whether natural or social or hybrid (Dominelli 2012a).

Community resilience is a property that facilitates community responses to disasters including climate change. Many communities focus on developing resilience in response to specific threats or vulnerabilities. Cutter, Barnes, Berry, Burton, Evans, Tate and Webb have defined resilience during disasters as:

> The ability of a social system to respond and recover from disasters and includes those inherent conditions that allow the system to absorb impacts and cope with an event, as well as post-event, adaptive processes that facilitate the ability of the social system to reorganize, change and learn in response to a threat.
>
> *(Cutter et al. 2008: 599)*

This definition identifies existing strengths that are useful in developing and harnessing resilience in particular communities. However, a danger is that a community that is deemed resilient will be unable to press claims for external assistance when resources are scarce or inaccessible and demand heavy. Indeed, the NGO, Planning for Resilience and Emergency Preparedness (PREP) that aims to create resilience amongst individuals and communities in the USA, is already advising people to develop their own resilience so that they can look after themselves for a minimum of 72 hours during an emergency. The organization '72 hours' concurs with this approach. The websites of both organizations offer specific advice on self-help options aimed at keeping people going in the first few days after a disaster when formal service providers are unable to reach victim-survivors. This self-help advice focuses on helping people to become better prepared and more resilient when confronting specified hazards. Unfortunately, such self-help approaches have to be treated with caution. For example, self-help might be particularly difficult for people who lack mobility or have health or other needs that mean that their lives are endangered within a few minutes or hours of a disaster striking. This could happen to an older person living alone and relying on oxygen tanks to assist breathing during an electricity outage when there is no access to a back-up generator. Another instance is that of a wheelchair user who cannot move to higher floors during a tsunami because lifts are inoperable and there is no obvious means of moving upwards unassisted.

Dominelli (2012a: 64–6) adds that resilience is an 'emerging property' which suggests that resilience is not a characteristic that once acquired is always there as a static feature. She suggests that resilience is stochastic and changes according to the specificities of event, time and place. Moreover, as circumstances change, there can be a loss of resilience, no change or its further development. A flexible, dynamic approach to resilience enables social and community development workers to engage communities in extending their resilience and strengthening their capacities to respond, cope with and adapt to calamitous events. Resilience, therefore, becomes the ability of a system to receive information about and absorb a shock while retaining its functions and structures. Adaptability refers to the system's capacity to deliberate and take action that will manage these strengths and thereby mitigate the impact of a disaster. This presupposes collective action which social workers can facilitate to ensure the effective use of existing resources and capacity to pull in additional ones. For systems that are no longer resilient or adaptable, their capacity to transform themselves into something new and different, that is, their transformability, becomes the key to their success or failure in building upon past events and change (Walker and Salt 2006).

Communities are not monolithic entities and the differentiated experiences of its inhabitants indicate that social positioning, economic conditions, political regimes, governance structures, the physical ecosystems and daily routines interact to produce disparate patterns of reaction, adaptation and recovery (Cutter et al. 2008; Dominelli 2012a). The BIOPICCC and 2004 Indian Ocean Tsunami in Sri Lanka projects revealed that those responding to questions about their futures stated their desire to return to the state of affairs that prevailed before the disaster took place. This wish exposes their determination to survive and retain their links to their previous communities, limiting their expectations to what was, rather than what might be. Because differentials exist in a community's capacity to organize to reduce the impact of disasters before they occur as well as respond to them when they strike, this attitude could re-produce existing inequalities. This state of affairs was evidenced in various disasters including Hurricane Katrina in 2005 (Pyles 2007), the 2004 Indian Ocean Tsunami and the Japanese Tohoku earthquake and tsunami of 11 March 2011 which also caused a failure in the nuclear power plant in Fukushima Daiichi (Holt et al. 2012). These three disasters in particular highlighted the importance of seeing building resilient capacity as an unending and constantly evolving process. Although Japan had one of the most well-prepared populations for earthquake disasters, existing preparations proved to be inadequate in handling the consequences of this one, especially in the short term, and nearly 20,000 people died, many of them older people. Older people, women and children are amongst the most vulnerable populations during disasters. In the case of Hurricane Katrina, 'race' and racism resulted in African American communities in the New Orleans neighbourhood called the Lower Ninth Ward being the worst affected. Some of these residents have yet to fully recover to their pre-Katrina status. Yet, getting back to where they were remains one of their objectives and is closely linked to the sense of place encapsulated in their imaginings of community – the place called 'home'.

Community responses cannot be assumed or taken for granted. Developing resilient capacities in systems is a specific aim that has to be worked for, and achieved if vulnerabilities around hazards are to be contained. Reducing vulnerability and enhancing resilience are activities that social workers and community workers can undertake by facilitating collective action and mobilizing the resources that allow communities to return to normalcy, however residents define this, in a process of (re)imagining communities as they used to be. Although returning to where they were can reproduce prevailing inequalities, achieving their goal of stability in a known environment is more likely to be realized if there is a sense of community in place (Chavis and Wandersman 1990). However, a return to normality does not necessarily mean going back to where one was before the disaster, despite this plea often being heard in humanitarian aid situations. Returning to normal may entail a repositioning of people and their communities. This might be extremely important in a situation in which communities seek to become more equal and demonstrate more solidarity after a disaster. Moreover, the development of new and different forms of resilience may be called for at points of upheaval and stress. Alternative visions of communities and the possibilities they offer can be a by-product of interactions with others during the aid giving process. For example, a young Sri Lankan in the 2004 Indian Ocean Tsunami project made this clear when interviewed about experiences of being an aid recipient by saying:

> I had a hope of combining sports and fashion together and [develop] … sport fashion. The experience … with [exchange students] taught me [about] the new world trend and … [I could] approach my goal more easily … [T]heir visit showed me a new path and I could [be] expose[d] to [new ideas and practices from other parts of] the world as I … never [was] before.

When asked what they would like to see happen, interviewees in post-disaster research projects such as the 'Internationalizing Institutional and Professional Practices' examining humanitarian aid in the context of the 2004 Indian Ocean Tsunami and BIOPICCC projects, raised other issues through their continuous requests to rescuers to 'put it back the way it was' (Dominelli 2012a). In Sri Lanka, for example, literally going back to one's previous physical geographical space proved particularly problematic because many of the homes and businesses which had been located on the coastline adjacent to the sea had been destroyed by the tsunami. Following the 2004 Indian Ocean Tsunami which caused around 40,000 deaths in the country, the government prohibited poor coastal dwellers from rebuilding dwellings within 300 metres of the shoreline. For those without land elsewhere, or lacking money with which to purchase it, this objective was meaningless. The only possible outcome would be that they would lose their homes and livelihoods if they were to observe this condition, as some did. As many people ignored this stipulation, the government was unable to enforce this injunction as required.

At the same time, the Sri Lankan situation indicates that finding suitable alternatives is difficult and in most circumstances impossible because it means addressing various structural inequalities, vested interests across the whole of a society and the procuring of resources from other communities where they may already be in scarce supply. Consequently, many poor people continue to be dispossessed of their homes and eking out a living in the interior of the country when they would rather return to the coast where they originated. Loss of community as place is complicated especially in the Sri Lankan case because others including business people from overseas are constructing houses, hotels and restaurants on what were lands that previously belonged to tsunami survivors. Such developments expose the interdependencies between peoples and places that are not always easy to disentangle. What one person does impacts upon another and highlights the local and the global and the interdependencies between them, particularly when (re)imagined communities exclude former residents.

In BIOPICCC, older people recovering from extreme weather events in Northern England were able to draw upon informal caring relations and community-based social capital to see them through failures in the built infrastructure. Care was provided by friends, relatives, neighbours, and public sector workers during cold snaps and flooding events when the transportation systems failed and private service providers were unable to reach affected communities. Whilst this community demonstrated resilience in these circumstances, the question arose as to how far informal caring can plug the gap between what older people needed and what could be provided informally if extreme weather events became long-lasting and their frequency rises as predicted (Dominelli 2012b). Moreover, this community was based in a rural area and was a former mining community where social bonds between its members were stronger and social capital was more extensive in its coverage than other rural communities or, as Florin and Wandersman (1990) have pointed out, in urban ones. Therefore, this level of informal caring might not be replicated elsewhere. The limitations of relying on informal carers in such circumstances become a serious policy issue for politicians to consider. A community may not have the resources or resilience necessary to cover the gap left by formal service providers. And this becomes an issue during disasters. Public providers responding to questions about future planning for extreme weather events expressed the sector's reliance on informal carers during periods of cuts in public expenditures. One said:

> when a person is being assessed we'll be asking about whether it is a family member [and] … what support they are willing and able to provide to that person … no sort of judgement [is] made that someone must provide something for their loved one, but we would ask them because we don't want to take that care away … this is something we think about – it is part of the contingencies.

Disasters expose the interdependencies between people and the environment. In the Japanese nuclear accident in Fukushima Daiichi, the links were between the earthquake, the tsunami and nuclear meltdown, and the impact of these events on local-global relations as radioactive debris spilled across territorial boundaries, making their interdependencies evident (Holt et al. 2012). These interdependencies have been exposed in other disaster situations and call for holistic action that considers systems as integrated and inter-related, even when thinking about vulnerabilities and the development of resilient responses. This is particularly relevant in poor communities where resources can be stretched more effectively and efficiently by drawing on the networks and links that people already have with each other and developing them further.

Industrialized countries are not immune from disasters. The interdependencies between people and their physical environments are important there too. For example, in a case of a severe cold snap that made roads treacherous in Northern England, local social connections, networks and interdependencies between different members of the community ensured that when formal providers were unable to reach the locality to provide health and social care services to older people, local authority employees, family and neighbours plugged the ensuing gaps and ensured that help was given to those needing it (Dominelli 2012b).

Linking local and global challenges

Addressing global challenges raised by climate change issues and drawing upon renewable energy technologies offers potential to address social issues and reduce energy consumption at the local level. This occurred in Misa Rumi in Argentina, for example, where local residents were assisted by community development workers and EcoAndina, an NGO interested in sustainable energy, to purchase and install solar panels. This action helped them to obtain solar energy for cooking, heating, lighting and other domestic purposes, thereby reducing demand for Yareta trees as firewood. Consumption of the Yareta tree as a fossil fuel had endangered its existence. By using solar panels, they reduced pressure on this resource. They also cut back on soil erosion and deforestation (Stott 2009). In Gilesgate in England, social workers promoted the use of Inflector Blinds[3] to address fuel poverty, curtail fossil fuel consumption and explore renewable energy opportunities for income generation projects (Dominelli

2010). This initiative involved partnerships between community workers, academics, private enterprise and local residents in developing community resilience. Both examples indicate how community participation produces results that attempt to tackle more than one problem simultaneously and aim for long-term sustainability.

Each project involved communities (re)imagining themselves to build their adaptive capacities by creating multi-stakeholder partnerships that empowered them in meeting their needs. And, each project contributes to meeting global targets set through the Kyoto Protocols that aim to reduce greenhouse gas emissions and keep rises in air temperatures to below 2°C (Dessler and Parsons 2010). These partnerships varied according to location, but involved practitioners and residents working with civil society organizations, policymakers, business leaders, universities and others as they deemed appropriate to build and enhance community resilience. For those social workers and community workers engaging with community groups to develop partnerships that are locality-specific and culturally relevant, ensuring that those affected by decisions are the ones who make them is a thread that links all parts of a project together. In this way, they co-produce solutions, take ownership of them and feel empowered by the process. They also demonstrate that local people can take action independent of the state as a direct player in their lives, especially if they are organized around other stakeholders. This approach is consistent with the appropriation of local energies to make good deficits brought about through the absence of publicly funded services. Plugging these gaps is important in the lives of individuals but cannot occur without making simultaneous demands on the state not to abrogate its responsibilities for the well-being of individuals and communities. Multi-stakeholder partnerships outside of state control could become genuine state-citizen ones like the ones in Misa Rumi and Gilesgate. The state could make more mileage cut of small demonstrator type project like these if it were to provide the funds and the skilled personnel to roll out such partnerships to other communities and expand such initiatives more widely.

The processes of building effective partnerships to reduce the consumption of fossil fuels involves a (re)imagining of communities based on making a contribution towards a reduction in the formation of greenhouse gases and their impact on climate change. Although these connect the local with the global and vice-versa, the empowering processes that social workers utilize affirm social justice and seek to realize human rights for marginalized groups. These are:

- Getting to know a community, its resources, decision-makers, and formal and informal networks.
- Forming effective alliances with the community and those outside it.
- Engaging residents in working together to solve common problems and meet needs.
- Mobilizing community members around agreed action plans.
- Carrying out the activities contained in an action plan.
- Evaluating the actions that have been carried out throughout the life of the project and at its end.

Each of these processes requires careful thought and open discussions among those participating in the development and implementation of the action plans if these are to enhance community cohesion. They do so by having communities look for and consolidate the common bonds that enable them to act together as a community, united by common interests and geography, if not identity. And, it requires communities to integrate vertically and horizontally, in what Gunderson, Holling and Ludwig (2002) call a 'panarchy'. In other words, an 'imagined community' (Anderson 1991) has to take form and shape and be constantly re-imagined and re-produced through everyday life practices that enable people to take action and promote their development as a community whether acting in isolation or acting in concert with others.

Developments that are linked to reducing greenhouse gases seek to achieve sustainability, or the capacity to develop and meet the needs of today's generations without undermining the capacity of future generations to meet their needs (Brundtland 1987). Sustainable development highlights the (re)imagining of communities based on a holistic approach to people, communities, built infrastructures and the natural or physical environment. It takes as its starting point intergenerational connectivities and interdependencies. The relations that exist between the generations may be complicated, but their presence is not in doubt. Children are dependent on adults for their survival during disasters and older adults are dependent on younger people to help them deal with such events. All age groupings are dependent on each other for their day-to-day existence. Indeed, one age group exists because the other does in a circle of interdependencies and connectivities that underpin communities – their strengths and their weaknesses. Intergenerational dependencies are also critical to re-imagining communities. The visions and dreams of the future are made of sustainable and sustained relationships.

Conclusion

Climate change and other disasters have challenged contemporary notions of communities – real and imagined. The movement is away from the strictly local and into a blurring of the local and the global – a unity of interdependencies within many variations. Communities are real but difficult to define. Communities exist as spatial, relational and interest-based groupings. Communities are imagined and re-imagined as people alter them and change them according to different circumstances. Communities may be re-imagined for altruistic purposes when people are brought together to transcend adversity. Or, they may be re-imagined for exploitative purposes as occurs when politicians abuse connectivities in social relations to make up for deficits in service provisions caused by their neglect or policies they enact to prioritize economic imperatives over people's basic human rights. Such decisions subordinate the well-being of their populations to fiscal crises that boil down to choices that politicians make about the type of development that they will follow or the path that they will take to ensure that they provide the conditions that will support human lives and the ecosystem in which they are situated. That politicians can either exacerbate or reduce vulnerabilities or destroy or enhance resilience in communities through their support or lack of it, is all part of this process and an outcome. That they have chosen to drag their feet on the issue of climate change and do little to ensure that temperature rises remain below 2°C is to their shame and the detriment of living things and the physical environment. Social workers and community workers have a duty to act under these circumstances, and mobilize residents to put pressure on their politicians to act in ways that promote sustainable development in (re)imagined, interdependent and sustainable communities. Tackling climate change is an important aspect of such activities.

QUESTIONS FOR REFLECTION

- Why should social workers be interested in promoting community resilience related to climate change?
- What kinds of partnerships can social workers develop with politicians to ensure that communities are able to meet their needs during times of fiscal crises when poor people become more excluded and marginalized than ever?
- How can social workers help poor communities re-imagine themselves as key players in envisaging a better future for all living things and the physical environment?

Notes

1. A 'portmanteau word' is a term used to describe the fluidity of a concept. For 'community', it means the diverse meanings and uses which are attributed to it. A portmanteau is literally a suitcase in which anything can be stuffed. The term was used with regards to community by Elizabeth Wilson in 1977.
2. The 'Internationalizing Institutional and Professional Practices' (IIPP) was a project funded by the Economic and Social Science Research Council (ESRC) into the 2004 Indian Ocean Tsunami in Sri Lanka; the 'Climate Change, Built Environment and Older People' (BIOPICCC) project was financed by the Engineering and Physical Sciences Research Council (EPSRC); and the International Association of Schools of Social Work (IASSW) supported people in disasters including the recent earthquakes in places like Chile, China and Japan. I currently head the Climate Change and Disaster Intervention Committee and have done so since its inception, albeit under several re-structurings.
3. Inflector Blinds are a special type of blinds to cover windows instead of curtains. These blinds are made of special material and have one side that is

dark to absorb solar energy that keeps dwellings warm and another that is light to reflect the sun's rays and keep a place cool. Although the effect is a slight tint, it is possible to see outside when these blinds are drawn, but not for people on the outside to look in.

Useful websites

Planning for Resilience and Emergency Preparedness (PREP). Online. Available HTTP: http://www.pdxprep.net/ (accessed 23 April 2012).

72 Hours. Online. Available HTTP: http://72hours.org/ (accessed 2 May 2012).

For tsunami-specific advice, refer to 72 Hours. Online. Available HTTP: http://72hours.org/tsunami.html (accessed 30 March 2012).

References

Anderson, B. (1991) *Imagined Communities: Reflections on the Origins and Spread of Nationalism*, London: Verso.

Bankoff, G., Frerks, G. and Hilhorst, D. (2004) *Mapping Vulnerability: Disasters, Development and People*, London: Earthscan.

Blair, T. (1998) *The Third Way: New Politics for the New Century*, London: The Fabian Society.

Brundtland, G.H. (1987) *The World Commission on the Environment and Development. Our Common Future*, Oxford: Oxford University Press.

Burton, C. (2007) *The Development of Metrics for Community Resilience to Natural Disasters*. Columbia, SC: University of South Carolina, Department of Geography.

Cameron, D. and Clegg, N. (2010) *Building the Big Society*. Online. Available HTTP: http://www.cabinetoffice.gov.uk/news/building-big-society (accessed 26 April 2011).

Chavis, D. and Wandersman, A. (1990) 'Sense of community in the urban environment: a catalyst for participation and community development,' *American Journal of Community Psychology*, 18(1): 55–81.

Cutter, S., Barnes, L., Berry, M., Burton, C., Evans, E., Tate, E. and Webb, J. (2008) 'A place-based model for understanding community resilience to natural disasters', *Global Environmental Change*, 18(4): 598–606.

Delanty, G. (2003) *Community*, London: Routledge.

Dessler, A. and Parsons, E. (2010) *The Science and Politics of Global Climate Change: A Guide to the Debate*, Cambridge: Cambridge University Press.

Dominelli, L. (2006) *Women and Community Action*, Bristol: Policy Press.

——(2010) *Social Work in a Globalizing World*, Cambridge: Polity Press.

——(2012a) *Green Social Work*, Cambridge: Polity Press.

——(2012b) '"Mind the gap": built infrastructures, sustainable caring relations and resilient communities in extreme weather events', *Australian Journal of Social Work*, 65(1): 1–14. Online. Available HTTP: http://dx.doi.org/10.1080/0312407X.2012.708764 (accessed 2 February 2013).

Florin, P. and Wandersman, A. (1990) 'An introduction to citizen participation, voluntary organizations and community development: insights for empowerment through research', *American Journal of Community Psychology*, 18(1): 41–54.

George, S. (2003) 'Globalizing rights?' in M.J. Gibney (ed.) *Globalizing Rights*, Oxford: Oxford University Press.

Gunderson, L., Holling, C. and Ludwig, D. (2002) *Panarchy: Understanding Transformation in Human and Natural Systems*, Washington, DC: Island Press.

Holt, M., Campbell, R. and Nikitin, M. (2012) *Fukushima Nuclear Disaster: CRS Report for Congress*, Washington, DC: Congressional Research Services.

Islamic Relief (2012) *Flooded and Forgotten: The Ongoing Crisis Threatening Lives and Livelihoods in Pakistan,* London: Islamic Relief.

Lewis, J. (1999) *Development in Disaster-Prone Places. Studies of Vulnerability,* Rugby: Practical Action.

Newby, H. and Bell, C. (1971) *Community Studies,* London: Alan and Unwin.

O'Carroll, E. (2008) 'US army seeking to reduce its CO_2 emissions', *The Christian Science Monitor,* 28 July. Online. Available HTTP: http://www.csmonitor.com/Environment/Bright-Green/2008/0728/us-army-seeking-to-cut-its-co2-emissions (accessed 28 July 2012).

Perez, E. and Thompson, P. (1994) 'Natural hazards: causes and effects', *Pre-hospital Disaster Medicine,* 9(1): 80–8.

Putnam, R. (2000) *Bowling Alone: The Collapse and Revival of American Community,* New York: Simon and Schuster.

Pyles, L. (2007) 'Community Organising for post-disaster development: locating social work', *International Social Work,* 53(5): 321–33.

Tönnies, F. (1957) *Community and Society;* trans. C. P. Loomis, New York: Harper and Row.

Stack, C.B. (1983) *All Our Kin: Strategies for Survival in a Black Community,* New York: Basic Books. First published in 1975.

Stott, K. (2009) 'Remote village turns to the sun for power', *The Vancouver Sun,* 26 October, p. B4.

UN (United Nations) (2006) *On Better Terms: A Glance at Key Climate Change and Disaster Risk Reduction Concepts,* New York: United Nations.

Walker, B. and Salt, D. (2006) *Resilience Thinking: Sustaining Ecosystems and People in a Changing World,* London: Island Press.

Wilson, E. (1990) *Women and the Welfare State,* London: Tavistock Publications. First published in 1977.

14

PACIFIC HERITAGE SPECIFIC CONCEPTUAL FRAMEWORKS AND FAMILY VIOLENCE PREVENTIVE TRAINING IN AOTEAROA NEW ZEALAND

Vaiolesi Passells

A small and diverse class group of first year Pacific Islands' social and community work students present a synopsis of what they perceive they have learned during a semester long professional development course: the curtains are drawn on a poignant farewell scene – that of a young Pacific Islands' girl dressed in traditional garments standing on a woven pandana mat and weeping as she is slowly pulled away from a shoreline representation. On 'the shore', a mother figure waves and sobs at the same time as she gestures encouragingly; while background ukulele music plays bon voyage music 'Now is the hour'. As the 'sea voyage' proceeds across the room the background music changes to the haunting rhythmic sound of a purerehua (Māori wind instrument), thereby signalling the girl's imminent arrival to the shores of Aotearoa New Zealand (curtain drop). After a brief interlude the curtains open again on the young girl, this time a little older, and wearing a blouse, a skirt and high heel shoes. Rock and roll music of the 1950s and 1960s plays in the background and as the story progresses, the music genre changes to reflect the progression of years. The demeanour of the young girl growing into a young woman, then into a mother is at first wide eyed and curious: agog at new sights and promising opportunities. As she stands straight and proud and excited, one at a time a number of placards are placed around her neck: 'long hours on the factory floor'; 'recession/redundancy'; 'overcrowded housing'; 'early hours of the morning cleaning office buildings' or 'State Services'; 'prejudiced landlords'; 'cheap fast food'; 'cheaper fatty cuts of meat'; 'plethora of neighbourhood liquor outlets'; 'inadequate access to health services'; 'growing rates of obesity'; 'diabetes'; 'suicide'; 'dawn raids';[1] 'poor educational outcomes'; 'pepper potting';[2] 'institutional racism'; 'over representation in prisons'; 'under-represented in the courts'; 'individual choice'; 'individual ownership' ... Each time a placard is placed around her neck the young woman becomes more and more bowed until she is kneeling on the floor, her face sunk to her chest. The impact of this non-verbal sociological imagination depiction of the experiences of Pacific

Islands' parents and grand-parents is not lost on the audience. However into the thoughtful silence interlopes the at first muted sound of islands' drums playing and then the added rising notes of guitar music, followed by Pacific Islands' Church choir harmonies. As the music grows, flowers are placed in the young woman's hair, and she lifts her face to smile her thanks and starts to rise from her knees. Plates of traditional food are brought before her; an elder weaving a basket comes to sit beside her; a paleu (sarong) is placed around her waist as she draws to a full standing position. The finale is islands' dance music playing and the 'girl', head held high, dances with her peers; restored, nurtured and no longer weighed down by deficits.[3]

Nga mihi (greetings)

I am a first generation New Zealand born Niue woman of mixed heritages. My mother is from the villages of Mutalau and Alofi on Niue Island and my father hailed from Portsmouth in England, UK.

An incentive for the following narrative has its roots in my own experience of family violence (spousal abuse) while raising four children (emotional harm). After actioning out of an abusive relationship some sixteen years ago, I went on to graduate from a four-year honours degree in social work during which time I was invited to contribute to a developing 'grassroots' Pacific Islands' community organization, by serving as a voluntary working Board member.

Sixteen years later I continue to serve Pacific Islands' Safety and Prevention Project (PISPP) (The Project) in that capacity, as a group supervisor and more recently as a member of a core group using Pacific specific conceptual frameworks to inform the development of Family Violence training programme(s). The aim of the programme(s) is to inform practitioners and service providers working with Pasifika victim(s), perpetrator(s) and families affected by family violence. This narrative acknowledges the privilege of being a small part of what has been coined a legacy event. My participation in the development of the Sāmoa training programme afforded me insight into emotions of discovery, recovery, and 'aha' moments of learning (my own and others). The learning from this participation is shared during the development of the Niue family violence training programme.

It is my authentic participatory working relationship with PISPP in tandem with experiential knowledge that enables me to be grounded in my praxis. In academic 'research' language it affords me privileged positions as, 'participant observer', complements my praxis as a cultural 'insider' community member and corroborates my professional 'outsider' role as a lecturer in social work and human services training and education. Since I am also not an expert, in all ways it allows for my on-going learning of Pasifika legacies.

Introduction

Much of contemporary literature and research around family violence continues to focus on western micro attributes – individual psyche (causation) and the onus of personal responsibility – for informing assessment and interventions. Alternatively macro considerations focus on gender/power analyses from notions of patriarchal norms. With this in mind my attention to historical antecedents establishes an irony of dual contexts for Pasifika. One context offers the potential for resolutions (heritage specifics) while the other is the ongoing potential for harm (by any other name domination is subjugation). Instead Pacific ethnic specific conceptual framework(s) from seven Pacific Islands' communities in Aotearoa centre on family and relational vā (concepts) which prioritise mutual respect for the quality of relationships; crucial when group unity is valued over individual satisfaction.

The advent of the framework(s) is a pinnacle of a tradition of community and cultural mobilisation by Pasifika peoples in New Zealand, over decades. It is genuinely unique in that seven diverse groups have come together in a concentrated commitment for change. It realises a valid approach to improving social practice by changing it. The intent for the ensuing development of heritage specific training Programme(s) is to enhance the ability of family violence practitioners and service providers to provide culturally appropriate engagement, assessment and interventions.

With regard to participation and community work, the way in which the Pacific ethnic specific conceptual framework(s) and subsequent training programme(s) have unfolded resonates with participatory and appreciative action and reflection (PAAR) (Ghaye et al. 2008: 361), as well as reflection and action methods used in Participatory Action Research (PAR) (Wadsworth 1997). Because this presentation is my academic perception and not a translation of the process, I have not used defining headings from these methodical frameworks. Suffice to say the aspects of PAAR that may be recognised in this narrative, favour

> development of appreciative insight, understanding the root causes of success and sustaining strengths based discourses in order to amplify those things that will inform a better future ... away from self-learning (individualism and isolation) and towards collective learning, through interconnectedness, appreciative knowledge sharing ... away from one way of knowing and one perspective on truth [...]
>
> *(Ghaye et al. 2008: 361)*

Further examples may be assumed from the five characteristics of the PAR framework in that it is: participatory, defined by a need for action, useful and meaningful, reflexive about creation and meaning, flexible and iterative (cyclical) (Wadsworth 1997: 79). It is important to note that this is not a research project in a western sense per se in that community action is carried out by Pasifika communities of practice (Pasifika) and not on them.

Throughout, there are many diverse collaborations (regional/national, intra/inter) and for it to occur a number of local and international rhythms, aligned. Not the least of which is the precedence setting outcomes of bi-cultural tenets that benefit multi-cultural interests in Aotearoa New Zealand.

The conceptual framework(s) with which to address family violence in New Zealand is referenced from seven Pasifika communities: Sāmoa, Cook Islands, Tonga, Fiji, Niue, Tuvalu and Tokelau. In a miasma of current national/ international economic and political 'rip tides', the framework(s) and subsequent training programme(s) signify a triumph for marginalized communities. The culmination of critical reflection from practical theorising, they provide a premise from which to launch training for Pasifika working in areas of family violence that is co-ordinated, evidenced, progressive and relevant (Wadsworth 1997: 79).

In short the chapter is structured to accommodate setting the scene with Pasifika diaspora and the politics of identity for a growing Pasifika youth population; as well as salient historical antecedents. Theoretic assumptions on family violence contrast with Pasifika theoretical assumptions on the subject. Some attention to the community and cultural mobilisation of diverse communities and cultures highlights the reflective and iterative aspects of the development rhythm of the Pacific Conceptual Framework(s) to address family violence. The Pacific Islands Safety and Prevention Project (the Project) takes the next iterative step in the legacy movement to design and deliver a training programme using the conceptual frameworks. Last but not least is an acknowledgement that the fruition of the community process thus far is testament to Treaty of Waitangi (1840) bi-cultural dynamics in a multi-cultural society.

Pasifika diaspora

Discussion of Pasifika responses to 'family violence' cannot take place without heeding the socio-cultural, economic and political realities of Pasifika communities and families from within which 'family violence' takes place.

For clarification, the use of the generic term Pasifika when referring to Pacific peoples from Pacific nations living in New Zealand, is 'in the spirit of unity through diversity' (McCaffrey and McFall-McCaffrey 2010: 87). Concerns about the potential for it to homogenise distinct ethnic and national identities have been raised (ibid). Here the term acknowledges the wealth of diversity within and between the distinct Islands nations. While they may share acculturation and assimilation experiences in common, it is vital that assumptions are not made about their respective world views and cultural practices. Inherent aspects of the term Pasifika also refers to 'politics of identity' realities. Varying disparate experiences are realised among: Pacific Islands' born and raised, Pacific peoples born in the Islands and who migrate to New Zealand with their parents and Pasifika born and raised in New Zealand.

The focus here is on the seven largest Pacific Islands' populations in New Zealand. Historic currents saw the majority of Pasifika living in New Zealand as having been born overseas. The majority now however are born in New Zealand, under fifteen years at the last census and account for a rapidly growing Pasifika youth population. It is also significant that the 2006 census found a significant number of New Zealand born Pasifika were less likely to speak their language.

Although the numbers differ for each of the Islands' groups the attenuation of heritage languages typifies a parallel weakening and sometimes loss of implicit cultural nuances, knowledge and wisdoms and spiritual dis-ease. There is however areas of shared knowledge with reference to Pasifika family violence. One of these is inherent aspects of vā concepts (Autagavaia 2001; Refiti 2002; Māhina 2004; Ka'ili 2005; Mila-Schaaf 2006, 2009; Airini et al. 2010) which is vital for understanding non-punitive (law and order) models for working with family violence.

Relational vā translations

Without entering into essentialist discourse (English speaking only) and with respect to the spiritual depths of relational vā it is vital to note that my translations and subsequent understanding of vā is not definitive. Relational vā spaces of wellbeing is about relationship protocols and spiritual covenants among family members, communities and at the public interface (Ka'ili 2005: 89, referenced in Mila-Schaaf 2006: 8). In 2006 Mila-Schaaf discussed the potential for vā-centred social work with regard to Pacific cultural approaches to wellbeing (ibid. 8–13). The centrality of relationships and relational vā as codes for conduct and understanding affirms family violence conceptual framework(s) as tool(s) for engagement, potential assessment and interventions. Relational vā tenets denounce violations upon the social, psychological and physical realms between individuals, families and communities (Refiti 2002, referenced in Mila-Schaaf 2006: 11). Related meanings of vā are to be found in many Pacific languages and identify relationship 'spaces' as entity contexts informed by elements of interconnected and interdependent spiritual, and intellectual behaviour such as mutual respect, mutual reciprocity, humility and servitude.

Historical antecedents

> 'Fuluhi ki tua ke kitia mitaki a mua'
> Niue fakatai (adage)
> (Turn backwards so that you may see forward well)

In the development of Pasifika responses to family violence an understanding of contemporary circumstances requires an analysis of what has gone before. Covering one-third of the planet, Moana Nui a Kiwa[4] is not measured by land mass(es) alone, but includes surrounding ocean seas, underworld(s) and heaven(s) above, sourced from traditional narratives, legends and cosmologies of Pacific peoples (Hau'ofa 1993: 7).

The arrival of explorers, entrepreneurs, missionaries and settlers from the west and northern hemisphere during the 1800s signalled the arrival of colonisation. Imperialists imposed archaeological, geographic, biographical and political boundaries (Melanesia, Micronesia, Polynesia). Instead of previous boundaries as normative points of entry constantly negotiated and or contested, Pacific peoples were limited to boundaries that saw them confined (Hau'ofa 1993: 7) and subjected to colonial machinations. Brookfield interprets colonisation as

> the thoroughgoing, comprehensive and deliberate penetration of a local or 'residentiary' system by agents of an external system, whose aim is to restructure the patterns of organisation, resource use, circulation and outlook so as to bring these into linked relationship with their own system and is revolutionary in the sense that it involves termination or diversion of former evolutionary trends [...]
>
> *(Brookfield 1972: 1)*

As the administrative conduit for imperial expansion, colonisation afforded imperial nations to lay claim to land and raw resources with which to furnish industrial economies (Connell 2007: 51). Missionary administrations sought the salvation of souls and facilitated 'civilising' tenets ushering Pacific societies into the 'era of light and civilisation' where before they languished in 'the era of darkness associated with savagery and barbarism' (Hau'ofa 1993: 3).

In New Zealand recruitment policies of the 1950s and 1960s facilitated a migrant influx of Pacific peoples. At a policy level the influx of labour was sought to facilitate an expanding manufacturing agenda which was part of a 'boom' economy after World War II. At an aspirational level it was the hope of many Pasifika that migration would realise their dreams of a land of 'milk and honey' prosperity (Mila 2001: 23).

Theoretic assumptions on family violence

'O le i'o i mata o le tama teine'
Sāmoa metaphor
(The pupil of a brother's eye is his sister)

In Falevitu conceptual framework(s) literature review; two widely held assumptions 'that violence is an acceptable part of ethnic specific cultures' and that 'Pacific Islanders are inherently violent' are mentioned. Each of the seven conceptual frameworks' worldviews refutes the accuracy of such beliefs. Family members who are violent towards their kin are not supported or authorised by cultural beliefs. On the subject of culture as a barrier to achieving health and well-being, the 'telling' response 'whose culture?' came from Tongan educationalist 'Ana Taufe'ulungaki (Peteru 2012a: 6).

It could be argued that Post-colonial and neo-colonial concepts are simply extensions of old 'colonial speak' to new 'market speak'. What once presented as the language of the coloniser may now be argued as contemporary meanings for metropolitan, instead of imperial access to labour resources with which to facilitate global market driven economies (instead of colonial raw resource intensive industries). At an organic level, experiences of subjugation remain, and resonate with 'whether urbane or harsh, cultural invasion is always an act of violence [...] the invaders are authors of and actors in, the process' (Freire 1970: 152).

Pasifika family violence continues to escalate both in New Zealand and in home islands (Abirafeh and Ryan 2011) and the argument for Pasifika family violence theory to heed historical contributing factors is nonetheless less than appealing to some. Connell (2007), for example, points to the erasure of colonisation experiences of subjugation in the modern sciences. She notes that some theorists go so far as to deny its relevance to the present. In a parody of family violence 'perpetrator' language, omissions and denials on such a grand scale simply serve to confirm the predisposition for 'northern metropolitan' theoretical assumptions – to assume various mantels of universal epistemologies and readily marginalise non-metropolitan experiences (Connell 2007: 65). The assumptions that underpin the causes of family violence and subsequent interventions are therefore, mainly based on values, beliefs and world views from the west, (North America and Europe) (Connell 2007: 31).

Nevertheless persistent resistance allows wide open oceans of opportunity for southern epistemologies to confirm and assert preferred knowledge waves.

By whose definition?

> 'How one defines domestic violence, its causes and impacts, will determine how one intervenes.'
>
> *(Crichton-Hill 2001: 209)*

International literature and research collaborations with indigenous research provide shifts for authenticating movements of Pasifika epistemologies (Autagavaia 2001: 72–84; Gray and Coates 2010). For the most part contemporary discourse hovers around western monopolies of orthodox social work. However current comparisons are being made about the validity of self-determining notions of social work in social developmental, community inspired and indigenous informed ways of addressing widespread injustices and poverty (Gray and Fook 2004: 634; Gray and Coates 2010).

Similarly, family violence frameworks used in Aotearoa New Zealand have traditionally been drawn from western social sciences disciplines (Lombard and McMillan 2013: 233). How well they might be applied to Pasifika family violence interventions remains dubious. If the status quo works, why doesn't it? (An acknowledgement that it may work for whom it is designed to work for, but not necessarily all who live within it.)

For example while offering suggestions for working with Sāmoa women and their communities, Crichton-Hill (2001: 203–9) states 'Sāmoan women need to be permitted to seek alternatives and make choices for themselves'. Furthermore feminist intelligence around 'power' and gendered analyses reflect women's experiences as premised from 'natural order' concepts that situates the abuser 'in a position of power over the victim and that makes the abuser feel he is legitimately entitled to obedience.'

Western 'natural order' analyses, with regard to Sāmoa family violence, serve to refute vā tapuia – sacred Sāmoan covenant relationships between parents and children, brothers and sisters, older and younger siblings, between Matai (male/female chief) and family members, elders and the young. Male and female relationships in Sāmoa are informed by fa'aSamoa (Sāmoa way of doing things), and the brother sister covenant also informs relational expectations for non-related females and males.

Unfortunately while explanations from Pakeha 'power and gender' platforms are removed in Pasifika heritage terms, ironically in 'real terms' they are reminiscent of experiences for Pasifika victims, perpetrators, families and communities. For instance where Pasifika heritages do not countenance the subjugation of women, because of disruption to the spiritual harmony and dignity of relational vā, nevertheless patriarchal mandates of the dominant New Zealand culture continue to assimilate. Hence over time with attrition, acculturation and assimilation, the natural order of Pasifika heritage relational vā roles is weakened, misconstrued, distorted and, in some instances, subsumed under dominant ideology.

Mafile'o captures this in essence when she notes that 'the function of service to family and community has been separated from integrated, holistic and communal contexts [...] to professional domains' (Mafile'o 2001: 117). By the same token, micro-orientated social learning motivations tend to explain family violence as the behaviour of interrelated individual, factors (Crichton-Hill 2010: 15), thereby perpetuating dis-connections upon societies that rely on continuity of 'in harmony/unity' behaviour of the collective for explanations and interventions.

There are however alternative rhythms for persistent resistance against adversity. It is neither about blame nor expectations of guilt; but rather about behaving responsibly with the information.

Pasifika theoretical assumptions

'Mai i te mamaetanga o mua
ka tupu te mamae o tenei ra.
Mai i te mohiotanga o mua
ko te maramatanga o te mamae'.
(Māori whakatauki (adage))
(From the sorrows of the past comes the pain of today.
In the wisdom of the past is the understanding of the pain)

For Pasifika, violence and violation are inseparable. Hau'ofa cites ecological time as having to do with rights for succession and inheritance rather than evolutionary development per se (2000: 459–61). His suggestion that we find ways to reconstruct our pasts resonates with ecologically based oral narratives. In much the same way, the Pasifika family violence conceptual framework(s), although not definitive, nevertheless provide a catalyst from which to facilitate the dissemination of Pasifika knowledge that was once learned through immersion and lived experiences. For some time, Pacific indigenous research imperatives recreated cultural nuances to un-silence 'Silenced Pasts' (Nabobo-Baba 2004). For those of us who haven't had implicit access to heritage aspects of wellbeing, 'seeking, learning, reclaiming and – to an extent – reimagining Pacific cultural approaches to wellbeing can be powerful and transformative work' (Mila-Schaaf 2006: 9).

There is therefore a growing body of literature and research and paradigms from distinguished Pasifika heritage approaches by Tamasese et al. 1997, Fusitu'a and Coxon 1998, Helu-Thaman 1998, Mulitalo-Lauta 2000, Autagavaia 2001, Pulotu-Endemann 2002 in Mafile'o (2005) to name a few. Their works inform a 'reaffirmation of the fact that groups who are strongly rooted in their own cultures, values and belief systems, and which enjoy reciprocal relationships, tend to sustain health and wellbeing' (Taufe'ulungaki 2004 in Mila-Schaaf 2006: 9).

With specific reference to family violence, Crichton-Hill (2001: 209; 2003: 13) highlights the paucity of Pasifika specific ethnicity data. Counting Pasifika as a homogenous group compromises definitions of the phenomenon (Family Violence) in question and in effect fails appropriate theory building, leaving instead, inaccurate generalisations (Herzberger 1993: 136, referenced in Crichton 2003: 13). Despite perceived inaccurate generalisations aside, from lived experiences of family violence impacts amongst their own, Pasifika communities of practice have nevertheless united in proceeding to address family violence issues in their respective communities.

'Nga vaka o kāiga tapu' (A Pacific conceptual framework(s) to address family violence in New Zealand)[5]

A private communication summed up 'Nga vaka o kāiga tapu – The Sailing Vessels of Sacred Families' (Peteru 2012b) as the culmination of a long legacy of community and cultural mobilisation (Ministry of Social Development 2002). It is unique in that it required and facilitated the mobilisation of large diverse groups of people, prompted by a shared commitment to addressing and preventing family violence. Over a period of two years the Pacific Islands' Advisory Group (PAG) to the Government Taskforce on Violence cast their nets widely and engaged with local and regional communities with regard to finding relevant and appropriate responses for sustainable resolutions to Pasifika family violence. After numerous meetings the cumulative findings from hundreds of people were discussed and overwhelmingly the themes calculated – the importance of culture and identity as a key part of the solution to preventing violence – and solutions lie within Pacific communities themselves. Thereafter PAG returned to Pasifika communities to engage their commitment. Core working groups Tuvalu, Tokelau, Fiji, Niue, Tonga, Cook Islands, and Sāmoa communities in New

Zealand deliberated to devise Pacific ethnic specific cultural frameworks for addressing family violence in New Zealand. In November 2011 a Pacific Conceptual Framework Fono was held, during which the nine framework documents (a literature review, a summary, and seven ethnic specific conceptual frameworks) were presented and consolidated. From among the heritage specific frameworks are guiding principles of working with Pasifika issues of family violence. They are premised on core relational cultural concepts that promote and protect the wellbeing of Pasifika families and individuals (Peteru 2012b: 3). Collectively the language used throughout the seven frameworks iterates the transformations, restoration and retention for collective wellbeing of families and communities premised from time-honoured heritage criterion.

The project

> Welfare programmes as instruments of manipulation ultimately serve as the end of conquest [...] distracting from the true causes of their problems and from the concrete solutions of these problems.
>
> *(Freire 1970: 152)*

A steadfast contributing trajectory for the training programme is the history of Pasifika 'coal face' working, grassroots community and service providers in Aotearoa New Zealand. Often following in the footsteps of volunteer elders from the 1950s and 1960s they sustain Pacific specific ways of knowing in their praxis (Autagavaia 2001; Mafile'o 2005; Anae et al. 2001). For example among the strengths of the Project (but not exclusive to) is its commitment to working from a strengths-based focus with regard to Pasifika premised praxis. As a community development social service, a Project mantra is to 'integrate cultural practices to enhance the well-being of communities.' Selected by the Ministry for Social Development (MSD) as the preferred provider to deliver the first phase of the Pacific Family Violence Training programme(s) (2012), the Project has been working for and with the seven Pacific ethnic specific groups. The focussed intent of the programme(s) is to establish the proficiency of Pasifika family violence practitioners and service providers to provide appropriate engagement, assessments and interventions for victims, perpetrators and their families.

Systemic and collaborative learning processes are integral to the development of an approach that involves people theorising, reflecting critically and making improvements. Each Pasifika group has a core working group, some of whom served on the conceptual frameworks core groups. Members are invited for their linguistic specific cultural knowledge (Elder expertise), some for programme development skills, as community representatives, Church Ministers, and so forth. The Programme(s) is not definitive in that it is always open for further input and discussion to avoid miscommunications and or misinterpretations of heritage specifics (evaluation).

Delivering services by Pasifika for Pasifika includes innate methods of engaging with client workers – instituted from shared experiences, comparable world views and implicit understandings of diverse Pasifika beliefs values and needs. Culturally relevant and appropriate ways of working in ways that ensure relational vā contexts insists on 'creative and innovative means' (corporate speak for making diverse praxis palatable). This commitment, while strengths based, Pasifika relevant and appropriate is not without its difficulties. Statutory funding bodies, who oversee contractual obligations and responsibilities, do so from the stance of western values and beliefs. Their measures of competency and 'to be qualified' are sourced from academic and professional qualifiers based on western values, beliefs and world views. In contrast, an adaptation of criterion for culturally appropriate theory/ model of practice, by Meemeduma (1994) as shown in Table 14.1, showcases the soundness of Pacific conceptual framework(s) in that they:

- Identify and are based upon beliefs and values of Pacific Islands' cultures.
- Explain problems and concerns in a manner that is relevant to Pasifika understanding.
- Use Pacific Islands' 'helping' traditions and practices.
- Incorporate Pacific Islands' understanding to change process.
- Can differentiate aspects of the behaviour which are associated with Pacific Islands' cultural patterns from those resultant in dominant Palagi cultural interpretations.
- Avoid pathological stereotyping.
- Encompass macro and micro levels of explanations and interventions.
- Incorporate the experiences of the community and individuals in Aotearoa New Zealand society.
- Can guide the selection of appropriate knowledge and practice skills from other cultures.

Using Pasifika centric paradigms to address Pasifika issues of family violence is not an action of separation or division. Nor does it exclude acculturation experiences and/or alternative values and beliefs, as changing cultural rhythms are likely to include. It is simply a normative and strategic approach for facilitating reasoned and pragmatic development for Pasifika specific praxis.

Bi-cultural/Multi cultural dynamics

Bi-cultural determinants in Aotearoa New Zealand speak to obligations and responsibilities to Tangata Whenua[6] by non-Māori. In New Zealand they are premised on the Treaty of Waitangi (1840), and includes the terms of reference (Treaty articles) by which diverse nations ought to be able to live together equitably.

Although comparable circumstances of marginalised social determinants are not a measure with which to ascertain Pasifika and Māori relations, multi-cultural dynamics fare well in the wake of Māori (as of right) endeavours. For example the

TABLE 14.1 Framework for Pacific Islands' theories and models of practice

Values	Concepts	Assumptions	Practice Principles
Collective kinship	emphasis on interdependence	basic unit of polity is the aiga/maga/kainga/family	work with the family/collective
	the sum total is more important than the individual	individual sees the world through the eyes of her/his family	family dynamics
		individual actions reflect upon the family	gender/aged/status based relationships
Secular & spiritual worlds	belief in a supreme being	physical actions spiritual guidance	power of prayer, chants
	primordial truths and metaphysical experiences inform physical world	events can be 'illogical' and unexplained	acknowledgement of primordial experiences
			deference of speaking rights/ decision making to sister, matai, fahu (Tonga older sister)
Respect for authority	authority and leadership	respect for authority figure	recognition of professional power
	collective good can be attained through good leadership	duality of respect	recognise other figures of authority
Deference & humility	servitude	the road to authority is to serve	approach the family/individual with humility
	lowering of self	the self is not the centre of the universe	uphold the rights of others

Adapted in agreement with Meemeduma (1994)

Māori language 'nests' (Kohunga Reo) movement initiated in the 1970s is a role model for subsequent Pasifika (and others') heritage language 'nests'. Furthermore Māori values and beliefs resonate with Pasifika where they are premised on holistic relational notions of psychological, physical, spiritual and whanau (family) health and wellbeing (Durie 1997). These stalwarts have not been echoed at macro government levels until now in the form of a Māori party (coalition partner to the governing party). Without doubt, in my mind the bi-cultural alignment is an example of Treaty terms of reference facilitating positive relational vā in political contexts. Unfortunately the nature of political rhythms is subject to the whims of the populace and it remains to be seen whether the same genuine support will be honoured in subsequent changes in government policies.

Conclusion

Looking back to the future historic antecedents heralded alignments of international and local family violence discourses, sustained Pasifika centric relational vā imperatives; and preferred community praxis tenets. Together they informed the unique movement of seven diverse Pasifika groups uniting in a common cause against family violence. An outcome presents in the legacy documents of heritage specific conceptual framework(s), a summary and literature review. A further alignment outcome is the development of training programme(s) informed by the conceptual frameworks and which continue to be reflective and iterative. A final (but not the last) alignment in this reflective cycle is that the movement came to fruition under the watch of Treaty of Waitangi adherents.

For me the use of Pacific specific conceptual frameworks with which to address issues of family violence is about reclaiming sustainability. It realises processes of restoration of heritage with which to manage and maintain healthy family relationships. Identity gains and transformative aspects are drawn from Pasifika community(s) preferences for a strength based focus inherent in heritage tenets and nuances that have prevailed and withstood tests of time. At its most basic the training programme(s) establishes tools for terms of engagement. At its fullest potential is the realisation of heritage specific family violence assessment and intervention foci.

QUESTIONS FOR REFLECTION

- What can be learned from the historical heritage of oppression described in this chapter?
- Do you recognise treads from oppressive history in your own culture and what affect does it have on gender issues today?
- How is family violence addressed in your culture/community?

Notes

1. 1970s recession and dawn raids by authorities on Pasifika suspected of overstaying visa conditions.
2. Dispersal of populations housing policy to prevent residential concentrations.
3. Thank you Charmain, Felicity, Ashlea Dee, Kris and Tangi.
4. Pacific Ocean, Oceania.
5. To be read in conjunction with Falevitu: A literature review on culture and family violence in seven Pacific communities in New Zealand (Peteru 2012b).
6. People of the land (Māori).

References

Abirafeh, L and Ryan, J (2011) *Ending Violence against Women and Girls: Evidence, Data and Knowledge in Pacific Islands' Countries,* 2nd edn., Victoria Parade Suva: UN Women Pacific.

Airini., Anae, M., Mila-Shaaf, K., Coxon, E., Mara, D. and Sanga, K. (2010) *Teu le vā – Relationships across Research and Policy in Pasifika Education* Wellington: Ministry of Education. Online. Available HTTP: http://www.educationcounts.govt.nz/__data/assets/pdf_file/0009/75897/944_TeuLeVa-30062010.pdf (accessed 9 March 2013).

Anae, M. Samu, T., Airini and Coxon, E. (2001) *Pasifika Education Research Guidelines.* Wellington: Ministry of Education.

Autagavaia, M. (2001) 'Social work with Pacific Island communities', in M. Connolly (ed.) *New Zealand Social Work: Contexts and Practice,* Auckland: Oxford University Press (pp. 72–84).

Brookfield, H. C. (1972) *Colonialism, Development and Independence: The Case of the Melanesian Islands in the South Pacific,* Great Britain: Cambridge University Press.

Connell, R. (2007) *Southern Theory: The Global Dynamics of Knowledge in Social Science,* Crows Nest NSW: Allen & Unwin.

Crichton-Hill, Y. (2001) 'Challenging ethnocentric explanations of domestic violence', *Trauma, Violence and Abuse,* 2(3): 203–14.

——(2003) 'The nature of violence in Pacific populations', *Te Awatea Review,* 1(1).

——(2010) 'Changing landscapes: responding to domestic violence in New Zealand', *Aotearoa New Zealand Social Work,* 22(4): 12–19.

Durie, M. (1997) 'Identity, nationhood and implications for practice in New Zealand', *New Zealand Journal of Psychology,* 26(2).

Freire, P. (1970) *Pedagogy of the Oppressed,* M. Bergman (trans), D. Macedo (introduction), New York: Continuum International Publishing.

Ghaye, T., Melander-Wikman, A., Kisare, M., Chambers, P., Bergmark, U., Kostenius, C. and Lillyman, S. (2008) 'Participatory and appreciative action and reflection (PAAR): democratizing reflective practices', *Reflective Practice,* 9(4): 361–97. Online. Available HTTP: http://keycenter.unca.edu/sites/keycenter.unca.edu/files/participator_and_appreciative_action_and_reflection_PAAR.pdf (accessed 9 March 2013).

Gray, M. and Coates, J. (2010) '"Indigenisation" and knowledge development: extending the debate', *International Social Work,* 53(5): 613–27.

Gray, M. and Fook, J. (2004) 'The quest for universal social work: some issues and implications', *Social Work Education: The International Journal,* 23(5): 625–44.

Hau'ofa, E. (1993) 'Our sea of islands', in E. Waddell, V. Naidu and E. Hau'ofa (eds), *A New Oceania: Rediscovering Our Sea of Islands,* Suva, Fiji: School of Social and Economic Development, The University of the South Pacific in association with Beake House (pp. 3–16).

——(2000) 'Epilogue: pasts to remember', in R. Borofsky (ed.) *Remembrance of Pacific Pasts: An Invitation to Remake History,* Honolulu: University of Hawai'i Press (pp. 453–71).

Ka'ili, T. O. (2005) 'Tauhi vā: nurturing sociospatial ties in Maui and beyond', *The Contemporary Pacific,* 17(1): 83–114. Online. Available HTTP: http://scholarspace. manoa.hawaii.edu/bitstream/handle/10125/13837/v17n1-83-114.pdf?sequence=1 (accessed 9 March 2013).

Lombard, N. and McMillan, L. (2013) 'Taking stock: theory and violence against women', in N. Lombard and M. Lesley (eds) *Violence against Women: Current Theory and Practice in Domestic Abuse, Sexual Violence and Exploitation,* London: Jessica Kingsley Publishers (pp. 233–244).

McCaffrey, J. and McFall-McCaffrey, J. (2010) 'O tatou ō aga'i i fea?/Oku tau ō ki fe?/ Where are we heading?: Pasifika languages in Aotearoa New Zealand', *AlterNative: An International Journal of Indigenous Peoples,* 6(2): 86–121.

Mafile'o, T. (2001) 'Social work and the Pasifika dimension', in M. Nash (ed.) *Social Work in Context: Fields of Practice in Aotearoa New Zealand,* Palmerston North New Zealand: School of Sociology, Social Policy and Social Work (pp.113–21).

——(2005) *Tongan Metaphors of Social Work Practice: Hangē ha Pā kuo Fa'u,* Massey University, Palmerston North.

Māhina, O. (2004) 'Art as ta-vā "time –space" transformation,' in T. Baba, O. Māhina, N. Williams and U. Nabobo-Baba (eds) *Researching the Pacific and Indigenous Peoples: Issues and Perspectives,* Auckland: Centre for Pacific Studies the University of Auckland (pp. 86–93).

Meemeduma, P. (1994) *Reshaping the Future: Cultural Sense and Social Work,* Townsville, Australia: James Cook University.

Mila, K. (2001) 'Flying foxes don't fit into pigeon holes: working as "Pacific Island" social workers: questions of identity', *Social Work Education Review,* 13(3): 23–4.

Mila-Schaaf, K. (2006) 'Va-centred social work: possibilities for a Pacific approach to social work', *Social Work Review/Tu Mau,* 18(1): 8–13.

——(2009) 'Pacific health research guidelines: the cartography of an ethical relationship', *International Social Science Journal,* 60(195): 135–43.

Ministry of Social Development (2002) *Te Rito: New Zealand Family Violence Prevention Strategy,* Wellington: Ministry of Social Development. Online. Available HTTP: http:// www.msd.govt.nz/documents/about-msd-and-our-work/publications-resources/ planning-strategy/te-rito/te-rito.pdf (accessed 9 March 2013).

——(2012) *E tu whanau. Strength-based Initiatives in Maori Communities to Support and Build Strong Families that are Free from Violence.* Wellington: Ministry of Social Development. Online. Available HTTP: http://www.familyservices.govt.nz/working-with-us/ programmes-services/whanau-ora/index.html (accessed 9 March 2013).

Nabobo-Baba, U. (2004) 'Research and Pacific indigenous peoples' in T. Baba, M. 'Okusitino, N. Williams and N. Nabobo-Baba (eds) *Researching the Pacific and Indigenous Peoples: Issues and Perspectives,* Auckland: Centre for Pacific Studies The University of Auckland (pp. 17–32).

Peteru, C. (2012a) *Falevitu. A literature review on culture and family violence in seven Pacific communities in New Zealand.* Online. Available HTTP: http://www.familyservices.govt. nz/documents/working-with-us/programmes-services/pacific-framework-literature- review-fa2.pdf (accessed 9 March 2013).

——(2012b) *Nga vaka o kaiga tapu: A Pacific Conceptual Framework to Address Family Violence in New Zealand,* Wellington: Ministry of Social Development. Online. Available HTTP: http://www.familyservices.govt.nz/documents/working-with-us/programmes- services/pacific-framework-fa2.pdf (accessed 9 March 2013).

Refiti, A. (2002) 'Making spaces: Polynesian architecture in Aotearoa/New Zealand', in S. Mallon and P.F. Pereira (eds) *Pacific Art in Niu Sila: The Pacific Dimension of Contemporary New Zealand Arts,* Wellington: Te Papa Press (pp. 209–25).

Taufe'ulungaki, A. M. (2004) 'Fonua: reclaiming Pacific communities in Aotearoa', *Keynote Speeches, Lotu Moui Pacific Health Symposium,* Counties Manukau District Health Board.
Treaty of Waitangi (1840). Online. Available HTTP: http://www.nzhistory.net.nz/files/documents/treaty-kawharau-footnotes.pdf (accessed 9 March 2013).
Wadsworth, Y. (1997) *Everyday Evaluation on the Run* (2nd edn), Australia: Allen and Unwin.

15

SOCIAL ACTION FOR COMMUNITY WORK IN INDIA

Grassroots interventions to face global challenges

Sanaya Singh and Prabha Tirmare

Introduction to the context

To give a picture of the challenges people in India meet, we start with this short story. In the small Plachimada village of Kerala, Coca Cola International set up a bottling plant in 1999. To meet the water requirements for the plant, the company procured vast stretches of land and dug deep wells using sophisticated technology. Since the company's wells are deep due to the modern machinery, water from the wells of poor farmers in the vicinity rushed to the company's wells and the farmers were deprived of water even to drink. Local people lost 510,000 litres of water a day and their daily subsistence farming was jeopardized. They suffered high crop loss leading to deaths and poverty. Locals had to walk a minimum of 5 kilometres twice every day to fetch water. For every 3.75 litres of water used by the plant, it produced one litre of cola and a large amount of waste water. The cola so produced is enjoyed by relatively richer people and the profits are transferred to the Coca Cola Company at the cost of people's sufferings. In this small hamlet, a movement started and organized by local tribal women unleashed a national and global wave of people's energy in their support. They started a 'dharna' (sit-up) at the gates of Coca-Cola, and huge rallies were organized to give an ultimatum to Coca Cola. On Earth Day 2003, they celebrated one year of their agitation. In the next year, the State under pressure of the growing movement and the aggravation of the water crisis due to a drought ordered closure of the Coca Cola plant. The victory of the movement in Plachimada is one among many in India and was the result of creating broad alliances and using multiple strategies of community mobilization and development (Bijoy 2006) (read more at http://www.righttowater.info).

Globalization and capitalism have in recent years led to an increasing level of social exclusion and marginalization of vulnerable groups in India. Within this context, community workers are employing a spectrum of strategies to achieve the goal of social justice. Indian community practices today are characterized by large diversities. People's grassroots movements work parallel with traditional top-down models of community change; mass mobilization for structural transformation is used, as are expert technical skills to guide the change process. In this chapter we will focus more on the emanipatory ideals and practices of community work.

India

India is the largest democracy and the second most populated country in the world, ranked 136th in the 2013 Human Development Report (United Nations Development Program 2013). The economy is predominantly based on the primary sector, the majority of the population being engaged in agriculture and allied small industries (Weiss and Welbourne 2007). There are eight recognized religions and approximately 3,000 castes, more than 2,000 ethnic groups with numerous sub groups. The 4,693 communities include several thousands of endogamous groups, speaking 325 functional languages and writing in 25 different scripts. With a population of 1,198 billion, the complexity increases as 72.2 per cent of the population lives in about 638,000 villages and the remaining 27.8 per cent in over 5,100 towns and over 380 urban agglomerations (Government of India 2003). This makes the society highly diverse and heterogeneous and the proud maxim 'unity in diversity' is often associated with India.

India is characterized by caste based atrocities, religion based genocide, gender based violence, poverty related issues like starvation deaths and malnutrition, street children, child labour, poor sanitation and health, land displacement, water inaccessibility, infant mortality rate, farmers' suicide, unemployment, illiteracy and HIV/AIDS (Andharia 2009). Additionally, capitalism continues to concentrate the world's wealth and resources into the hands of the few, increasing disparity between the haves and the have-nots. This further pushes entire communities and cultures into displacement, poverty and marginalization (George and Marlowe 2005).

Marginalization is deeply rooted in Indian society where discrimination is prevalent from centuries based on caste, class, religion and gender. The 'untouchables' or Scheduled Castes (see the Constitution of India Article 341, 366) constitute around 16.5 per cent of the Indian population; 8.5 per cent of the population consists of the 'tribal' or Scheduled Tribe (see the Constitution of India Article 342, 366) who remain cut from the mainstream due to their confinement in largely secluded, inaccessible forests and hilly regions. Almost 4 per cent called the 'denotified and nomadic tribes' are constantly on the move from the periphery of one mainstream community to another in search of a daily wage. Fifty-seven per cent of the total Indian population is recognized as 'Other Backward Classes' with similar status like the other marginalized. Thus, more than 80 per cent of the population is discriminated against and is powerless with limited resources and inaccessibility to basic needs like food, water and shelter. In addition to this, more than 90 per cent of the population works in the unorganized sector (Government of India 2012). Thus the urban marginalized are the urban poor, rag pickers, scavengers, daily wage earners, small vendors, mill labourers, domestic workers and physical labourers. In rural areas, the rural artisans, landless labourers, marginal and small farmers, bonded labourers and the workmen in the unorganized sectors constitute the marginalized communities. Women and girl children are the largest marginalized groups. All these groups are in search of an identity, security and basic amenities of life. Politically they are powerless, economically deprived and resourceless, socially backward and, therefore, easy victims of oppression, exploitation, privatization and globalization (Tirmare 2006, 2007).

In India community workers have been an important resource in terms of the mobilization and integration of marginalized communities (Shragge 2003). The history of India reflects a nation replete with organizing, asserting, demanding and fighting for rights, an example being the process of India's independence from British colonization (Andharia 2009). Community work in India is focused on the empowerment of disadvantaged and marginalized populations as well as on changing power relations, social institutions and structures to better benefit the marginalized (Lee 1999; Shragge 2003). According to Lee (cited in Moffatt et al. 2011), community work addresses the dual goals of empowerment and social justice through five objectives that include citizen involvement, organizational development, facilitation of a sense of community, social learning and the attainment of concrete benefits. To understand the nature of community work in a globalization impacted India, it is crucial to get an overview of globalization in India. This is presented below.

Globalization in India

In early 1991, India went through an economic–political crisis. The economic crisis comprised a steep fall in the foreign exchange reserve, galloping inflation, large public and current account deficits and mounting domestic and foreign debts. Two governments fell in a span of four months, a long interregnum until the elections and assassination of a former prime minister reflected an unprecedented crisis. These events led to a sharp erosion of confidence in India among foreign lenders, downgrading of India's credit rating and consequently snapping of international credit lines from private or commercial sources (Teltumde 2001).

At this time, many nation states were adopting the 'Reforms' promoted by international bodies such as the World Trade Organization, the World Bank, the Brettonwood Institute with their Structural Adjustment Programs and free trade agreements as a local initiative (George and Marlowe 2005). In India the adoption of these economic reforms were linked with conditions accepted as a rescue package to manage the crises that had erupted. The neoliberal conditions imposed a reduction in the role of state on social welfare, eliminated the concept of public good, increased deregulation, and established a general replacement of public with private services and institutions. Like in most countries around the world, globalization was accompanied with privatization of public companies and resources and the weakening of state intervention in the areas of social welfare, which led to increased social inequality and intensified marginalization of communities (Parada 2007; Moffatt et al. 2011). In particular, the privatization of natural resources due to globalization that were previously considered to be collective resources has had a detrimental effect on indigenous people in India. In this manner, indigenous people are alienated from traditional sources of production (Nathan and Kelkar 2003). In the name of development and industrialization, marginalized communities sustaining on agriculture and natural resources have borne the brunt of ill-conceived 'development' projects and new unconstitutional and anti-people enactments and policies like Special Economic Zones (SEZs). SEZs are aimed at stimulating foreign direct investment and rapid, export-led, industrial growth. Establishment of a SEZ generally requires the forced acquisition of land and the eviction of its previous users. While the state is required to compensate previous owners for the value of land and dwellings, such compensation is woefully inadequate to the loss of land and non-land assets, the loss of livelihood opportunities and the disruption to traditional rural life (Rawat et al. 2011). This has led to displacement and disruption of livelihood on a massive scale (Aravinda 2000). The slum dwellers, fish workers in coastal regions, farmers, dalits, tribals and artisans in rural and sub-urban areas and all the unorganized sector workers are left without physical or political space. The right to life, livelihood and participation in the development planning process is denied to all these communities.

Community organizers in India have done a thorough analysis with respect to the impact of globalization on local communities and they have a clear political understanding of how global changes have led to increasing marginalization of communities (Moffat et al. 2011). As a result of these changes, the guiding principles of community practices in India are being rethought (ibid). However, to understand the evolving practices of community work in India, it is important to see the history of community work in the country.

Community development in India

Community work as a major national rural development strategy was formally introduced in 1952 in India, six years after its independence from British colonization, as it was also an upcoming strategy in many western countries. The community development scheme in India, in a nutshell, aimed at providing increased employment and increased production by the application of latest methods of agriculture, self-help and self-reliance of the village community. It was also during this period that the Department of Urban and Rural Community Development was established in the first school of Social Work in India, generating several scholars and practitioners espousing diverse perspectives and ideologies (Andharia 2009). In the 1960s there were more than 2,000 community development blocs, each one consisting of 100 villages, and they were expected to serve about 194 million villagers all over the country. Huge administrative machinery engaging hundreds of officials was involved (Korten 1980).

However, challenges were faced to reach the desired goals, as existing power structures were accepted as a given and no attempt was made to change them. Responsibility for implementation of community development was placed in administratively separate ministries or agencies and targets were formulated with little regard to the willingness or capability of the locals. When working with the community, the field worker easily fell into the pattern of directing local level programs and little was done to build independent member controlled local organizations able to solve local problems and make demands on the broader system (ibid).

A new emergence

The failure of the governmental community development program to impact the poverty levels or people excluded from health, education, housing, sanitation and infrastructure services forced social workers and community organizers to re-examine the excessive emphasis on local development issues. They began to recast their work to include structural factors that shape local realities (Andharia 2009). A generation of teachers and activists from the 1980s onwards began to associate themselves with mass-based struggles, discovered different strategies and questioned conventional moorings of western forms of institutionalized social work and its relevance to India (ibid). Grassroots empowerment took precedence over community organization and saw greater involvement of community workers and scholars in issues of exclusion, violation, assertion of rights and discrimination. Today mobilizing communities against atrocities and domination is evident in almost all parts of India. The social work fraternity began to review its curriculum and the choice of field-work agencies. Modes of intervention were revised, tools of analysis underwent a shift and political frameworks were consciously used, in more fundamental ways to shape both the practice and education in community work in context of the local and indigenous realities (ibid).

Overarching theoretical framework

New ideologies in community practice gave rise to different critical and radical approaches for community work in India. One popular and important theoretical framework that is used today within community work is the 'structural social work approach'. Structural social work is one form of radical and emancipatory approach to social work that holds the fundamental transformation of an inequitable society as its primary goal (Longres 1986). This approach challenges the individual level focus of conventional social work and emphasizes emancipation and social justice of the masses. 'Structural social work questions the legitimacy of institutions and systems, suggesting that real advances in social welfare cannot be achieved without fundamental changes to the way in which global society organizes the distribution of resources and power' (Gray and Webb 2008: 87). It holds an analysis of the social structure at its core, which views social inequalities, rather than individual deficiencies, as the root of people's problems (Gil 1998; Healy 2000). The twofold goal of structural social work is to alleviate the negative effects of an exploitative and alienating social order while simultaneously working to transform society through social reforms and fundamental social change (George and Marlowe 2005). This theoretical approach is deciphered and popularly put into practice in the Indian context through 'the social action model' for community development. Social action is seen as an endeavour to bring about or prevent change in the social systems through a process of making people aware of the socio political and economic realities conditioning their lives and by mobilizing them to organize themselves to bring about the desired change, or to prevent the change that adversely affects them, through the use of whatever strategies they may find workable, with the exception of violence. In the process of social action, group work, group knowledge and skills are utilized along with a very thorough understanding of the political and economic forces operating in a society as well as a very clear understanding of the goals to be achieved and probable strategies to be followed (Siddiqui 1984). The social action model commonly applies key concepts like empowerment, critical consciousness, issue selection, community capacity, social capital, participation and social action in practice.

In addition to this theoretical approach, it is important to realize that every community practice is specific to its context. These overarching goals of structural social work are used in combination with Indigenous practice, which is local practice that is unique to a given culture or society. Indigenous practice means the practice wisdom applied by the people is of local origin and in tune with the socio-economic and cultural realities at the ground level (Singh 1984) and places emphasis on inclusion, interconnectivity and holistic ways of being. Indigenous practice systems are dynamic, and are continually influenced by internal creativity and experimentation as well as by contact with external systems. If we as social workers can reach clients where they eat, live and play, if we can encounter them in the systems that are meaningful to them and understand the relevance of their cultural beliefs and practices, then our practice can be relevant to their needs.

Sarvahara Jan Andolan is one such people's movement, which engages social action at grassroots for structural changes in a unique context. Below we present a case study based on this movement.

Sarvahara Jan Andolan: the movement of the one who has 'lost' everything

Sarvahara Jan Andolan (SJA), which more appropriately denotes the 'agitation or struggle of those who from whom everything has been snatched away', is a people's organization of the tribes and other oppressed communities based in the Raigad district of Maharashtra, India. It was formed in 1990 and today works in more than 750 villages in Maharashtra. SJA started by taking up the issue of 'landlessness' of the local tribes and then moved on to take up livelihood related issues like atrocities against tribes and proper implementation of government programmes for people's welfare and development.

Community profile

Raigad is part of an industrial belt between Mumbai and Goa and has stretches of productive land and natural resources. The small villages along the national highway are fertile for agriculture and small-scale industries. These features of Raigad make it a perfect place for the establishment of multinational companies, SEZs, free trade zones and large scale industries that wipe out large masses of people and their livelihood. More than 12 per cent of the population in Raigad belongs to the *Katkari* tribal community (Mahajan n.d.). The Katkaris have been cultivating 'dali' land in the forest since the times of British colonization. The word 'dali' is derived from the local dialect, meaning cultivating the slopes. Under colonization, the Katkari tribes were given some tracts of sloping land on the periphery of the forests for a dual purpose, that the forests should be protected and the tribe's livelihood should be taken care of. However, the Katkaris had no proprietary ownership rights over this land and paid rent for it. Thus, the land could be and often was taken away from them at the whim of the government. After independence from the British, there were tribal uprisings in various parts of India on the issue of land rights. There was no such uprising in Raigad since the Katkari tribe were never organized. Governments changed and the issue of this tribe's livelihood was forgotten (ibid). Today these tribes have to shift from season to season in search of a means of livelihood and are dependent on daily wages earned as labourers and bonded slaves. The children are left uneducated and individuals without any papers of registration, housing, sanitation or health care (ibid). SJA is a movement of the Katkari tribe struggling to sustain control on natural livelihood resources like land and forest for social justice.

The beginning: critical consciousness

SJA was founded by two young social work graduates who had done their field placement in Raigad as students. These activists thus had background knowledge of the contextual issues and most significant problems. But when the locals were confronted, the activists were intrigued by the social issues identified by the people. The locals listed that they wanted electricity, water, roads, kindergarten schools, houses, roof tiles, crematoriums and small bridges. These issues were indicative of what people wanted from the government. This awareness about what role the government should be playing in their development stemmed from the tutoring by high caste leaders. Rarely did people mention that they had no land to cultivate or no access to forest land. They never mentioned low wages as an issue; nor did they mention that their lands were usurped by the upper castes and government or that they were beaten up and their women were raped. It was as if these issues were part of their daily routine, their life and hence did not deserve any special mention – they were not even considered as issues.

SJA was hence challenged to raise the consciousness of the tribes not only to realize the importance of a struggle and aspiration for a 'humane' existence but also to create a sense of identity, an understanding of themselves as the 'labour' or 'exploited' class. It was necessary therefore to enable the people to think independently and critically (Mahajan n.d.).

Critical consciousness is a mental state by which members in a community recognize the need for social change and are ready to work to achieve those changes. This is a step completely necessary in achieving community involvement for social action. As consciousness of injustice grows, marginalized people begin to identify social causes of their oppression and become less likely to accept their situation as it is. SJA began to extend its work on the principle that developing awareness of the structural causes of oppression and building strengths reinforces each other. These insights help people to develop analyses of their marginalization as well as to build confidence and capacity for seeking social changes. It is argued that the most effective mode of consciousness-raising occurs in groups who share the same oppressive situations (Mullaly 2009).

Making a pathway: issue selection

Even as steps for consciousness-raising of the tribes were taking effect, threats to their livelihood were a reality. The activists from SJA realized early on that the tribes were employed as labourers and were indebted to the higher caste landlords of the villages. Not only wages, there were innumerable socio-economic ties between the tribal and his landlord, which had endured over years and generations at times. Right from advancing financial and other help during the marriages held in the labourers' family, to lending money in times of crisis, petty issues like allowing the tribes and untouchables to fish in the ponds that were created in the landlords' fields during monsoon, facilitating the labourers to access some government schemes, to ensuring bail in the case of arrest by police – all these reasons led to dependency and indebtedness of the low caste and tribal labourer to the landlord. For the labourer, therefore, opposing the master and confronting him on any issue was like axing one's own feet.

This meant that if SJA began their work in Raigad with focus on an issue like caste based atrocities, they would not be able to garner the support and involvement of the downtrodden victims, as people could not become involved in an issue which would sever all their immediate livelihood support; especially when they did not have a new support system to replace the old one nor the self confidence to face the repercussions. In the social action model as well as in anti-oppressive practice, 'issue selection' is another key concept wherein communities identify winnable, specific goals that unify and build community strength. In this process, individuals work together to select issues they feel are beneficial and relevant to the entire community (Minkler et al. 2008). SJA initiated this process with the locals and came to a conclusion that the issue they chose to begin with would be one where the 'enemy' would be distant and perhaps nebulous, but also an issue which would call upon all the tribe to participate and be involved in 'their issue'. The issue that fitted these criteria was the issue of landlessness – the dali land. It was close to their heart and the confrontation would be with the government, which was a relatively distant opposition and which would not resort to overt, anti–people actions overnight. Also, if the government put attention towards these tribes, they could slowly start getting access to other state benefits. After this, SJA was confronted by many other issues like growing industrialization, threats arising out of globalization, issues arising from caste and gender differences etc. Selecting the appropriate and pressing issue still remains an important challenge.

Community mobilization

Community mobilization is considered as a participatory process through which members of the community are empowered towards collective action for changes that could benefit the community as a whole. This has been the basis to all of SJA's activities. In the beginning, the activists went to the locals and explained to them the cause of mobilization and how it was their 'issue'. After the meetings they would ask the locals to contact others and inform them about SJA. By snowballing, information was disseminated and people collected one at a time. Slowly the number increased and in July 1990, about 250 people marched in the first morcha (protest march) in the Katkari community. The people's confidence and enthusiasm increased and people from neighbouring villages began to participate in SJA's activities. Efforts were made by SJA for people to understand the strength gathered from the collective action at various stages of the movement. As the founding activist of SJA argues:

> The role of movements like ours is to create memories of struggles which will feed fire and inspire not only those who participate but will also be carried forward to the next generation of the oppressed. Especially in the case of communities that do not have struggle-oriented histories, no tradition of conquering conflicts, such memories have a special role – they inspire people to fight against injustice.
>
> *(Mahajan n.d.)*

Social action for empowerment

Since 1990, SJA and its people have taken action in various forms for social change through structural transformation. When the government and other structures overlooked the people's justice and rights, SJA and the people themselves took to social actions for their development, using the structural social work theory as its crux.

Land rights

Once the community began to get organized to address the issue of dali land, non-violent mass protest marches were organized to all the concerned government official's offices. These protests continued in the form of fasts until death undertaken at the doorsteps of the officials who were keeping information from the people.

These actions by mobilized groups of people pressurized the state government to undertake surveys to implement the resolution that the land would be restored to the tribes. As things stand today the state government has agreed in principle to transfer the land to the tribes.

Prevention of land alienation

SJA has successfully taken up numerous cases of land alienation by companies, hotels and real estate investors and developers with similar non-violent protests and discussions. Various frauds in connivance with corrupt government officials have been perpetrated by the companies to dupe the people of their land, illegally use government land and illegally withdraw water for industrial use. Many times the cases would only come to notice when the construction would start and the companies would forcibly take over land from the tribes.

In a small village SJA fought against a giant Indian private company to get justice for the tribal hamlet whose land was taken without any compensation. After almost a four year long struggle the company had to provide alternate land and construction expenses for the displaced families. In this case the sangathan (collective mobilization) achieved full success.

Public distribution system

The public distribution system (PDS) is an Indian food security system established by the Government of India, which distributes subsidized food and non-food items to people living in poverty. However, the food grains supplied by the ration shops are not enough to meet the consumption needs of the poor and are of inferior quality. The PDS is infested with corruption and is criticized for its urban bias and failure to serve the poorer sections of the population effectively. These lacunae became more prominent after impact of globalization.

SJA has taken up the issue of streamlining the PDS in Raigad in collaboration with the state and other organizations, thus networking to create pressure. Along with networking, SJA conducted large-scale training sessions for various people's organizations to educate locals on PDS and raise awareness. However, with increasing privatization, the PDS system has become more inaccessible to people. SJA is working on the issue of PDS in a big way even today. For instance, SJA participated in a state level seminar on challenging the government's definition of the poverty. Several trade unions and representatives of political parties participated in this seminar. The struggle still continues at policy and structural level as well at grassroots in streamlining the functioning of ration shops.

Electoral politics

SJA has made it a point to become involved in the policy making of the marginalized for their welfare. In the initial years due to lack of finances and non-recognition of

SJA as pro-poor resulted in no political recognition. But over the years SJA has become a political entity and the votes of the tribals are considered essential by all candidates to win the elections. SJA takes up voter awareness campaigns and serious discussions are held on which ideology to support. This is a way of including the marginalized into the important state systems and making their voices heard, an important strategy used in community work in India.

The case study of SJA shows the crucial role of direct action, hunger strikes, mass protests and legal action in bringing about societal transformation. From this perspective, such interventions need to be considered as an added and an inevitable dimension to the community work model to strengthen its pursuit of social change. The work of SJA includes immediate engaging core components of direct social action interventions. Had these actions not been an integral part of the intervention of SJA, the fundamental change in the situation of tribes and other oppressed of Raigad would not likely have been as significant.

Conclusion

With India going through a phase of socio-economic policy changes, challenges for practitioners working with marginalized communities changed. National and international forces are increasingly shaping realities in local communities. The state has withdrawn from fundamental responsibilities toward the citizens of India. In the absence of accountability by the state, community practitioners are left to themselves for solving problems that impact their communities. Local practitioners have constructed a thorough analysis with respect to the impact of globalization on marginalized communities. It is argued that community practitioners have a clear political understanding of their practice that is tied to the perception that global change has led to increasing marginalization of communities in India (Moffatt et al. 2011).

As a result of the new issues engendered by corporate globalization, the foundations of community development practices are changing. Movements that existed prior to the onset of the global economy have shifted agendas to incorporate responses to globalization (Armstrong 2004; Singh Gill 2004; Natarajan 2005; Pattenden 2005). For example, farmers' movements and rural development organizations have developed explicit anti-globalization policies. Various movements that support the rights of the poor have united on the issues of globalization, collaborating in rallies and demonstrations, and are exploring the use of legal channels to challenge negative developments associated with globalization (Sheth 2004). These processes remain indigenous to avoid the historical failures in community work in the Indian context. SJA is an excellent example of the use of social action strategies like mass mobilizations, peaceful protests and awareness-raising about the impact of globalization. Community workers are responding to the current challenges through a number of strategies including a dual focus on capacity building within communities and a consciousness of the effects of globalization. The workers are interested in working within broad-based opposition movements to develop proactive strategies of political change. The determination of workers and activists to reframe resistance in the context of globalization is hopeful not only to the workers but to the marginalized populations within India. The workers are attentive to change and as shown here keen to express how changing social conditions are affecting the foundations of their practice.

QUESTIONS FOR REFLECTION

- Is there any example of social action in the form of mass mobilization that you can identify from your country? What was the social issue leading to such a collective movement and how can you analyze its success and/or failure?
- Can you recognize some marginalized communities in your country? What kind of marginalization do they face? Has globalization empowered or further marginalized these communities?
- What are your suggestions for altering community work practices to suit current global situations?

References

Andharia, J. (2009) 'Critical explorations of community organization in India', *Oxford University Press and Community Development Journal*, 44(3): 276–90.

Aravinda, L. S. (2000) 'Globalisation and Narmada people's struggle', *Economic and Political Weekly*, 11–17 November 2000. Online. Available HTTP: http://www.epw.in/commentary/globalisation-and-narmada-peoples-struggle.html (accessed 12 November 2012).

Armstrong, E. (2004) 'Globalization from below: AIDWA, foreign funding, and gendering anti-violence campaigns', *Journal of Developing Societies*, 20(1–2): 39–55.

Bijoy, C. R. (2006) 'Kerala's Plachimada struggle: a narrative on water and governance Rights', *Economic and Political Weekly*, 41(4): 4332–9.

George, P. and Marlowe, S. (2005) 'Structural social work in action', *Journal of Progressive Human Services*, 16(1): 5–24.

Gil, D.G. (1998). *Confronting Injustice and Oppression: Concepts and Strategies for Social Workers*, New York: Columbia University Press.

Government of India (2003) *The Genome Project, Anthropological Survey of India*, New Delhi. Online. Available HTTP: http://www.igvdb.res.in/references.php (accessed 3 July 2012).

——(2012) *Report of the Committee on Unorganised Sector Statistics*, National Statistical Commission. Online. Available HTTP: http://mospi.nic.in/mospi_new/upload/nsc_report_un_sec_14mar12.pdf?status=1&menu_id=199 (accessed 5 January 2013).

Gray. M. and Webb. A.S. (2008) *Social Work Theories and Methods*, Los Angeles: Sage Publications.

Healy, K. (2000). *Social Work Practices: Contemporary Perspectives on Change*, London: Sage Publications.

Korten, C. D. (1980) 'Community organization and rural development: a learning process approach', *Public Administration Review*, 40(5): 480–511.

Lee, B. (1999) *Pragmatics of Community Organization*, Mississauga: Commonact Press.

Longres, J.F. (1986) 'Marxian theory and social work practice', *Catalyst: A Socialist Journal of the Social Services*, 5(4): 13–34.

Mahajan, U. (n.d.) 'For Justice … For Dignity … For Equality.' A Story of the Katkaris of Raigad, Maharashtra: Sarvahara Jan Andolan.

Minkler, M., Wallerstein, N. and Wilson, N. (2008) 'Improving health through community organization and community building', in K. Glanz, Health Behavior and Health Education: Theory, Research, and Practice, San Francisco: John Wiley & Sons.

Moffatt, K., George, P., Alphonse, M., Kanitkar, M., Anand, V. and Chamberlain, J. (2011) 'Community practice at a crossroads: the impact of the global on the local in India', Oxford University Press and Community Development Journal 46(1): 104–21.

Mullaly, B. (2009) Challenging Oppression: A Critical Social Work Approach. Don Mills, Ont.: Oxford University Press.

Nathan, D. and Kelkar, G. (2003) 'Civilisational change: markets and privatization among indigenous peoples', Economic and Political Weekly, 17 May 2003. Online. Available HTTP: http://www.epw.in/special-articles/civilisational-change-markets-and-privatisation-among-indigenous-peoples.html (accessed 23 May 2012).

Natarajan, T. (2005) 'Agency of development and agents of change: localization, resistance, and Empowerment', Journal of Economic Issues, 39(2): 409–18.

Parada, H. (2007) 'Regional perspectives from Latin America, social work in Latin America, history, challenges and rewards', International Social Work, 50(4): 560–9.

Pattenden, J. (2005) 'Trickle-down solidarity, globalisation and dynamics of social transformation in a south Indian village', Economic and Political Weekly. Online. Available HTTP: http://www.epw.in/search/apachesolr_search/Pattenden (accessed 7 May 2012).

Rawat, V.B., Bhushan, M.B. and Surepally, S. (2011) The Impact of Special Economic Zones in India: A Caste Study of Polepally SEZ, paper presented at the International Conference on Global Land Grabbing: University of Sussex.

Sheth, D.L. (2004) 'Globalization and new politics of micro-movements', Economic and Political Weekly, 3 January 2004. Online. Available HTTP: http://www.epw.in/special-articles/globalisation-and-new-politics-micro-movements.html (accessed 3 July 2012).

Shragge, E. (2003) Towards a Conclusion: Community Organizing and Social Change, in Activism and Social Change: Lessons for Community and Local Organizing, Peterborough: Broadview Press.

Siddiqui, H.Y. (ed.) (1984) Social Work and Social Action: A Developmental Perspective, New Delhi: Harnam Publications.

Singh, R.R. (1984) 'Social action: some reflections reorienting social work education' in H.Y. Siddiqui (ed.) Social Work and Social Action: A Developmental Perspective, New Delhi: Harnam Publications.

Singh Gill, S. (2004) 'Punjab farmers' movement: continuity and change', Economic and Political Weekly, 3 July 2004. Online. Available HTTP: http://www.preservearticles.com/ (accessed 6 October 2012).

Teltumde, A. (2001) Globalisation and The Dalits, Nagpur: Sanket Prakashan.

The Constitution of India, Government of India Ministry of Law and Justice (modified 2007). Online. Available HTTP: http://lawmin.nic.in/coi/coiason29july08.pdf (accessed 5 January 2013).

Tirmare, P. (2006) 'Empowerment of the weaker sections need to establish interlinkages between social work profession and people's organizations', in R.B.S. Verma, H.S. Verma and R. K. Singh (eds) Empowerment of the Weaker Sections in India: Interface of the Civil Society Organizations and Professional Social Work Institutions, New Delhi: Serials Publications.

——(2007) 'Violation of human rights of dalit women: issues, factors and concerns Indian', The Indian Journal of Human Rights and The Law, 4(1–2): 139.

United Nations Development Program (2013) Human Development Report 2013. Online. Available HTTP: http://hdr.undp.org/en/media/HDR2013_EN_Summary.pdf (accessed 2 May 2013).

Weiss, I. and Weilbourne, P. (eds) (2007) Social Work as a Profession: a Comparative Cross-national Perspective, Birmingham: Venture.

16

COMMUNITY WORK AND THE CHALLENGES OF NEOLIBERALISM AND NEW MANAGERIALISM

Resistance, the Occupy Movement and the Arab Spring

Vishanthie Sewpaul

Introduction

From small-scale protest actions in various parts of the world to the Arab Spring with its beginnings in Tunisia and the international Occupy Movement that began in New York, rest the core-underlying theme of citizen intolerance of political authoritarianism, poverty and inequality, exclusion in its various forms and violation of human rights. The problems engendered by neoliberal capitalism and new managerialism, with their focus on trade liberalization; cut backs in state expenditure on health, education, housing and welfare; on increased consumerism and the commodification of every facet of human life; the profit motive above human well-being and dignity; and the focus on efficiency with the aim to do more for less place huge stress on participatory community work processes. Over the past few decades we have been witnessing an increasing dominance of neoliberalism and new managerialism, as discourse and practice on a global level which have been re-moulding health, education and welfare and more particularly social and community work education and practice (Abramovitz and Zelnick 2010; Schram and Silverman 2012; Sewpaul 2008). With these influences some of our most cherished values and principles in relation to social justice, human rights and our critical and radical approaches to community social work are under attack.

New managerial emphases on getting the job done, with checks and balances in the shortest space of time, impacts relationship building, the requisite empathic tuning into the life worlds of people for effective community intervention, and the use of emancipatory people-driven processes toward social change and development. While grassroots involvement and development is important, we need to recognize that the enormous consequences of neoliberalism and new managerialism mean that single small-scale community based initiatives are, in themselves, insufficient to challenge the power of capital, of centralized, authoritarian governments, and of the International Monetary Fund, the World Bank and the World Trade Organisation (WTO).

Despite the devastating effects that the austerity measures, imposed by the World Bank and the International Monetary Fund, and that liberalization of trade have on people, neoliberalism persists as the dominant ideology. In this chapter I begin with an elucidation of the ideological hegemony of neoliberalism, and I discuss the consequences of neoliberalism in relation to poverty, inequality, trade liberalization and unemployment. This is followed by a discussion on neoliberal and new managerial discourses and practices in welfare. The chapter concludes by deliberating the hope born out of resistance as reflected in the International Occupy Movement and the Arab Spring.

Neoliberalism as dominant ideology and practice

The global economic crisis that began in 2008 held the potential to create cracks in the consciousness of people about the limits of a system regarded as sacrosanct. However, the opportunities were lost and the 'world failed to shake the "Washington Consensus"' (Bond 2010: 59) – a consensus between the International Monetary Fund, the World Bank and the United States Treasury that fostered fiscal austerity, privatization and market liberalization (Stiglitz 2006). The failure to disrupt the Washington Consensus is understandable given that the mass media colludes with the corporate world and political elites to fabricate consent in support of neoliberalism (Fortunato Jr 2005). Capitalism succeeds through ideological control of consciousness that makes us believe that neoliberalism is in our interests and that it is inevitable. Neoliberalism was engineered and gained ground primarily on account of the lure of the language of liberal theory with its emphases on individualism, ownership, choice, flexibility and competition (Harvey 2007).

While most theorists are quick to comment on the dangers of neoliberalism, few are willing to critique the liberal democracy that underpins it. There is a general taken-for-granted assumption of a convergence between the market and democracy, with American liberalism and capitalist hegemony being erroneously pushed as the source of morality and democratic practice (Amin 2001; Fortunato Jr 2005; Tabb 2003). As previously indicated (Sewpaul 2006) as social workers we need to reflect on some critical questions posed by Amin (2001). If democracy is about human rights, social justice, people participation and respect for human dignity where is its convergence with the marketplace that has no room for justice and compassion, that creates indifference to inequality, hunger, exploitation and suffering; that excludes the voice of the *Other*, with highly centralized power negotiated by the World Bank, the International Monetary Fund, the WTO and by the world's superpowers? If information is central to a deepening democracy how can there be democracy, when information and the very ideas that we generate are commodified? What is the convergence of democracy and the market when intellectual property rights, incorporating patent laws, designed purely in the interest of profit (e.g. those of the multi-national pharmaceutical companies), allow people to die? What is liberal, individual freedom if such freedom means constricted choice to illness, starvation, hunger and death for a large proportion of the world's population? Harvey (2007) points out that the values of individual freedom and social justice may be incompatible with each other. The pursuit of social justice, he argues, 'presupposes social solidarities and a willingness to submerge individual wants, needs, and desires in the cause of some more general struggle for, say, social equality or environmental justice' (Harvey 2007: 50).

According to Vrasti (2012) the market is a socially embedded institution that cannot exist without ideological and institutional support. Neoliberalism endures as we all actively participate in its reproduction. Haiven (2011: 1) avers that 'we all consume, we all work, many of us employ or manage; we all participate in hierarchies of race, class gender and privilege. No one is a pure victim in this economic system, though almost everyone is ultimately a loser.' Gramsci (1977) and Harvey (2007) describe how neoliberal capitalism penetrates our daily consciousness so much so that we normalize it, and we consider it necessary for social order. It is important that community social workers understand such normalization dynamics if they are to work toward consciousness-raising and helping community members deconstruct the legitimating power of capitalism. In doing so they might inspire local communities to challenge neoliberal policies and practices that engender poverty and inequality, as so cogently addressed by Singh and Tirmare in chapter 15.

Neoliberalism, poverty and inequality

Neoliberalism has contributed to distorted development between the North and the South, to greater levels of inequality within nation states, to the further marginalization of women and to a greater feminization of poverty, especially among Black women (Gibson 2009; Lara 2011; Sewpaul 2004; 2005a). Skewed development within and across nation states and continents reflect that race, class, gender and other factors such as ethnicity, sexual orientation and disability intersect in powerful ways to influence people's access to power, prestige, status and resources. While the Global South has long been the biggest loser with global capitalism with austerity measures imposed as structural adjustment programmes (Rowden 2009; Bond 2005a; 2005b), patterns of capital accumulation and consumption are now becoming more complex with huge disparities existing both in the Global North and the Global South. With new configurations of global power, particularly with the rising economic power of China, we are finding growing pockets of poverty in the developed North and increasing pockets of richness in the South. Hoogvelt (1997) points out that the North-South divide is giving way to a new international division of labour, characterized no longer by a geographic but a social division of the global economy. The 'North and South, First World and Third World, are no longer "out there" but nestled together within all the world's major cities' (Held et al. 1999: 8). The Nobel Prize winner, economist Paul Krugman (2009: 190) concluded that financial globalization 'has definitely turned out to be even more dangerous than we realized'.

In the wake of the global economic crisis, it is the increasing levels of poverty, unemployment and inequalities that we must be concerned about as community social workers. In a recent update of 8 April 2012 by Anup Shah, the following levels of poverty and inequality were shown to characterize the world:

- Almost half the world's seven billion people live on less than $2.50 a day.
- The GDP (Gross Domestic Product) of the 41 Heavily Indebted Poor Countries (567 million people) is less than the wealth of the world's seven richest people combined.
- Nearly a billion people entered the 21st century unable to read a book or sign their names.
- Less than 1 per cent of what the world spent every year on weapons was needed to put every child into school by the year 2000 and yet it didn't happen.
- One billion children live in poverty (1 in 2 children in the world).
- 640 million live without adequate shelter.
- 400 million have no access to safe water.
- 270 million have no access to health services.
- 10.6 million died in 2003 before they reached the age of five (or roughly 29,000 children per day).

(Shah 2012)

Writing about the penalization of poverty, which disproportionately affects people of colour, Wacquant discusses the 'liberal-paternalist' state as follows:

> It is liberal at the top, towards business and the privileged classes, at the level of the causes of rising social inequality and marginality; and it is paternalistic and punitive at the bottom, towards those destabilised by the conjoint restructuring of employment and withering away of welfare state protection or their reconversion into instrument of surveillance of the poor.
>
> *(Wacquant 2001: 402)*

Trade liberalization and unemployment

Trade liberalization and unfair trade have often resulted in massive imports, which undermine local production and prices, and increases unemployment. This places enormous strains on the poor, contributing to children dropping out of school, women and child trafficking, engaging in dangerous work, starvation and xenophobic outbursts, all of which are key concerns for community social workers. John Maynard Keynes in 1933 argued that commodities such as ideas, knowledge, science and travel should be internationalized but that, as far as possible, economics should remain domestic and we should seek to stimulate local production and manufacturing. The salience of his reflections for our contemporary world is expressed in the following:

> Experience accumulates to prove that most modern processes of mass production can be performed in most countries and climates with almost equal efficiency [...]. National self-sufficiency [...] though it costs something, may be becoming a luxury, which we can afford, if we happen to want it.
>
> *(Keynes 1933 unpaged)*

Contrary to the above we have ever-increasing imports of foreign goods and transnational ownership of capital (Bichler and Nitzan 2012). The McKinsey Global Institute (cited in Bichler and Nitzan 2012) found that between 1990 and 2006 the global proportion of foreign-owned assets increased from 9 per cent to 26 per cent of all world assets. Foreign ownership of corporate bonds rose from 7 per cent to 21 per cent of the world total, foreign ownership of government bonds rose from 11 per cent to 31 per cent and foreign ownership of corporate stocks rose from 9 per cent to 27 per cent.

The influx of Chinese trade across the globe is engendering a great deal of anger at the destruction of domestic livelihoods. Local producers cannot compete against a range of cheap Chinese imports. In South Africa, as in many other parts of the world, trade liberalization and the relocation of manufacturing to areas of least labour costs have seen the shutdown of local industries. The subsidies offered to farmers in the US and Europe also contribute to importation of cheaper agricultural products that African farmers cannot compete with. The neoliberal macro-economic framework of Growth Employment and Redistribution (GEAR) was introduced in South Africa in 1996, with the promise of stimulating employment (Ministry of Finance 1996). However, contrary to this millions of people have been losing their jobs, with the rising level of unemployment being one of the greatest challenges for post-apartheid South Africa. The official unemployment rate is said to be about 25 per cent. The estimate goes up to 34 per cent if the expanded definition with discouraged work-seekers is included. According to Jenkins (2012) the crisis has been exacerbated in the manufacturing sector on account of increasing competition from Chinese imports. China's share of South African imports of manufactured goods increased from 2 per cent in 1995 to over 18 per cent in 2010. This was accompanied by marked loss of employment to Chinese goods, at a cost of 77,751 jobs between 2001 (when China joined the WTO) and 2010, compared with a loss of 24,117 jobs to Chinese imports between 1992 and 2001. These are only in terms of direct losses with lay-offs and closure of companies in labour intensive sectors such as clothing, footwear, leather and furniture manufacturing and do not take into account indirect losses such as those incurred by China crowding out South African imports into Sub-Saharan Africa. China's imports to Sub-Saharan Africa rose from $4.1 billion in 2001 to $53.3 billion in 2011 (Jenkins 2012), a pattern that is being replicated in various parts of the world.

According to Autor, Dorn and Hanson (2012) the value of goods imported from China into the USA rose by a staggering 1.156 per cent from 1991 to 2007. Through a comprehensive analysis they concluded that:

> Chinese import competition affects local labour markets along numerous margins beyond its impact on manufacturing employment [...] Chinese imports reduces manufacturing employment in exposed local labour markets. More surprisingly, it also triggers a decline in wages that is primarily observed outside of the manufacturing sector. Reductions in both employment and wage levels lead to a steep drop in the average earnings of households.
>
> *(Autor et al. 2012: 41)*

With growing intolerance for lack of government regulation, people are taking measures into their own hands with, unfortunately, violence and threats of violence. One Malawian merchant was reported to have said: 'One day there will be blood' (Reuters 2012: 13). In South Africa xenophobic attacks, linked to socio-economic deprivations (Misago 2011; Nieftagodien 2011), has seen blood and this seems to be spilling over to Chinese migrants. In November 2011 four Chinese were murdered in South Africa (Reuters 2012). In August 2012, Kenyans protested with placards that said: 'Chinese must go'. With an unemployment rate of above 25 per cent, a growing recession and pernicious austerity measures, there are similar backlashes against Chinese immigrants in Spain (Roman 2012). If no attempts are made to regulate trade, it is likely that we will see increased backlashes against cheap Chinese imports. It is unfortunate that ordinary people, who cross borders in search of better life prospects, often making huge sacrifices in the process of doing so, are on the receiving end of failed national and international trade policies. Political leaders go against their own professed understandings. In July 2012, Jacob Zuma, the President of South Africa during an official visit to Beijing, talked about the importance of exercising caution 'when entering partnerships with other economies', saying that the trade relationship was 'unsustainable in *the long term'* (Hook 2012: 1, my emphasis). People in positions of power to influence change need to appreciate that people have to feed, clothe, educate and care for themselves and their children in *the immediate and short term.*

Neoliberal and new managerial discourse and practices in welfare

According to Clarke (2007) neoliberalism has been the ideological base for the restructuring, privatization and retrenchment of social policy and welfare programmes. It is a discourse and practice, which rarefies individual interests where transnational corporations and its elites dominate the market primarily interested in profit making. Following this individualistic logic, neoliberal social policies allow the state to abdicate its responsibilities in relation to the welfare of its people.

The most dominant neoliberal discourses in welfare have been on the promotion of self-reliance: the importance of individuals, families and communities taking responsibility for their own wellbeing; and shifting responsibility from the state to local communities, as reflected in key welfare policy documents in South Africa (Sewpaul and Holscher 2004; Sewpaul 2005b; Desai et al. 2010) such as the Financing Policy for welfare released in 1997 (Department of Welfare 1997) and the draft Family Policy released in 2005. Sewpaul and Holscher (2004) highlighted how the Financing Policy is replete with managerial and market discourses. It speaks of business plans, contracts, affordability, efficiency, outputs, performance audits, outsourcing, venture financing and service purchasing, thus effectively reconstructing the people whom we work with as *customers*. One of the authors of the Policy said:

> The State is an entrepreneur of its own. It must make a profit where it can [...]. The state must be minimalist, it must really do the least and the last. Civil society, empowered civil society is to do the most.
>
> *(Sewpaul and Holscher 2004: 84–5)*

Sewpaul (2005b) identified two major issues related to the conservative and neoliberal discourses in the Family Policy. Firstly, the burden of coping with South Africa's huge problems is reduced to the level of individuals and families, without recognition of the structural sources of unemployment, poverty, exclusion and inequality and the profound impacts of society and state on family living. Secondly, rebuilding the moral fibre of individuals and communities appears to be the panacea for all of the problems mentioned. These ideologies are manifest in policies such as community home based care for persons who are HIV+ and kinship care for orphans, where the burdens of care are often transferred to poor black women (Gibson 2009; Lara 2011).

Banks (2001) observes an increasing dominance of the technical/bureaucratic model in social work. This dominance has manifested in a growing 'specification of tasks [...], attempts to reduce indeterminacy in decision-making, the adoption of competency-based approaches to education and training, [...] the growth of interest in 'evidence-based practice' (Banks 2001: 146), an intensification of 'procedures, measurement and centrally defined targets', and the adoption of de-personalised ethics that focus on pre-determined standards, contracts and procedural manuals (Banks 2011: 10). New managerialism relegates the importance of other ethical values such as autonomy, critical reflection, care, equality, solidarity, inter-dependence, reciprocity, respect and trust in favour of narrowly defined economic priorities (Bottery 2000). Under such circumstances case management and administration take precedence over constructionist, radical and participatory approaches to community work.

While neoliberalism guarantees personal and individual freedom, each person is held responsible for his or her own actions and wellbeing. Thus poverty and hardships are seen as personal failings rather than being attributed to any structural barriers in people's lives, such as structural determinants of unemployment and the impact of exclusions based on race, class, caste, gender and/or disability. The impact of the financial crises that began in 2008, which saw marked decreases in the living standards of people, had reverberating effects in all parts of the globe, as reflected in the crises of Wall Street, the deepening of the Eurozone crisis, the economic slowdown of some of the Asian counties, the entrenching of uneven development and greater inequality within and across countries. Economic growth in some parts of the world, like Africa, belies the uneven development and inequalities across the continent and within countries. The Africa Development Bank (2011) recorded that despite Tunisia's economic growth and being one of the most robust performers in Africa, widening disparities within Tunisia and increasing unemployment, paved the way for revolution that saw the end of the 23-year rule of President Ben Ali. The African Development Bank (2011) refers to the increasing depredations and dishonesty under privatization in Tunisia and links the discontent and revolutionary movement, in part to the corruption of the Ben Ali regime.

Resistance to neoliberalism: the Occupy Movement and the Arab Spring

Given the manufacture of consent around neoliberalism we are generally filled with a sense of hopelessness of a possibility of a better world. However Graeber (2011) warns that killing the radical imagination supports the very nihilism that capitalism instils in us, entrenching Thatcher's doctrine: 'there is no alternative'. The Occupy Movement and the Arab Spring serve to negate this by highlighting inequalities, popularizing radical theory and providing hope that something can be done. Wight asserted that

> The Arab Spring, looting in London, riots in Greece, wars across the Middle East and beyond, the Global Financial Crisis (GFC), and the Occupy Movement are all connected [...]. What connects them is a corrupt, degenerative, immoral, sexist, and racist global capitalist political-economic system.
>
> *(Wight 2012: 161)*

The Occupy Movement began in September 2011 when a group of activists encamped in a park in New York and began a protest called Occupy Wall Street. They took a stand against corporate greed, social inequality and the destructive power of major banks and multinational corporations (New York Times 2012). Within weeks, similar demonstrations spread to other American cities and to cities in other parts of the world. Although the Movement lost momentum since its inception, the protesters managed to popularize the slogan, 'we are the 99 per cent' and heightened awareness of inequalities. The 1 per cent refers to the haves i.e. those in banks, the mortgage industry, the insurance industry and the 99 per cent refers to the have-nots (New York Times 2012). Tormey (2012: 136) argues that Occupy Wall Street asks us 'to re-imagine democracy as an instrument of the

99 per cent as opposed to something that operates as the handmaiden of global capitalism, and the 1 per cent'. The outcome of the Occupy Movement is difficult to predict; it was at once both coherent and fragmented. But for Hozic:

> The most fascinating aspects of the movement are precisely its Situationist roots; its amorphous, malleable nature; its anarchist trust in diffusion and dissolution of power; its carnivalesque features – a lived experience of space and time that could be otherwise; its belief in process rather than outcomes; its embodiment of non-instrumental action.
>
> *(Hozic 2012: 151)*

The Arab Spring had its genesis in Tunisia in December 2010. One worker Mohammed Bouazizi, who would not tolerate his indignities any longer, began, by setting himself alight, a revolution that toppled autocratic regimes in Tunisia, Egypt and Libya and sent warning bells across the world that ordinary people were willing to die to secure their civil, political and socio-economic rights. Civil uprisings had also erupted in Bahrain and Syria; major protests broke out in Algeria, Iraq, Jordan, Kuwait, Morocco and Sudan and minor protests occurred in Mauritania, Oman, Saudi Arabia, Djibouti and Western Sahara. The hope borne out of the Arab spring, what Filiu (2011) also calls the Arab renaissance and the Arab revolution, was echoed in the Occupy Movement.

Reflecting the power of civil society, broad-based inclusive and democratic efforts, and the power of the Internet in engineering and supporting socio-political change, Slim Amamou, the Minister of Youth and Sports in Tunisia (post revolution) said on 11 February 2011, soon after the resignation of Egyptian President, Hosni Mubarak:

> They [the Tunisian and Egyptian uprisings] are both ONE uprising. One world, one revolution [...] We have been ready, we people of the Internet, for a revolution to start anywhere in the Arab world. We've been supporting each other and trying hard [...] Egyptians actively supported the Tunisian revolution as any Tunisian national did [...]. And now Tunisians are doing the same for Egyptians. *It's really a new citizenship.*
>
> *(Amamou cited in Filiu 2011: 1; highlights and brackets mine)*

The Arab revolution, the Occupy Movement and the on-going protests in different parts of the world against austerity measures are acute reminders that economic growth in itself does not ensure development. Economic growth must be accompanied by sound social policies in relation to gender equality, redistributive justice, employment creation, and ensuring universal and free access to basic services. In concluding his detailed analysis of the Arab revolution, which he says is a fight for democracy over chaos and corruption, and inclusivity over the sectarian divide between Muslims and secularists fostered by autocrats, Filiu asserts:

> The Arab revolution is a democratic renaissance. It will suffer backlashes, betrayals, defeats and vicious repression. Once the initial enthusiasm fades away, this uprising and its actors will be slandered, vilified and caricatured. Even if its most radical demands are to be fulfilled in the political arena, the rehabilitation of governance will only be one part of a daunting challenge to cope with the deficits in the labour market, in the housing sector or in the public infrastructures ... History is in the making. The Arab renaissance is just beginning.
>
> *(Filiu 2011: 147–8)*

Having succeeded in changing governments through the Arab revolution, these countries must be careful that those taking over the reign do not compromise democracy and revert to the oppressive practices of their predecessors, as so characteristic of post-colonial states as Fanon (1963) so cogently warned about.

Conclusion

This paper detailed the consequences of neoliberalism in relation to unfair trade policies, poverty and inequality and how neoliberal and new managerial discourses and practices have found their way into welfare and community social work practices. The individualizing, pathology based paradigm promoted by these ideologies do not augur well for collective community based interventions that promote participation, solidarity, respect for human dignity, human rights, social inclusion and social justice. However, against the power of corporate greed and capital, imposed by the world's global financial institutions and authoritarian and demoralizing national regimes, ordinary people across the world are beginning to stand up. From individual actions such as those of Mohammed Bouazizi and small-scale protest actions in localized communities to global resistance movements, what manifests is people's anger against human atrocities and injustice.

There is hope borne out of such anger and of the on-going resistance and struggle of the Arab revolution. There is also hope in people becoming aware of the legitimating power of neoliberal capitalism as seen in the international Occupy Movement. As discussed in this paper, the problems of local communities in contemporary society are almost always located beyond their borders. Thus, effecting change will depend on our ability to build alliances and bridges across similarities and differences; to network across borders; and on joining and supporting global social justice movements. Contrary to the demands of neoliberalism and new managerialism, there are calls in community social work for the envisioning of another world based on social activism, on popular people participation and on emancipatory politics (Sewpaul 2006; Fergusson and Lavalette 2006).

Community social work does have a role to play in bridging the gap between the global and the local (Ife 2000; Haug 2004; Sewpaul 2006). The problems experienced by people whom we work with are, in large measure, linked to structural sources of oppression, exclusion and poverty at the global level, and if we are to seek adequate solutions we need to engage with global structural forces. Community social workers can use Freirian strategies of consciousness raising and praxis (Freire 1970) to get people to understand the impact of structural oppression and of privilege (Pease 2010); to develop a 'counter-hegemonic consciousness' to neoliberal capitalism (Tabb 2003: 10); to explore alternatives and to support advocacy for an alternative world (Sewpaul 2006); and drawing on the benefits of the globalization of people and global communication we can mobilise, support and link 'communities of resistance' (Wilson and Whitmore, cited in Haug 2004: 133). Like the Occupy Movement, the idea is to 'build a resistance – both hi-tech and grassroots, both focussed and fragmented – that is as global, and as capable of coordinated action, as the multinationals it seeks to subvert' (Klein 2000: 446).

QUESTIONS FOR REFLECTION

- How has neoliberal capitalism affected employment in your country?
- What might the potential benefits and risks be for educators and/or community social workers that resist new managerial influences in their workplaces?
- What can community social workers do to support advocacy and lobbying on a global level?

References

Abramovitz, M. and Zelnick, J. (2010) 'Double jeopardy: the impact of neoliberalism on care workers in the Unites States and South Africa', *International Journal of Health Services*, 40(1): 97–117.

African Development Bank, (2011) *The revolution in Tunisia: economic challenges and Prospects.* Online. Available HTTP: http://www.afdb.org/fileadmin/uploads/afdb/Documents/Publications/Northpercent20Africapercent20Quaterlypercent20Analyticalpercent20 Anglaispercent20ok_Northpercent20Africapercent20Quaterlypercent20Analytical.pdf (accessed 3 June 2012).

Amin, S. (2001) 'Imperialism and globalization', *Monthly Review* 53: 2, June 2001.

Autor, D.H., Dorn, D. and Hanson, G.H. (2012) *The China Syndrome: Local Labour Market Effects on Imports in the United States.* Online. Available HTTP: http://economics.mit. edu/files/6613 (accessed 4 February 2013).

Banks S. (2001) *Ethics and Values in Social Work* (2nd edn), Houndmills, Basingstoke, Hampshire: Palgrave.

——(2011) 'Ethics in an age of austerity: social work and the evolving new public management', *Journal of Social Intervention: Theory and Practice* 20(2): 5–23.

Bichler, S. and Nitzan, J. (2012) 'Imperialism and financialism: A story of nexus', *Journal of Critical Globalisation Studies* (5): 42–78.

Bond, P. (2005a) *Elite Transition: from Apartheid to Neoliberalism in South Africa,* Scottsville: University of KwaZulu-Natal Press.

——(2005b) *Fanon's Warning: A Civil Society Reader on the New Partnership for Africa's Development,* Trenton, New Jersey: Africa World Press, Inc.

——(2010) 'Limits to class apartheid', in B. Maharaj, A. Desai and P. Bond (eds) *Zuma's Own Goal: Losing South Africa's War on Poverty,* Trenton: Africa World Press (pp. 1–57).

Bottery, M. (2000) *Education, Policy and Ethics,* New York: Continuum.

Clarke, J. (2007) 'Subordinating the social? Neoliberalism and the remaking of welfare capitalism', *Cultural Studies,* 21(6): 974–87.

Department of Welfare (1997) *Financing Policy: Developmental Social Welfare Services,* Pretoria: Government Gazette.

Desai, A., Maharaj, B. and Bond, P. (2010) 'Introduction: poverty eradication as Holy Grail', in B. Maharaj, A. Desai and P. Bond (eds), *Zuma's Own Goal: Losing South Africa's War on Poverty,* Trenton: Africa World Press, (pp. 1-35).

Fanon, F. (1963) *The Wretched of the Earth,* London: Penguin Books.

Ferguson, I. and Lavalette, M. (2006) 'Globalisation and global justice: towards a social work of resistance', *International Social Work* 49(3): 309–18.

Filiu, J.P. (2011) *The Arab Revolution: Ten Lessons from the Democratic Uprising,* London: Hurst and Company.

Fortunato Jr, S.J. (2005) 'The soul of socialism: connecting with the people's values', *Monthly Review,* 57: 3, July–August 2005. Online. Available HTTP: http://www.monthlyreview.org/0705fortunato.htm (accessed 30 June 2012).

Freire, P. (1970) *Pedagogy of the Oppressed,* Hammondsworth: Penguin.

Gibson, C. C. (2009) *Neoliberalism and Dependence: A Case Study of the Orphan Care Crisis in Sub-Saharan Africa,* Graduate School Theses and Dissertations. Online. Available HTTP: http://scholarcommons.usf.edu/etd/1983/ (accessed 1 November 2012).

Gramsci, A. (1977) *Selections from Political Writings 1910–1920,* London: Lawrence and Wishart.

Graeber, D. (2011) *Hope in Common, Revolutions in Reverse: Essays on Politics, Violence, Art, and Imagination,* London: Minor Compositions.

Haiven, M. (2011) '*From NYC: "Occupy Wall Street has no agenda" is an alibi for apathy*', Halifax Media Co-op. Online. Available HTTP: http://www.mediacoop.ca/blog/max-haiven/8378 (accessed 1 November 2012).

Harvey, D. (2007) *A Brief History of Neoliberalism,* New York: Oxford University Press.

Haug, E. (2004) 'Critical reflections on the emerging discourse of international social work', *International Social Work,* 48(2): 126–35.

Held, D., McGrew, A., Goldblatt, D. and Perraton, J. (1999) *Global Transformations: Politics, Economics and Culture,* Cambridge: Polity Press.

Hoogvelt, A. (1997) *Globalization and the Postcolonial World: The New Political Economy of Development,* London: Macmillan.

Hook, L. (2012) 'Zuma warns on Africa's ties to China'. Online. Available HTTP: http://www.ft.com/cms/s/0/33686fc4-d171-11e1-bbbc-00144feabdc0.html#axzz27MqYq8Us (accessed 26 September 2012).

Hozic, A. A. (2012) 'Return to the real', *Journal of Critical Globalisation Studies,* (5): 149–52.

Ife, J. (2000) 'Localised needs and a globalized economy: bridging the gap with social work practice', in B. Rowe (ed.) *Social Work and Globalization,* Canada: Canadian Association of Social Workers.

Jenkins, R. O. (2012) 'Chinese competition and the restructuring of South African manufacturing', *Dev. Research Briefing 4,* International Development, University of East Anglia. Online. Available HTTP: http://www.uea.ac.uk/international-development/research/research-themes/globalisation-and-csr/research-projects/chinese-competition-and-the-restructuring-of-south-african-manufacturing (accessed 11 February 2013).

Keynes, J. M. (1933) 'National self-sufficiency', *The Yale Review* 22(4): 755–69. Online. Available HTTP: https://www.mtholyoke.edu/acad/intrel/interwar/keynes.htm (accessed 25 September 2012).

Klein, N. (2000) *No Logo.* Hammersmith: Harper Collins Publishers.

Krugman, P. (2009) *The Return of Depression Economics and the Crisis of 2008.* New York: W.W. Norton.

Lara, M. S. (2011) *Kinship Care Policy: Exacerbating Women's Oppression through Neoliberal Familialization*, Open Access Dissertations and Theses. Paper 6375. Online. Available HTTP: http//digitalcommons.mcmaster.ca/opendissertations/6375 (accessed 23 July 2012).

Ministry of Finance (1996) *Growth, Employment and Redistribution: A Macroeconomic Strategy.* Online. Available HTTP: http://www.treasury.gov.za/publications/other/gear/chapters.pdf (accessed 11 February 2013).

Misago, J.P. (2011) 'Disorder in a changing society: authority and the micro-politics of violence', in L.B. Landau (ed.) *Exorcising the Demons Within,* Johannesburg: Wits University Press.

New York Times (2012) 'The Occupy Movement', 29 September. Online. Available HTTP: http//topics.nytimes.com/top/reference/timestopics/organizations/o/occupy_wall_street/index.html (accessed 29 September 2012).

Nieftagodien, N. (2011) 'Xenophobia's local genesis: historical constructions of insiders and the politics of exclusion in Alexandria Township' in L.B. Landau (ed.) *Exorcising the Demons Within,* Johannesburg: Wits University Press.

Pease, B. (2010) *Undoing Privilege: Unearned Advantage in a Divided World,* London: Zed Books.

Reuters (2012) 'Chinese test limits of friendship', *Daily News,* 13 September 2012.

Roman, D. (2012) 'Spain's Chinese feel backlash from tax case', *Europe News,* 19 November 2012. Online. Available HTTP: http://online.wsj.com/article/SB10001424127887323551004578116994254071124.html (accessed 4 February 2013).

Rowden, R. (2009) *The Deadly Ideas of Neoliberalism: How the IMF has Undermined Public Health and the Fight against AIDS,* London: Zed Books.

Schram, S.F. and Silverman, B. (2012) 'The end of social work: neoliberalizing social policy implementation', *Critical Policy Studies* 6(2): 128–45.

Sewpaul, V. (2004) 'Globalization, African governance and the new partnership for Africa's development', in N.T. Tiong and A. Rowlands (eds) *Social Work Around the World,* Berne: IFSW Press.

——(2005a) 'Feminism and globalization: the promise of Beijing and neoliberal capitalism in Africa', *Agenda* 64: 104–13.

——(2005b) 'A structural social justice approach to family policy: a critique of the draft South African family policy', *Social Work/Maatskaplike Werk,* 41(4): 310–22.

——(2006) 'The global-local dialectic: challenges for African scholarship and social work in a post-colonial world', *British Journal of Social Work* 36: 419–34.

——(2008) 'Social work education in the era of globalization', *Caribbean Journal of Social Work* Vol. 6/7: 16–35.

Sewpaul, V. and Holscher, D. (2004) *Social Work in Times of Neoliberalism: A Postmodern Discourse,* Pretoria: Van Schaik Publishers.

Shah, A. (2012) *Global Issues: Causes of Poverty.* Online. Available HTTP: http://www.globalissues.org/issue/2/causes-of-poverty (Accessed 1 November 2012).

Stiglitz, J. (2006) *Making Globalization Work,* London: Penguin Books.

Tabb, W. K. (2003) 'After neoliberalism', *Monthly Review* 55: 2. Online. Available HTTP: http://hmb.utoronto.ca/HMB303H/weekly_supp/week-08-09/Tabb_Neoliberalism.pdf (accessed 11 February 2013).

Tormey, S. (2012) 'Occupy Wall Street: from representation to post-representation', *Journal of Critical Globalisation Studies* (5): 132–7.

Vrasti, W. (2012) 'Mic check, reality check', *Journal of Critical Globalisation Studies,* (5): 121–6.

Wacquant, L. (2001) 'The penalization of poverty and the rise of neoliberalism', *European Journal on Criminal Policy and Research* 9: 401–12.

Wight, C. (2012) 'Riot, why wouldn't you?', *Journal of Critical Globalisation Studies* (5): 161–6.

17

COMMUNITY DEVELOPMENT

Towards an integrated emancipatory framework

Vishanthie Sewpaul and Anne Karin Larsen

Introduction

The sixteen chapters in this book collectively highlight the power of community work in addressing a multiplicity of challenges confronting communities at various system levels. From community organization, with its focus on neighbourhood development in Bergen, Norway to asset based community development through a community garden project in Bhambayi, South Africa; from the use of consciousness-raising strategies with children on the streets of Durban and the dispossessed peoples of Kerala to the use of art in Holland and Portugal, the various chapters underline the centrality of *context* in community development initiatives. The descriptions of working with disadvantaged communities in Bergen, Norway and Bhambayi, South Africa and the pictures showing the stark contrasts emphasize the importance of context. Poverty and structural disadvantage do have different meanings for the peoples of Norway and of South Africa, and the context does play an important role in determining the choice of community work strategies. In traditionally well-developed welfare states the focus might be more on participatory neighbourhood organizing than on community development aimed at structural changes, while oppressive and authoritarian regimes might make it difficult to adopt authentic participatory approaches in development.

Context shapes the ideological underpinnings of the concept 'community', and the values that we imbue it with, thus determining who gets to be included or excluded and the ways in which we choose to engage with communities. Consistent with existing literature, 'community' is used by the various authors to reflect a geographic community and/or a community of interests. The community development programmes, described in this text, often reflect the inclusion of communities of interest within defined geographic areas. Thus geographic communities and communities of interest do not have to be mutually exclusive categories. Context also shapes our conceptualization of community organization and community development and their implementation, with the former having gained primacy in the United States of America and Canada, the latter in Europe, Australia and much of the developing world.

Although there are some commonalities across the different chapters in this book, reflecting an adherence to the basic values and principles of community work, varying contexts and living conditions often contribute to the adoption of different approaches and solutions. Contextual features also influence meanings attached to participation and its substantive operationalization, as seen in the SW-VirCamp project with its emphasis on the co-construction of knowledge among teachers and students across several European countries, the place of positive reframing in the Imagine Chicago project, and the use of critical social theory and research and participatory learning in action techniques in South Africa.

Global challenges that profoundly impact the lives of families and local comm-unities call for innovative ideas for development and practices. In theorizing around this and making proposals for a more radically and ecologically oriented community development practice we need to ask: How can we link local change initiatives to macro level structural issues, and to global strategies that challenge systems of injustice and oppression and unsustainable ecological development? What is the relationship between structure and agency, and how might this relationship influence our perceptions and expectations of the community worker? What implications do these questions have for community work as a participatory strategy for collective change? In this concluding chapter we attempt answers to these questions, and we provide alternative definitions of the key concepts: community work, community organization and community development. Drawing on the strengths of some of the existing models in community work and our critique of them, we propose a radical ecological approach that integrates eco-systems theory with structural and emancipatory theories, with the latter falling within the broad rubric of critical theory.

Understanding community work, community organization and community development

In many parts of the world community development and related concepts such as community organization, community work, community social work, social action, development practice and community practice have merged and are often used synonymously, so it is difficult to ascertain the ideologies underscoring the specific terminologies simply by their use. Conradie contends that community work is seen by some to be

> a similar intervention to community development – claimed in the past by social work [...] and as a means by which a professional facilitator can assist a local group or 'community' in achieving social goals formulated by them or with them or for them.

(Conradie 2011: 311)

Conradie's approach perhaps reflects the pragmatism of a community social worker who recognizes that there are instances, for example, in working with severely intellectually disabled people where development goals may have to be formulated *for* them. The qualifier that the facilitator be a professional is refuted in some development quarters that challenge professionalism, asserting its equation with elitism, and a detached neutral, outside expert who may counter development efforts (Sewpaul 2010). Akimoto (2007) argues that the emphasis on professionalism represents a Western unipolarity.

According to the Younghusband Report (1959) community organization is:

> primarily aimed at helping people within a local community to identify social needs, to consider the most effective ways of meeting these and to set about doing so, in so far as their available resources permit.
>
> *(cited in infed http://www.infed.org/community/b-comwrk.htm)*

It is interesting that the Merriam Webster online dictionary defines community organization as 'social work concentrating upon the organized development of community social welfare through coordination of public and private agencies'. This definition reduces the role of the practitioner to that of coordinator, thus ignoring the multiple roles of the community worker. Community organization, as seen in the Younghusband report, focuses on locality development, and meeting community needs 'in so far as their available resources permit.' Given the enormous challenges facing communities it is not possible for any one discipline or sector to claim dominion in the field of development. If community work has to make meaningful changes impacting individual consciousness *and* broader structural systems of injustices in relation to race, class and gender we need broad-based initiatives involving a range of disciplines and sectors. This also means that community work need not necessarily take place within the constraints of 'available resources'. It is important that we mobilize external resources when necessary, so that communities can achieve their objectives and aspirations. Community work has historically been, and continues to be, a method that is taught and practised within the discipline of social work. However, there have been shifts in some countries over recent years, where community work/development is regarded as a separate discipline. At the University of KwaZulu Natal, South Africa, for example, there are community development modules within the social work programmes at under- and post-graduate levels, as well as separate bachelor and post-graduate education in community development. At Bergen University College, community work as a subject is implemented in the social work bachelor programme, as well as in an optional international online course, and an interdisciplinary Master in Community Work.

Conradie (2011) claimed that community social work came to suffer some of the limitations of community development, as government or specific groups of people appropriated it for their own partisan interests. Citing Kothari, she asserts that:

Community development has [...] been shaped, among other things, as a colonial and post-colonial construct [...] throughout the developing world, and there is a constant danger that it could be associated with a secondary political agenda of the funding government, of larger development organizations, or of donor agencies – serving as a vehicle for bringing people 'in line' with policies.

(Conradie 2011: 312)

In addition to the above we need to be mindful about the relationship between power and the construction and dissemination of knowledge (Foucault 1977). In view of dominant discourses and North-South power dynamics, knowledge that emerges within Western contexts become valorized and universalized, while the voices of the 'other' are silenced, and indigenous knowledge remain marginalized and submerged. Assumptions about what constitutes valid knowledge and good practices have contributed to professional imperialism (Midgley 1981). Modernization theory constructed societies in particular ways, creating dominant ideological frames about inferiority and superiority and what constitutes development, which were taken for granted and not questioned (Midgley 1981). Conradie (2011: 313) avers that: 'The questions "why," "by whom" and "for whom" were [...] only asked much later, after a set of North American and Eurocentric assumptions and values had already been internalized as global norms for development.'

As we are dealing with ideological struggles, we need to adopt a critically reflexive approach where we deconstruct and strip community development from its colonial legacies and, as we propose in this chapter, imbue it with meanings consistent with an emancipatory approach that has – at its heart – people centred empowerment, consciousness raising, participation and ecological development. A simple change in terminology is not going to change the history of the world. It would neither undo the ideological battlefield that characterizes the development field, nor would it challenge or change prevailing patterns of exclusion, marginalization and discrimination. Sewpaul (2013) argues; 'Because language plays a powerful role in maintaining ideological hegemony, we have to analyze and deconstruct language – and deconstruct stereotypes and attributes attached to certain categories.' As Stuart Hall emphasized;

Ideological struggle actually consists of attempting to win some new set of meanings for existing term or category, of dis-articulating it from its place in a signifying structure. For example it is precisely because 'black' is the term which connotes the most despised, the dispossessed, the unenlightened, the uncivilized, the uncultivated, the scheming, the incompetent, that it can be contested, transformed and invested with a positive ideological value.

(Hall 1985: 112)

As reflected in chapter one, Bracht, Kingsbury and Rissel (1999: 86) define community development as 'a planned process to activate a community to use its own social structures and any available resources to accomplish community goals that are decided on primarily by community representatives and that are generally consistent with local values.' Twelvetrees' (2008: 1) definition of community development work is 'the process of assisting people to improve their own communities by undertaking autonomous collective action.' As with the definitions of community organization, these definitions presuppose the existence of resources sufficient enough for communities to realize their aspirations through independent activity. The latter might seem to indicate that community development, facilitated by external development workers, is not community development. It does beg the questions: Who helps? What does *autonomous collective action* constitute in view of the complex relationship between structure and agency?

Existing models of community work

There are several existing models of community work and it is not within the scope of this chapter to review all of them. Indeed, Boehm and Cnaan (2012) claim that the field is saturated with models, but they include as model single ideas, for example doing for or with people. One of the early best-known practice frameworks of community work is that of Jack Rothman who in 1967 wrote about three models, which are locality development, social planning and social action. With locality development the goals are primarily self-help and capacity building, with a focus on small local communities. The roles of the community worker are mainly those of enabler, catalyst, coordinator and teacher of problem-solving skills. The social planning model uses fact-finding and rational decision-making as the basis for change. The emphasis is on technical skills and roles in research, analysis and programme implementation, with no focus on active participation of people. In the social action model the focus is on changing power relations and the basic institutions of society. The roles of the practitioner are mainly those of activist and advocate. Legerton and Castelloe (1999) rightly point out that people from various political persuasions use social action to protect their interests and that social action can pose as barriers to social justice. Boehm and Cnaan (2012: 144) argue that while 'comprehensive and refined', Rothman's three models 'left a wide range of practice activities undefined and outside the model'. It is difficult, perhaps impossible for a single framework to incorporate the full range of complexities, diversities and contextual realities in community development.

Another is the feminist model of community practice (Hyde 1989). Weis (cited in Meenaghan and Gibbons 2000: 98–9) asserts that the feminist model is underscored by the following principles: support of female values and principles; emphasis on process and on product that emerges from process; commitment to consciousness-raising; affirming the diversity of women's experiences while working toward wholeness and unity; the empowerment of women through reconceptualization of power and through democratization of organizations and systems; politicization of issues in order to achieve collective solutions to oppressive situations; and commitment to bring about structural changes in organizations and institutionalized systems such as sexism, racism and classism. The feminist model has much in common with the empowerment model of community work, particularly with its emphasis on consciousness raising, challenging structures and institutionalized forms of oppression and discrimination, and on both process and product.

Legerton and Castelloe (1999) propose an organic model based on the Gramscian idea of worldviews and practices being developed through people's direct experience of social reality. They use the concepts social action and community practice interchangeably, and what they call a social action process is actually a synonym for a community work process. They identify ten components with key characteristics of what they call a social action process as synthesized in Table 17.1. The first three components constitute the organizing phase and the rest the implementation phase. The social learning component spans the entire social action process.

The phases do not occur in a linear manner; there are overlaps and practitioners continue organizing, researching and deliberating throughout the implementation phase. Legerton addresses the issue of process and product as meaning and purpose. Meaning is achieved through 'quality relationship-building and community-building [...] a sense of belonging', while purpose refers to 'the accomplishment of

TABLE 17.1 Synthesis of Legerton and Castelloe's (1999) organic model

Component	Key characteristics
1) Social organization	Groups organize themselves, build their capacities, and build community.
2) Social research	Investigation of a social situation or issue of concern.
3) Social deliberation	Critically reflecting on the situation that has been researched. Selecting a strategy to improve it.
4) Social relief	Meeting of basic needs by providing food, shelter, money on a temporary basis to alleviate suffering.
5) Social support	Strengthening capacities through education and resources e.g. support groups, consciousness-raising groups, child care.
6) Social development	Building capacity with the aim of modifying a social situation.
7) Social reconstruction	Change in social systems and institutions through changes in policies, procedures, practices and/or values.
8) Social witness	Appealing to the conscience of people e.g. pro-life protests, hunger strikes, anti-privatisation protests.
9) Social disruption	Rebellion against the present order e.g. riots, wildcat strikes to highlight discontent.
10) Social learning	Diffused throughout the social action process and cuts across the organizing and the implementation phase.

tasks, and relates to how successful we are [...] in meeting our goals [...] In the ideal situation, people find both meaning and purpose' (Legerton cited in Legerton and Castelloe 1999: 10).

Legerton and Castelloe (1999) use social development to refer to strategy, while Elliot (1993) uses it as a social policy model that is more proactive and radical than the institutional model. Social development from Elliot's perspective is an over-arching concept that allows for assessment and intervention across methods, incorporating therapy, organizational change and community development.

Boehm and Cnaan (2012) offer one of the latest models. They claim that theirs is a genuinely participatory, process-oriented and reflexive approach based on Habermas' deliberative democracy and dialogue. While acknowledging the contributions of the various models, they conclude that 'community practice models are often less community-oriented and conceptually more top-down' (Boehm and Cnaan 2012: 143). They propose a model based on binary opposites, which are put to communities that choose one or the other. In their words 'each issue is a paradox and the stakeholders must choose the position they wish to take [...] it presents sets of polarities that the community chooses from' (Boehm and Cnaan 2012: 154). These binaries are briefly presented in Table 17.2. (For a full outline of the binary concepts see Boehm and Cnaan 2012.)

The model is reflective of dualistic thinking and practice. Community initiatives are characterized by complexity, with more 'and/or', rather than 'either/or' choices. Communities e.g. might choose to use both collaborative and confrontational strategies to deal with the same issues, and one may work with communities of interests within defined geographic spaces.

TABLE 17.2 Illustration of Boehm's and Cnaan's model for community practice based on binary opposites

geographical-based community	versus	community of interest
enhancing community integration	"	maintaining group identity
focusing primarily on activists	"	appealing to indifferent community members
integral/comprehensive change	"	targeted focused intervention
intra-community-focused change	"	external change
collaboration with government	"	collaboration with nonprofit organizations
technical-rational approach	"	organizational-political approach
incremental process	"	breakpoint change
mass mobilization	"	small action system
collaborative strategy	"	confrontational strategy
directive approach	"	nondirective approach for the professional
routine activity	"	activity in crisis

Based on the strengths of some of the models and gaps identified, particularly in relation to the lack of emancipatory approaches, we propose a framework that integrates ecological theory with structural and emancipatory theories.

Proposed definitions: community work, community organization and community development

In the following we proffer three connected definitions on community work, community organization and community development which accord with our emancipatory ethos.

> Community work is a broad umbrella concept referring to a method of working with groups of people that include a range of community organization and community development strategies for the purpose of enhancing human wellbeing and fundamental freedoms, optimizing opportunities and human capabilities, and ensuring sustainable species biodiversity and ecological development.

Much of the above definition is self-explanatory. The enhancement of human wellbeing refers to the holistic, bio-psychosocial and spiritual development of people against the background of their total environment and the educational, health, political, economic, religious, cultural, and labour market systems that have an impact on them (Tesoriero 2010).

The human capability approach constitutes the seminal works of Amartya Sen (1999) and Martha Nussbaum (2011) as they discuss the potentials that people have and the personal and/or structural factors that might hinder realization of such potential. Sen (1999: 10) argues that the freedom to think is one of our most fundamental freedoms and asserts that there are five instrumental freedoms that 'help to advance the general capability of a person.' These freedoms are: political and democratic freedoms, economic facilities, social opportunities, transparency guarantees and protective security. As he asserts an identifiable relationship between responsibility and freedom, he posits a strong case for the removal of what he calls substantial unfreedoms, such as hunger, insecurity, homelessness and unemployment. Sen (1999: xi–xii) argues that individual agency and freedom are central to addressing social, economic and political deprivations, but that 'the freedom of agency that we individually have is inescapably qualified and constrained by the social, political and economic opportunities that are available to us.'

Nussbaum (2011) asserts that human flourishing requires the protection of ten central capabilities: life; bodily health; bodily integrity; senses, imagination and thought; emotions; practical reason; affiliation; other species; play; and control over one's environment.

Human development cannot take place in the absence of consideration for the environment. The interdependence between people and the flora and fauna means that we respect and promote the existence of all species, and that we take measures to curb carbon emissions, save water and electricity, and promote the use of renewable energy to halt global warming. Our inability to do so will deplete the earth's resources and increase phenomena such as floods, droughts, tsunamis and earthquakes that have devastating effects on the lives of people. The focus on opportunities and human capabilities means that we are cognizant of the need for both equality of opportunities and equality of outcomes, as we take into account people's initial starting situations.

Our suggested definition for community organization is this:

> Community organization represents valuable strategies, often externally mediated for engaging people in dialogue and action to work towards their preferred goals, and/or the negotiation of conflicting and competing goals, through capacity building, and/or organizational, infrastructural development and the mobilization of resources from within or outside of the community.

We have not subscribed to the notion of locality development only in community organization. We acknowledge that much of community organization takes place within local communities. However, in view of the global challenges facing communities such as the threats of terrorism, nuclear testing and warfare, environmental pollution and global warming, and the impacts of global economic crises linked to neoliberalism, locality development, in itself, might be insufficient to bring about meaningful and enduring change. Ideally locality development should be complemented by cross-border dialogue and sharing, and the development of links with people-to-people movements. Ledwith asserts,

> The local community development agenda has to think on a global level [...] whilst capitalism is reorganizing in the form of globalization, there is the need for reorganized challenge [...] locating ourselves on the complex, political terrain of New Times.
>
> *(Ledwith 2001: 174)*

Ledwith emphasize that 'radical community development is committed to collective action for social justice and environmental justice' (2011: 2). Participatory practice in community work embraces a diversity of roles where community development is 'at the heart of the process' (Ledwith and Springett 2010: 14).

Our umbrella definition of community work includes community organization and community development. We define community development as:

> Community development, which may include community organization strategies and goals, from a radical and critical perspective has, as its key trust, consciousness raising by engaging people in reflective dialogue and activities to understand the sources of oppression and/or privilege on their lives, and in doing so increasing people's hope, self-esteem and creative potential to confront and challenge oppressive power dynamics and structural sources of injustices.

By offering the above definition we divest community development from its historically conservative-liberal strands discussed earlier. Consistent with our definitions we reflect a paradigmatic shift from step-by-step traditional approaches to problem solving, with a focus primarily on community development as an end product to community development as a people-centred process, where subjectivity, meaning and the ethical imperatives of active and authentic people participation, take centre stage. The latter does not deny the importance of ends and the need to work toward the achievement of clearly identifiable objectives. A people-centred participatory approach to community development acknowledges the messiness of the real world, the importance of flexibility of approach and how the complexities of power play themselves out in development initiatives. In considering the process-product dialectic important questions that need to be asked are: Who defines the objectives? Why? By what means and strategies are they to be achieved? How does our theoretical and ethical analysis influence our conceptualization of community, of community work and how we engage with communities? What are the main principles of community development?

Community development and participation: key principles

There is often a danger of stating ideal notions of participation, with fundamental principles being violated on account of factors such as the imposition of donors; meeting national government imperatives; practitioners' inability or unwillingness to relinquish power or the role of expert; and fear of challenging authority, authorised truths and oppressive systems can be seen. Practitioners may also lack the necessary knowledge and facilitation skills that promote participation and the mobilization of communities. Irrespective of context and in order to obviate some of the barriers to authentic participation there are some core principles that we need to adhere to:

- Begin where people are. But, as the goals are development and change, people must make shifts in their thinking, values, attitudes and behaviour and/or in structural conditions.
- Respect local practices and cultures and the tacit knowledge of communities. However, as community development practitioners we have an ethical responsibility to ensure that certain universal standards with regard to human rights are upheld (Ife and Fiske 2006). Culture is all too often used as a guise to keep certain groups of people, for example women and children, in check and to abuse them. Authoritarian political leaders often use culture and as an excuse to violate human rights. The Global Standards for Social Work Education and Training (Sewpaul and Jones 2004) addresses this complex issue by advocating that social workers be schooled in a basic human rights approach, with an explanatory note that reads as:

Such an approach might facilitate constructive confrontation and change where certain cultural beliefs, values and traditions violate peoples' basic human rights. As culture is socially constructed and dynamic, it is subject to deconstruction and change. Such constructive confrontation, deconstruction and change may be facilitated through a tuning into, and an understanding of particular cultural values, beliefs and traditions and via critical and reflective dialogue with members of the cultural group vis-à-vis broader human rights issues.

(Sewpaul and Jones 2004: 512)

- Recognize the existing strengths and capacities of people and build on these.
- Set defined goals and objectives and the strategies by which these are to be achieved, but do so with flexibility as there are often unanticipated events to be dealt with.
- Understand the mutually constitutive relationship between power and participation. While it takes power to participate, participation engenders power. Indeed, participation is power. We need to stimulate the most marginalized and silenced groups into participation by enhancing self-esteem, confidence and power, and enhance these qualities through participation.
- The ability of the community facilitator/leader, whether internal or external to the community, professional or non-professional, to stimulate people's passions and imaginations to realize their strengths, and to envision and influence change and development.
- Be, what Meenaghan and Gibbons (2000) call, a collaborative leader, not a traditional top-down leader.

An integrated emancipatory framework for community development

We propose a radical ecological approach, which integrates eco-systems theory with structural and emancipatory theories. From an eco-systems perspective, individuals, families and communities do not exist in isolation (Bronfenbrenner 1979). They are surrounded by a number of systems that constitute obstacles and/ or resources to the realization of full potential. The eco-systems approach allows for systematic and comprehensive assessment, and helps us to order and to make sense of our relatively untidy world (Hartman 1970). Thus the major contribution of the eco-system perspective is positioning person-in-environment – an episte-mology that has shaped social work broadly, and community work more specifically in profound ways (Gitterman and Germain 2008). The environment as reflected in Figure 17.1 ranges from the micro context of the family to the global. Yet, the eco-systems approach is not without its limitations. Authors such as Coates (1991) have argued that the eco-systems approach, with its emphasis on goodness of fit between the individual and society, reflects liberal values and an individualistic bias. The approach is epistemologically different from critical and radical approaches that call for structural changes, rather than the adjustment or adaptation of people to the environment.

The adaptation discourse is so powerful that it finds its way into policy documents where people are expected to *adapt* to huge structural problems like poverty, unemployment, crime, family and gender-based violence, child abuse and neglect, rape, child-headed households, and the effects of migration and urbanization in engendering unstable family and sexual relationships (Sewpaul 2005). The eco-systems approach also does not, in any overt way, address power imbalances in society. It does not consider how systemic problems like racism, sexism and class issues intersect to influence people's access to resources, power and status, and it places no moral imperative on the practitioner to challenge structural injustices. Given these limitations, we propose a model that integrates the strengths of the eco-systems approach with radical ecology and structural and emancipatory theories that fall within the broad rubric of critical theory.

The model we present provides a conceptual framework, positioning people within micro, mezzo, exo, macro and chrono systems, to facilitate understanding of the inter-connectedness among several interacting factors (Zastrow and Kirst-Ashman 2010). The ecological component refers to the natural, geographic environment that impacts human life and development on one hand, and the power and intersectional influence of systems including the individual and family at the micro level and those broader educational, political, health, labour market, cultural, religious, information and communications, legal, and economic systems that surround them affecting people's life in a global scale (see Figure 17.1). The figure depicts the mutually reinforcing and continuous relationships across all system levels and between individuals and systems. While the environment exerts enormous influence on individuals and families, individual consciousness, values and behaviours also influence societal consciousness and practices. Issues regarding power and intersectionalities cut across all system levels and systems. The interdependence between the natural environment and species diversity and the various systems is also depicted.

Producing a neologism to reflect a radical ecological approach Dobson (1995: 2) asserts that, 'Ecologism holds that a sustainable and fulfilling existence presupposes radical changes in our relationship with the non-human natural world and in our mode of social and political life'. Embracing such radicalism, the Norwegian philosopher Arne Næss (2008: 309–13) discusses the unsustainablilty of present patterns of consumption and challenges conventional views on development. He classifies ecologically sustainable countries as developed and ecologically unsustainable countries as underdeveloped. 'The richest industrial country is not a developed country if it is not in a process of ecologically sustainable development' (Næss 2008: 295). Such an approach addresses the wider ecological system to include the power relations and geo-political social structures and the resource distribution in the world. The lack of holistic thinking and of environmental justice, lack of democracy, authoritarian regimes and war causes huge problems with a global domino effect. Chapters in this book have described how oppressive

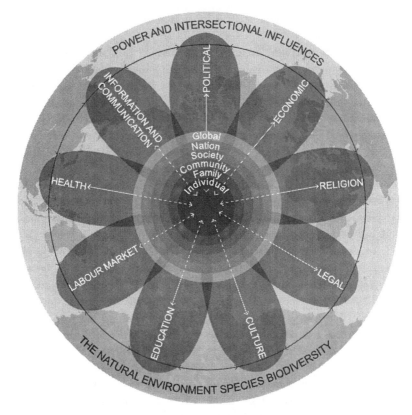

FIGURE 17.1 An integrated emancipatory framework for community development

forces cause violation of human rights with regard to basic resources like water, safety and shelter. In what she calls green social work, Dominelli (2012) calls for

> the reform of the socio-political and economic forces that have deleterious impact upon the quality and life or poor and marginalized populations, to secure the policy changes and social transformations necessary for enhancing the well-being of people and the planet today and in the future, and advance the duty to care for others and the right to be cared by others.
>
> *(Dominelli 2012: 25)*

Our emancipatory framework is also born out of our awareness that the requisites for maximum and meaningful participation presuppose the ability of people to be actively involved. Pretty (1995) for example, who regards self-mobilization without external intervention as the highest level of participation, presumes that everyone has the capacity to participate on an equal basis. The reality is often far from the rhetoric, and this idealized notion of participation negates the impact of power imbalances in society. People often cannot and do not participate on account of structural barriers linked to race, class, caste, gender, nationality and sexual orientation or personal factors such as severe mental illness or intellectual disability, or incapacities related to age. Also on account of the internalization and normalization of poverty and oppression, people may not recognize the need for structural change. Ledwith (2001: 171) discusses how right wing conservatives have appropriated the language of liberation, empowerment and participation and in doing so weakened community work's radical tradition, 'transferring the collective responsibility of the welfare state to the individual, the family, the community as a moral responsibility.'

Ideological hegemony contributes to people internalizing societal oppression and blaming themselves for their problems, contributing to withdrawal, fatalism, self-depreciation, helplessness or engagement in self-destructive behaviour. This, in turn, contributes to societal rejection, which reinforces the already low image that the oppressed have of themselves. Loving the oppressor and an unexplained attraction to the oppressor is another characteristic among some oppressed people (Fanon 1968; Freire 1970; Mullaly 2010), thus contributing to the possible legitimization of oppression. Underscored by radicalism, structural and emancipatory theories emphasize the links between the personal and the political. The individual versus society is seen as a false dichotomy as private troubles cannot be understood and dealt with outside of their socio-economic, political and cultural contexts (Ife 1999; Mullaly 2010; Dominelli 2002). Also given the dialectical relationship between structure and agency we recognize the power of dominant societal discourse on individual consciousness and the ability of individuals to influence dominant discourse and the structures of society (as illustrated in Figure 17.1).

In proposing our emancipatory framework, we draw on Freire's (1970; 1973) popular education and Gramsci's (1971) thesis of the organic intellectual to argue that all too often development cannot take place without a skilled facilitator on account of the internalization and normalization of oppression and of privilege, and of the common sense, taken for granted assumptions that we carry. Community development does depend on a sense of collective agency, but skilled facilitators are central to its success. Sewpaul (2013) argues that, as ideology is socially, culturally and politically constructed, if people are provided with alternative learning experiences, whether formal or informal, they do have the ability to disrupt dominant thinking. An organic intellectual plays an important role in this by creating counter hegemonic discourses.

Empowerment through consciousness-raising is one of the central themes in structural and emancipatory theories. Such empowerment, which occurs through education, validation and politicization of powerless people, contributes to liberation, heightened feelings of self-esteem, efficacy and control (Freire 1970; 1973). Despite the power of ideological hegemony, such an empowerment perspective supports the view that people have the capacity to reflect and to act. Through theoretically informed praxis (Ledwith and Springett 2010) that enables an understanding how external structural conditions contribute to oppression (Freire 1970; 1973) and/or privilege (Giroux 1997; Pease 2010) we are able to accept or reject certain elements, reframe issues and articulate change. Thus development cannot occur through macro level intervention alone. A critical reflection on one's own thinking and on one's social and political realities and the capacity to develop action strategies consequent upon these reflections is central to development (Freire 1970; 1973; Gramsci 1971; Giroux 1997). Our efforts must be directed at helping people to be emancipated from both the constraints of their own common sense assumptions and from the structural constraints on their lives.

Conclusion

In this chapter we have highlighted the power of context in the conceptualization of community and community work, and we propose definitions of community work, community organization and community development, and an integrated framework that accord with our emancipatory philosophy. In doing so we highlight the importance of understanding and undoing power and oppressions linked to race, class, gender and sexual orientation. We argue that the calls for autonomous action by communities without external resources are reflective of liberal, individualistic discourse of self-reliance that deny the impact of structural conditions in maintaining people in poor and disempowered positions. This is perhaps best summed up in the adage: people cannot pull themselves up by their own bootstraps if there are no bootstraps to pull. Based on our understanding of the power of ideological hegemony on the collective identities of people, determined by the ruling class elite, we challenge popular notions that rarefy community development from within. Skilled facilitators of the Gramscian ilk play a profound role in engaging people in consciousness raising exercises, enabling them to reflect on the external structural sources of oppression and/or privilege, and on the constraints of their own thinking. Such praxis validates people and it makes them appreciate that they are much more than that defined by their social circumstances; it enhances their sense of self, increases self-confidence, belief in themselves and instils hope that change is possible, which are all requisites for constructive engagement and participation. These can be tapped into and, complemented by skills development and other pragmatic capacity building and social action initiatives advocated by the various models reviewed in this chapter and from the outline of methods in the cases presented in previous chapters in this book, people can gain power to confront and change structural conditions.

QUESTIONS FOR REFLECTION

- What do you understand by the concept 'organic intellectual' and how can community development practitioners fulfil this role?
- What issues/concerns exist in your community and how might the integrated emancipatory approach proposed by the authors help to deal with them?
- What are the potential limitations of the emancipatory framework proposed by the authors?

Note

Figure 17.1 was made by graphic designer Lisbeth Thomassen Larsen, at the Centre for New Media, Bergen University College, at the request from the editors.

References

Akimoto, T. (2007) 'The unipolar world and inequality in social work: a response to James Midgley: global inequality, power and the unipolar world: implications for social work', *International Social Work* 50(5): 686–90.

Boehm, A. and Cnaan, R. A. (2012) 'Towards a practice-based model for community practice: Linking theory and practice', *Journal of Sociology and Social Welfare*, XXXIX(1): 141–68.

Bracht, N., Kingsbury, L. and Rissel, C. (1999) 'A five-stage community organization model for health promotion', in N. Bracht (ed.) *Health Promotion at the Community Level: New Advances*. 2nd edn. Thousand Oaks, California: SAGE Publications, pp. 83–104.

Bronfenbrenner, U. (1979) *The Ecology of Human Development: Experiments by Nature and Design*, Cambridge, Mass.: Harvard University Press.

Coates, J. (1991) 'Putting knowledge for practice into perspective', *Canadian Social Work Review*, 8(1): 82–96.

Conradie, I. (2011) 'Human development and development intervention: can community development increase capabilities?' *The Social Work Practioner-Researcher*, 23(3): 310–26.

Dobson, A. (1995) *Green Political Thoughts*, 2nd edn, New York: Routledge.

Dominelli, L. (2002) *Anti Oppressive Social Work Theory and Practice*, London: Palgrave Macmillan.

Dominelli, L. (2012) *Green Social Work, from Environmental Crisis to Environmental Justice*, Cambridge, UK: Policy Press.

Elliot, D. (1993) 'Social work and social development: towards an integrative model for social work practice', *International Social Work*, 36(1): 21–36.

Fanon, F. (1968) *The Wretched of the Earth*, New York: Grove Press.

Foucault, M. (1977) *The Archaeology of Knowledge*, London, Tavistock Publication.

Freire, P. (1970) *The Pedagogy of the Oppressed*, Harmondsworth: Penguin Books.

Freire, P. (1973) *Education for Critical Consciousness*, New York: The Seabury Press.

Giroux, H. A. (1997) *Pedagogy and the Politics of Hope: Theory, Culture and Schooling*, Colorado: Westview Press.

Gitterman, A. and Germain, C.B. (2008) *The Life Model of Social Work Practice*, New York: Columbia University Press.

Gramsci, A. (1971) *The Archaeology of Knowledge*, trans A. Hoare and G.N. Smith (eds), London: Lawrence and Wishart.

Hall, S. (1985) 'Signification, representation, ideology: Althusser and the post-structuralist debates', *Critical Studies in Mass Communication*, 2(2): 91–114.

Hartman, A. (1970) 'To think about the unthinkable', *Social Casework*, 51(8): 467–74.

Hyde, C. (1989) 'A feminist model for macro-practice: promises and problems', *Administration in Social Work*, 13: 145–81.

Ife, J. (1999) *Community development: Creating community Alternatives – Vision, Analysis and Practice*. NSW: Addison Wesley Longman.

Ife, J. and Fiske, L. (2006) 'Human rights and community work: complementary theories and practices', *International Social Work*, 49(3): 297–308.

Infed, *The Encyclopaedia of Informal Education, Community Work*. Online. Available HTTP: http://www.infed.org/community/b-comwrk.htm (accessed 3 March 2013).

Ledwith, M. (2001) 'Community work as critical pedagogy: re-envisioning Freire and Gramsci', *Community Development Journal*, 36(3): 171–82.

Ledwith, M. (2011) *Community Development. A Critical Approach*, 2nd edn, Bristol: The Policy Press.

Ledwith, M. and Springett, J. (2010) *Participatory practice: Community-based action for Transformative Change,* Bristol: The Policy Press.

Legerton, M. and Castelloe, P. (1999) *An Organic Model for Community Practice,* Lumberton: Centre for Community Action. Online. Available HTTP: http://www.uncp.edu/home/marson/personal/syllabi/385legerton_paper.doc (accessed 24 March 2012).

Meenaghan, T.M. and Gibbons, W.E. (2000) *Generalist Practice in Larger Settings: Knowledge, Skills and Concepts,* Chicago: Lyceum Books.

Merriam Webster dictionary, *Community Organization.* Online. Available HTTP: http://www.merriam-webster.com/dictionary/community%20organization (accessed 3 March 2013).

Midgley, J. (1981) *Professional Imperialism. Social Work in the Third World,* London: Heineman.

Mullaly, B. (2010) *Challenging Oppression and Confronting Privilege,* Ontario: Oxford University Press.

Næss. A. (2008) *Ecology of Wisdom: Writings by Arne Næss,* [(eds) A. Drengson and B. Devall], Berkeley, CA: Counterpoint Press.

Nussbaum, M. (2011) *Creating Capabilities: The Human Development Framework,* Cambridge: Harvard University Press.

Pease, B. (2010) *Undoing Privilege: Unearned Advantage in a Divided World,* London: Zed Books.

Pretty, J. (1995) 'Participatory learning for sustainable agriculture', *World Development* 23(8): 1247–63.

Rothman, J. (1967) *Three Models of Community Organization Practice,* New York: Columbia University Press.

Sen, A. (1999) *Development as Freedom,* Oxford: Oxford University Press.

Sewpaul, V. (2005) 'A structural social justice approach to family policy: a critique of the draft South African Family policy', *Social Work/Maatskaplike Werk* 41(4): 310–22.

——(2010) 'Professionalism, postmodern ethics and global standards for social work education and training', *Social Work/Maatskaplike Werk* 46(3): 253–62.

——(2013) 'Inscribed in our blood: confronting and challenging the ideology of sexism and racism as possible seeds of liberation and radical change', *Affilia, The Journal of Women and Social Work,* DOI:10.1177/0886109913485680. Online. Available HTTP: http://aff.sagepub.com/content/early/2013/04/17/0886109913485680.full.pdf+html (accessed 2 May 2013).

Sewpaul, V. and Jones, D. (2004) 'Global standards for social work education and training', *Social Work Education* 23(5): 493–513.

Tesoriero, F. (2010) *Community Development, Community-based Alternatives in an Age of Globalisation,* French Forest: Pearson Education Australia.

Twelvetrees, A. (2008) *Community Work,* Basingstoke: Palgrave.

Younghusband, D.E. (1959) 'Younghusband Report: Report of the Working Party on Social Workers', *Local Authority Health and Welfare Services,* London: Ministry of Health.

Zastrow, C.H. and Kirst-Ashman, K.K. (2010) *Understanding Human Behaviour and the Social Environment* (8th edn), Belmont, CA: Brooks Cole.

INDEX

accountability 127, 138, 162, 214

action learning 92–4

action research 11–12, 46, 50, 59–60, 73; art projects 166, 170; e-learning courses 92–4; family violence 190; power 107, 110; strengths 77–9

activism 161–2, 210, 224, 226

adaptability 127, 179, 183, 241

Addams, J. 2, 10, 19

Adelman, C.B. 12, 120–32

advocacy 98, 108–9, 160, 162, 227

Afghanistan 177

Africa 59, 74, 160, 221, 224

Africa Development Bank 224

African Charter on the Rights and Welfare of the Child 107

African-American people 177, 180

after-modernism 35–7

after-postmodernism 30

agency 11, 23–4, 27, 59, 74, 124–5; climate change 178; contextual issues 130, 231; emancipatory frameworks 234, 237, 243

AIDS 9, 62–3, 205

Akimoto, T. 232

Albatross 137, 141

Algeria 225

Ali, B. 224

alienation 4, 74

Alinsky, S. 19, 27–8

Alonso, A. 11, 30–40

Alonso, D. 11, 30–40

altruism 116, 184

Amamou, S. 225

Amin, S. 218

ancestor referencing 44

Annan, K. 24

antiretroviral (ARV) drugs 64

Aotearoa 188–203

apartheid 72–3

Appreciative Inquiry (AI) 48, 124, 131

Arab Spring 98, 217, 224–9

architecture 35–6

Argentina 120, 182

Aristotle 31

Arnstein, S.R. 7, 19, 25–6, 109

art 159–72

Arte Povera 159

artists 163–5

Asia 2, 160, 224

Asian Tsunami 24–5

assessment 91, 166

Asset-Based Community Development (ABCD) 11–12, 72–3, 75–85, 131

assets 72–87
Associação Hemisférios Solidários 168, 170
associations 75–6, 83, 85
assumptions 10, 42, 59, 99, 107; climate change 177; contextual issues 122, 124, 127; emancipatory frameworks 233, 243; family violence 191, 193–7; neo-liberalism 218; power 109, 117
Astray, A. 11, 30–40
asylum seekers 136, 138
austerity measures 218–19, 222, 225
Australia 5, 120, 163, 231
Autagavaia, M. 196
authoritarianism 217
autonomy 11, 13, 23, 33, 35; art projects 161; co-construction 41, 46; emancipatory frameworks 234, 244; neo-liberalism 223; post-modernism 37
Autor, D.H. 222

Bahrain 225
balance 20–1
Bambanani Women's Group 63–4
banking 100, 122, 224
Banks, S. 223
Barnes, L. 178
Bartolomei, L. 11, 19–28
Basic Income Grants 117
Bauman, Z. 113
behavioural change 120–1
Bell, C. 176
Beresford, P. 108
Bergen 12, 146–7, 230
Bergen Housing and Urban Renewal Company 147, 149
Bergen University College 232
Berry, M. 178
Bhambayi Reconstruction and Development Forum (BRDF) 78, 80, 230
Bhopal 177

Big Society 176
BIOPICCC 177, 179–80
Black people 219, 223
blogs 49, 89–92, 98
Boal, A. 167
body mapping 62–4
Bodymaps for Khayalitsha Hospital Art Project 62
Boehm, A. 234, 236
bonding strategies 154–5
Borrup, T. 161
Bouazizi, M. 225–6
bourgeoisie 33
Bozalek, V. 11, 57–71, 111
Bracht, N. 6, 233
Brady, M. 165
brainstorming 64
Brazil 167
Bretton Woods Institute 206
Brewer, J.D. 108
bridging strategies 154–5
Brookfield, H.C. 193
Browne, B. 12, 120–32
Budapest Declaration 156
Building Communities from the Inside Out 75
bureaucracy 6, 27, 35–6, 129–30, 137, 141, 223
Burton, C. 178
Butterflies project 109

Cameron, D. 176
Canada 5, 231
capacity building 80–3, 155–7, 162–3, 234, 244
Cape Town 120
capitalism 9, 12, 36, 175, 205, 217–19, 224–7
case studies 41, 45, 47–8, 137–8, 145–58, 214
Case Western Reserve University 124
caste system 205, 210–12, 223
Castelloe, P. 234–6
Chambers, R. 58

Chappati diagrams 67
charity 32–3, 133
Chicago 120–5, 127–31
Chicago Historical Society 130
child-paths mapping 146
children 107–17, 126, 135–6, 138,
    146–7; climate change 180;
    emancipatory frameworks 239, 241;
    family violence 189, 195;
    neighbourhood renewal 148, 150,
    152, 154–6; neo-liberalism 220,
    222; social action 206, 210
China 68, 219, 221–2
Christianity 32
Church City Mission 147
Citizen Leaders 128–9
citizenship 114, 116, 124, 129, 163,
    165, 170, 225
civil rights 23–4, 225
civil society 37, 145, 223, 225
Clarke, J. 222
class 13, 22, 35, 59, 107; art projects
    161; emancipatory frameworks 232,
    235, 241, 243–4; grassroots
    interventions 205; neo-liberalism
    219–20, 223; social action 211
Cleveringa, S. 164, 167
climate change 175–87
Cnaan, R.A. 234, 236
co-construction 11, 38, 41–53, 88,
    99–100, 127
Coates, J. 240
Coca Cola International 204
Cohen-Cruz, J. 162
cohesion 1–2
Coimbra 169
collective action 130–1
colonialism 12, 24, 73–4, 193–4, 233
commodification 217–18
communication skills 91–2, 94
communitarianism 31, 33–4, 36–8,
    176
communities 4–6, 175–87; definitions
    3–4, 175–7

communities of practice 11, 43–50, 63,
    68, 91; definitions 42; family
    violence 190, 196; neighbourhood
    renewal 155
community art 161–5
community development 47–8, 57,
    231–4; climate change 182, 184;
    definitions 4–6, 13, 145, 231,
    233–4, 237–9; emancipatory
    frameworks 230–46; key principles
    239–40; social action 207–9;
    strengths/assets 72–87
community knowledge 30–40
community organization, definitions
    4–6, 13, 232, 237–9
community rights 23–4
community work 19–28, 94–9; art
    159–72; definitions 4–6, 13, 231,
    237–9; e-learning courses 88–103;
    knowledge base 30–40; models
    234–7; neighbourhood revival
    145–58; neo-liberalism 217–29;
    online course 41–53; participatory
    learning 88–103; PLA techniques
    57–71; power 107–19; social action
    204–16; welfare state 133–44
comparative advantage 73
competence-based approaches 25, 28,
    50, 89, 94, 223
computer literacy 130
confidentiality 114
connectivity 175–7, 184, 209
Connell, R. 194
Conradie, I. 231–3
conscientization 57, 60, 68
consensus 94
consent 113, 224
constructivism 38, 42–3
contextual issues 120–32, 230–1, 244
Convention on the Rights of the
    Child 107
Cook Islands 191, 196
Cornwall, A. 7, 153
coursework 88

Cox, D. 4
Coxon, E. 196
creation management 163–5
creativity 128–9, 161–2, 166–7
Crichton-Hill, Y. 194, 196
critical theory 12, 107, 118, 231, 241;
    consciousness 210–11; power 114;
    questioning role 99; reflection 1–2,
    10–11; social research 108–10
culture 4, 12, 22–4, 27, 36; art projects
    159–60, 162–4, 166–7, 169–70;
    climate change 183; co-construction
    47; contextual issues 120, 126,
    130–1; definitions 160–1;
    emancipatory frameworks 239–40;
    family violence 189–200;
    mobilization 73; neighbourhood
    renewal 147, 149, 151–3, 156; PLA
    techniques 59; social action 208
Cunningham, G. 74, 76, 84–5
curriculum development 41–3, 46–7,
    50, 89, 93, 100–1
Cutter, S. 178
Cuylenburg, G. 160

Dadaisme 159
databases 43
De Beer, F. 74–5, 84
debt 206
deconstruction 36–7, 109, 159, 164,
    169, 219, 233, 240
deficit-based approaches 122, 124, 131
Delanty, G. 176
Delft 167
Delgado, M. 165
democracy 1, 99–101, 128, 133, 153;
    art projects 160, 163, 169;
    emancipatory frameworks 236, 241;
    grassroots interventions 205;
    neighbourhood renewal 146;
    neo-liberalism 218, 224–6
Democratic Republic of the Congo
    177
demographics 61, 98

Department of Urban and Rural
    Community Development 207
Derrida, J. 36
Descartes, R. 33
descriptors 126
development 21, 37, 120, 126,
    128–31; art projects 163; climate
    change 178, 180–1; emancipatory
    frameworks 232–4, 241; family
    violence 191, 196; neighbourhood
    renewal 156–7; neo-liberalism 217,
    225; online courses 97; social action
    207, 209; welfare state 133, 137
developmental psychology 120
Dewey, J. 2
dharna 204
dialectics 47, 50
diasporas 191–2
disasters 175–87
disciplinary process 138–42
discourse 36, 59, 83, 116, 122; art
    projects 159, 164, 169; contextual
    issues 126; emancipatory
    frameworks 233, 243; family
    violence 190, 192, 194; neo-
    liberalism 217, 222–4, 226
dissonance 121, 163
diversity 9, 156, 191, 237
Djibouti 225
Dobson, A. 241
dominant discourse 59–60, 233, 243
Dominelli, L. 3–4, 9, 12, 154, 175–87,
    242
door-openers 98
Dorn, D. 222
drought 204, 238
Drucker, D. 25, 27
drug abuse 134–7, 146
Dublin Accords 136
Durban 12, 107, 110, 112, 117, 230
Dutch language 167

e-cases 45
e-learning 12, 88–103

e-portfolios 91
Earth Day 204
East 20
Eastern Europe 162
Ebadi, S. 24
eco-systems theory 240–1
EcoAndina 182
ecological theory 21, 73, 237, 240–4
economics 11, 21–3, 30, 32, 37–8; art
    projects 160, 162, 165, 170; climate
    change 184; contextual issues 121,
    129; emancipatory frameworks
    237–8, 241–3; family violence 191;
    mobilization 72–3, 75–8, 80, 83,
    85; neo-liberalism 218–21, 223–5;
    PLA techniques 57, 60, 68; social
    action 206, 208, 211, 214; welfare
    state 138
Egypt 225
elders 197
electoral politics 213–14
elites 160, 218, 222, 232, 244
Elliot, D. 236
empathy 59, 113
empowerment 22–6, 34, 85, 110,
    114–17; art projects 161, 163–4,
    168–9; climate change 178, 183;
    emancipatory frameworks 233–5,
    243; neighbourhood renewal 148,
    151–4, 156; online courses 88, 91,
    94–5, 97, 99–101; social action 206,
    208, 212–14; welfare state 133,
    140–1
England 2, 181–2, 189
Enlightenment 33–8
entitlement 23
environment 4, 12, 22, 176, 238, 241
epistemic frameworks 30–40
epistemology 4, 6, 11, 30, 36–7, 50,
    73, 194, 240
ethics 10–11, 19–28, 30, 33, 38; art
    projects 169; emancipatory
    frameworks 239; neo-liberalism
    223; online courses 94, 98–9;

power 112–14; strengths 80; welfare
    state 138–9, 142
ethnicity 22, 121, 146, 154, 190–1;
    family violence 193, 196–7;
    neo-liberalism 219; social action
    205
ethnocentrism 41
ethnos 38
Eurocentrism 233
Europe 2, 5, 31–2, 41, 48; co-
    construction 50; emancipatory
    frameworks 231; neo-liberalism
    221; online courses 88–9; welfare
    state 136, 141
'Europe Magazine' 92, 98
European Credit Transfer System
    (ECTS) 89
European Union (EU) 41, 46
Eurozone 224
Evans, E. 178
Every Block is a Village 129
evidence-based practice 223
exclusion 1, 4, 8, 10, 34–5; art projects
    161, 163, 168–9; climate change
    176, 181, 185; co-construction 41;
    contextual issues 121; emancipatory
    frameworks 230; neo-liberalism
    217, 223, 227; post-modernism
    37–8; power 114; social action 204,
    208; welfare state 133, 139–40
experiential learning 166, 189

Facebook 98, 138
facilitators 48, 57, 59, 65, 69;
    emancipatory frameworks 231–2,
    240, 243; neighbourhood renewal
    155; online courses 94–7, 100–1;
    power 110, 115–16; roles 94–7, 101
Family Policy 223
family violence prevention 188–203
Fanon, F. 226
feminism 195, 234–5
fieldwork 59, 78, 208
Fiji 191, 196

Filiu, J.P. 225–6
Financing Policy 223
fiscal crises 184–5, 224
Five-Stage Community Organization
    Model for Health Promotion 91
Flatau, P. 165
Florin, P. 181
flow and impact diagrams 67–8
focus groups 78–9, 83, 93, 111, 114,
    116, 148
Fook, J. 10
Fordism 34
fossil fuels 182–3
Foucault, M. 35, 109
fragmentation 73, 154, 160, 165, 177,
    227
frameworks 128–31, 188–203, 230–46
Frameworks for Inspiring Change 131
Fraser, N. 57
Freire, P. 2, 10, 49, 57–8, 91, 100–1,
    111, 116, 152, 156, 227, 243
French Revolution 33
Fukushima Daiichi 179–80, 182
Fusitu'a, L. 196
future development 122–5
future generations 175, 184

Gandhi, M. 2–3
garden projects 72–87
Gemeinschaft 3–4, 176
gender 12–13, 22, 24–5, 36–7, 58–9;
    emancipatory frameworks 232, 241,
    243–4; family violence 190, 195,
    200; neo-liberalism 219, 223, 225;
    PLA techniques 62; power 107,
    110; social action 205, 212;
    strengths 73
generations of rights 23–4
generative frameworks 130–1
Germain, C.B. 10
Gesellschaft 4, 176
Gibbons, W.E. 234, 240
gift economy 32
Gilesgate 182–3

Giroux, H.A. 111, 116
Gitterman, A. 10
Global Agenda 140
global challenges 204–16
Global Financial Crisis (GFC) 224
Global Social Work Congress 112
Global Standards for Social Work
    Education and Training 239
global warming 9, 12, 238
globalization 9, 12, 73, 162, 175;
    neo-liberalism 220, 227; social
    action 204, 206–7, 212–15
glue people 123
Goa 210
Gonzalez, D.A. 11
Google 91, 116
Government Taskforce on Violence
    196
Graeber, D. 224
Gramsci, A. 10, 13, 57–8, 111, 116,
    219, 235, 243–4
grassroots interventions 204–16
Greece 224
Green Park Community 47–9, 89, 91,
    96–8
greenhouse gas emissions 176, 183–4
Grimen, A.L. 12, 145–58
Gross Domestic Product (GDP) 220
Growth Employment and
    Redistribution (GEAR) 221
Gunderson, L. 184

Habermas, J. 236
Hall, S. 233
Hanson, G.H. 222
Harkavy, I. 114
Harman, G. 38
Harper, W. 114
Harris, J. 11, 41–53
Harvey, D. 219
Hau'ofa, E. 195–6
Hawkes, J. 160
health care 23, 34–5, 43, 64, 114;
    climate change 182; contextual

issues 130; social action 210; welfare
  state 135
Health and Care Act (Norway) 134–5,
  140
hegemony 13, 35, 218, 227, 233,
  243–4
Helu-Thaman, K. 196
Henriksbø, K. 12, 145–58
heritage specifics 188–203
Hermansen, O.F. 5
Higher Education Institutions (HEI)
  41, 61, 88–9
Hlwele, N. 64, 69
Hogstad, R. 141
Hole, G.O. 1–15, 41–53, 88–103
Holling, C. 184
Hölscher, D. 35
Hoogvelt, A. 219
hope 121–2, 125, 127, 131, 149, 162,
  225
hospitality 32
72 Hours 178
Hozic, A.A. 225
Hugman, R. 11, 19–28
Hull House, Chicago 2
Human Development Project 205
human rights 1, 3, 9–11, 20, 22–4;
  climate change 177, 183–4;
  emancipatory frameworks 239–40,
  242; ethics 26–7; neo-liberalism
  217–18, 226; online courses 94;
  PLA techniques 61; post-
  modernism 33–4; welfare state 141
humanism 4
Humphries, B. 112
Hurricane Katrina 177, 179
Hutchinson, G.S. 12, 133–44

iatrogenesis 35
identity 45–6, 129–30, 191, 196, 210
ideology 9–10, 13, 30, 34, 60; climate
  change 176; emancipatory
  frameworks 230, 233, 243–4;
  grassroots interventions 207–8;

heritage specifics 195; neoliberalism 218–19, 222, 226; social
  action 214; strengths 72, 74
Ife, J. 19, 22, 75, 84
IkVrouw (I Woman) 167–8
Illich, I. 35
Imagine Chicago 12, 120–2, 125,
  127–31, 231
imagined communities 3–4, 175–87
imperialism 12, 192–4, 233
Inanda Child Welfare 84
India 2, 9, 12, 109, 120, 177, 204–16
Indian Ocean Tsunami 177, 179–81
indigenous people 12, 83, 194, 196,
  207–8, 233
individualism 4, 13, 165, 168, 190;
  emancipatory frameworks 240–1,
  243–4; neo-liberalism 218, 222, 226
Industrial Revolution 34
industrialization 2, 6, 9, 182, 207, 212
inequality 4, 22, 36–7, 57, 72–4; art
  projects 160; climate change 176,
  179, 181; mobilization 85; neoliberalism 217–20, 223–4, 226;
  power 114, 117; social action
  207–8; welfare state 140
inflation 206
Inflector Blinds 182
information and communications
  technology (ICT) 98
innovation 124, 162, 167, 198
integrated emancipatory frameworks
  230–46
intellectual property rights 218
interdependence 175, 181–2, 184, 192,
  223, 237
interdisciplinarity 122, 232
internalization 60, 68, 121, 126, 243
international community work courses
  41–53
International Monetary Fund (IMF)
  218
International Neighbours' Day 152
international style 35

'Internationalizing Institutional and Professional Practices' 180
Internet 4, 49, 98, 225
Inworldz Dreamz and Visionz Art Fest 169
Iran 167
Iraq 177, 225
issue selection 211–12

Japan 179–80, 182
Jenkins, R.O. 221
Jordan 225

Kant, I. 33
Katkari people 210, 212
Kenny, S. 21, 26–7
Kenya 63, 222
Kerala 204, 230
Keynes, J.M. 220–1
Khayelitsha Hospital 64
Kingsbury, L. 6, 233
knowledge 41–53, 152–3
Kohunga Reo 200
Komi Republic 89
Kothari, - 232
Kretzmann, J. 72, 75
Kroken, R. 138
Krugman, P. 220
Kuwait 225
KwaZulu-Natal 11, 73

'Labyrinth: Checkmate Poverty' 169
land art 159
land rights 212–13
Landry, C. 162–3
language 126–7, 131, 155, 162, 191–2, 200, 233, 243
Larsen, A.K. 1–15, 41–53, 88–103, 230–46
Latour, B. 38
Lave, J. 42
leadership 21, 23, 65, 72, 94; contextual issues 123, 125, 128–30; emancipatory frameworks 239–40;

neighbourhood renewal 149, 152; online courses 97, 99–100; power 110, 115–16
leading lights 99
Ledwith, M. 8, 57–8, 69, 74, 154, 156, 238, 243
Lee, B. 206
legacy events 189, 191
Legerton, M. 234–6
Leibowitz, B. 58
Leonard, P. 3–4
Lewin, K. 120
liberalism 13, 240, 244
librarians 43
Libya 225
lifelines 65–6
linkages 76, 84–5
literacy skills 129–30
living conditions 134–6, 142, 156
locality development 234, 238
London 120, 224
Long, R. 159
Ludwig, D. 184

McIntosh, P. 166
MacIntyre, A. 38
McKinsey Global Institute 221
McKnight, J. 72, 75
Mafile'o, T. 195–6
Malawi 89, 222
man-made disasters 175–87
Mandela, N. 3
manufactured resources 75
Māori people 198, 200
mapping techniques 60–4, 80, 83, 85, 91; contextual issues 128; neighbourhood renewal 146, 153, 156; online courses 98
Marcuse, H. 162
marginalization 1, 4, 9–10, 21, 25; climate change 176, 183, 185; contextual issues 123, 131; emancipatory frameworks 233, 240, 242; family violence 191, 194, 198;

mobilization 74, 77; neighbourhood renewal 155; neo-liberalism 219–20; PLA techniques 57, 59–60; post-modernism 35; power 109; social action 204–7, 211, 213–15; welfare state 133, 141
Marques, E. 12, 159–72
Marxism 37
Matarasso, F. 160, 163
Mathie, A. 74, 76, 84–5
Mathiesen, T. 138, 140
matrix ranking 64–5
Mauritania 225
Mayo, P. 57
Mead, G.H. 2
means-end connections 26–7
media 98, 116, 121, 138, 141, 218
mediation 94
Meemeduma, P. 198
Meenaghan, T.M. 234, 240
Melanesia 193
Memory Box 63–4
mentors 130
Merli, P. 166
Mhone, C. 12, 107–19
Micronesia 193
Middle East 224
Mila-Schaaf, K. 192
Miller, R.L. 108
Ministry for Social Development (MSD) 197
Misa Rumi 182–3
Moana Nui a Kiwa 192
mobilization 72–87, 98, 121, 156–7, 164; art projects 169; climate change 183, 185; emancipatory frameworks 232, 242; family violence 190–1, 196; neo-liberalism 227; social action 204–5, 208, 212–14
modernism 4, 11, 30–40
Montana 120
mood 65–6
Morgan, J. 62–4
Morocco 225

Mtshali, M. 83
Mubarak, H. 225
Mulitalo-Lauta, P.T. 196
Mullaly, B. 111
multiculturalism 4, 150, 167, 190–1, 198–200
multidisciplinarity 135
multinational corporations 73, 210, 219, 224, 227
Mumbai 210
Muslims 225

Næss, A. 241
natural disasters 175, 177
needs-based approaches 75
neighbourhood revival 145–58
neo-colonialism 193
neo-conservatism 37
neo-liberalism 12, 37, 73, 175–6, 206, 217–29, 238
neo-Marxism 38
Nepal 120
Netherlands 159, 167–70, 230
networking 98
new managerialism 12, 217–29
New Orleans 180
New Public Management 138
New York 217, 224
New Zealand 12, 188–203
Newby, H. 176
Nga vaka o kāiga tapú 196–7
Nietzsche, F. 35
nihilism 224
Niue 189, 191, 196
Nobel Prize 2, 219
non-governmental organizations (NGOs) 3, 61, 137, 151–3, 168, 178, 182
Non-Profit Organizations (NPO) 84, 120
Nordic countries 5, 10, 133
North 24, 60, 192, 194, 219, 233
North America 233
Norway 5, 12, 133–46, 152, 230, 241

Norwegian Data Protection Authority 94
Norwegian Directorate of Health 135
Norwegian Immigration Appeals Board 138
Norwegian State Housing Bank 147, 149
Nussbaum, M.C. 24, 60, 237

Occupy Movement 3, 12, 217, 224–9
OECD 178
Oman 225
online courses 88–103
ontology 30, 32, 34–7, 50
oppression 1, 3–4, 9–10, 13, 27; art projects 159, 164, 167, 169; emancipatory frameworks 230, 234–5, 238, 241, 243; neighbourhood renewal 154; neo-liberalism 226–7; online courses 101; PLA techniques 58; post-modernism 36–7; power 117; social action 206, 211–12, 214; strengths 74; welfare state 140
oral narratives 196
organizational learning 44
Østhus, I. 12, 107–19
Other 35–6, 218, 233
outcomes 21–2, 25, 27, 42, 46; art projects 163, 165–7, 169; climate change 178, 181, 185; co-construction 49; family violence 200; mobilization 85; neighbourhood renewal 147; neo-liberalism 225; online courses 89, 96; power 115
outreach services 137

Pacific Conceptual Frameworks 191, 197
Pacific Islands 188–203
Pacific Islands' Advisory Group (PAG) 196

Pacific Islands' Safety and Prevention Project (PISPP) 189, 191
Pakistan 177
Pan, R.J. 75
panarchy 184
paperless migrants 134, 136, 138, 141–2
participation 1–15; art projects 159–70; definitions 7–9; ethics 19–28; key principles 239–40; learning 88–103; online courses 88–103; power 107–19; strengths 72–87
participatory action learning (PAL) 46–7
participatory action research (PAR) 46–7, 50, 59–60, 73, 77–9; art projects 170; family violence 190; online courses 92–4; power 107, 110
participatory and appreciative action and reflection (PAAR) 190
participatory learning and action (PLA) techniques 57–71
participatory parity 57, 59
partnerships 83–5, 159–72, 183
Pasifika 189–98, 200
Passells, V. 12, 188–203
patents 218
paternalism 220
patriarchy 36, 190, 195
Pawar, M. 4
pedagogy 41, 58, 69, 91
philosophy 31–2, 35, 38, 88, 162, 241, 244
pilot courses 47, 49, 93–4
pilot studies 76
pioneers 130
Plachimada 204
Planning for Resilience and Emergency Preparedness (PREP) 178
Plato 31
pluralism 5, 36, 38, 128, 169
Poland 167

police 113, 115
political rights 23, 57
pollution 9, 177, 238
Polynesia 193
Portugal 159, 167–70, 230
positivism 35, 108–9, 166
positivity 122–5, 131
post-colonialism 193, 226, 233
post-modernism 4, 11, 30–40
post-structuralism 35
poverty 1–2, 4, 9, 12, 32; art projects
    168–70; climate change 176–7,
    181–2; contextual issues 121, 230;
    emancipatory frameworks 243;
    family violence 194; mobilization
    80–1; neo-liberalism 217–20, 223,
    226–7; PLA techniques 59–60;
    post-modernism 34, 37; power 114,
    117; social action 204–5, 208, 213;
    strengths 72–4
power relations 68–9, 74, 77, 85, 95;
    emancipatory frameworks 233,
    238–43; family violence 190, 195;
    online courses 100–1; research
    107–19; social action 206
praxis 13, 57, 100–1, 152, 156;
    emancipatory frameworks 243–4;
    heritage specifics 189, 197–8, 200;
    neo-liberalism 227
pre-modernity 11, 30–4, 38
Presley, F. 5
pressure groups 5, 156
Pretty, J. 7, 242
prisons 135
privatization 206–7, 213, 218, 222,
    224
professional development 89, 188
professionalism 25, 232
profit 204, 217, 219, 222–3
proportional piling 65
psychology 120, 156
public distribution system (PDS) 213
public goods 206
public relations (PR) 98

public works programmes 67
Pulotu-Endemann, F.K. 196
Putnam, R. 72, 75, 83, 177
Pyles, L. 78–9, 81, 85

question types 122–5, 128
questions for reflection 13, 28, 39, 51,
    69; art projects 170; climate change
    185; contextual issues 131;
    emancipatory frameworks 244;
    heritage specifics 200;
    neighbourhood renewal 156–7;
    neo-liberalism 227; online courses
    101; power 118; social action 215;
    strengths 85; welfare state 142

racism 60, 62, 72, 121, 180;
    emancipatory frameworks 235, 241;
    heritage specifics 188; neo-
    liberalism 224
Raigad 209–11, 213–14
Raniga, T. 11, 72–87
Rapid Rural Appraisal (RRA) 60
rationality 33–6
Reading Chicago and Bringing It
    Home 130
reading lists 48, 69
reciprocal research 22
reciprocity 72, 116, 120, 150, 192,
    196, 223
Red Cross 147
refugees 22
Rembrandt 159
Renaissance 31
renewable energy 182, 238
representational roles 98
resilience 178–83, 185
resistance 38, 58, 108, 195, 215, 217,
    224–9
rights 21, 23–4, 26
'Ring der Nibelungen' 159
Risen from the Ground (Levantados
    do chão) 168–70
Rissel, C. 6, 233

River of Life exercise 65–6
Rohleder, P. 91
role models 200
role play 50, 91, 113, 129
Ronnby, A. 99
Rothman, J. 34, 234
Rubin, M. 32
rural areas 59–60, 181, 206–7, 214
Russia 89
Rwanda 177
Ryen, A. 113

Sāmoa 189, 191, 194–6
Sarvahara Jan Andolan (AJA) 209–14
Saudi Arabia 225
Scheduled Castes 205
Scholastics 32
Scotland 120
second modernity 30–40
Second World War 35, 193
seed articles 44
Seed, P. 34
segregation 121
Sen, A.K. 60, 237
Sewpaul, V. 1–15, 35, 107–19, 217–46
sexism 224, 235, 241
sexual orientation 13, 244
Shah, A. 220
shared frameworks 128–9
shocks 177, 179
Silenced Pasts 196
Simpson, B. 80
Singapore 120
Singh, S. 9, 12, 204–16, 219
situated learning 43–5, 47–8, 50
Situationism 225
Siyazama 76, 78–81
Skype 91, 96
Slettebakken Neighbourhood Renewal
    Project 145–58
SMART outcomes 96
Smit, W. 76
snowball sampling 111
social action 204–16, 234–5, 244

social animation 94
social capital 22, 72–3, 75, 83, 85; art
    projects 163; climate change 175,
    177, 181; neighbourhood renewal
    152, 155; neighbourhood revival
    148–9; social action 208
social construction 42–3, 126–7, 131,
    240
social engineering 36
social justice 1, 9–11, 20–2, 24, 26–7;
    art projects 160; climate change
    183; emancipatory frameworks 234,
    238; neo-liberalism 217–18; PLA
    techniques 57; post-modernism 34;
    power 110; social action 205–6,
    208, 210; strengths 74; welfare state
    141
social learning theory 42–6, 48, 50
social media 4, 58
social networks 75–6, 83, 150, 163, 167,
    182
social planning 34, 234
social psychology 120
social sciences 120, 194
Social Services Act (Norway) 134–6,
    140
social work 41, 46, 57, 59, 72–3; art
    projects 159–60, 162–3, 167; climate
    change 176–9, 182–3, 185;
    emancipatory frameworks 232, 239;
    family violence 188, 194;
    mobilization 75, 78, 81, 84; neo-
    liberalism 217; online courses 89, 98;
    power 109, 114–17; social action
    208; welfare state 133–4, 136–42
Social Work-Virtual Campus project
    (SW-VirCamp) 11, 41–4, 46–50,
    88, 94, 231
Social Workers Union 141
sociology 188
solidarity 3–4, 34, 37, 73, 84; climate
    change 177; contextual issues 123;
    neo-liberalism 223, 226; online
    courses 100; power 114, 116

South 24, 59–60, 194, 219, 233
South Africa 3, 11, 21, 59, 61;
  emancipatory frameworks 230–2;
  neo-liberalism 221–3; PLA
  techniques 64, 67–8; power 117;
  strengths 72
South America 59
Spain 222
Special Economic Zones (SEZ) 207,
  210
Springer, J. 154
Springett, J. 8
Sri Lanka 24–5, 177, 179–81
Stack, C. 177
stakeholders 78, 83–5, 89, 91, 94; art
  projects 163–4; climate change 183;
  emancipatory frameworks 236, 243;
  neighbourhood renewal 152; online
  courses 97–9
Starr, E.G. 2
state responsibilities 175–87, 222
Stellenbosch University 65
stereotypes 116, 126, 160, 198, 233
stigmatization 140, 147
strengths 47, 72–87
Stringer, E.T. 77
structural adjustment programmes 206,
  219
structural social work 208
structuralism 35
structure of online courses 89–91
student-centred learning 48
Sub-Saharan Africa 221
Sudan 225
Surinam 167
sustainability 9–10, 12, 22, 27, 44; art
  projects 163, 170; climate change
  178, 182–5; contextual issues 124,
  128; family violence 196, 200;
  mobilization 72–3, 75–6, 83, 85;
  neighbourhood renewal 155–7;
  online courses 97; PLA techniques
  68
Swanepoel, H. 74–5, 84

Swiss Cultural Program (SCP) 162
synchronic chats 89–91
Syria 225
systems thinking 130

Tamasese, K.C. 196
Taos Institute 126
Tate, E. 178
Taufe'ulungaki, A.M. 193
Taylor, M. 5
Taylorism 34
technical roles 98–9
technocracy 81
Tenant Representative Forum 156
tenant representatives 149–50, 153,
  155–7
Tesoriero, F. 10, 27, 75, 84, 91, 94,
  98, 101, 155
Thatcher, M. 224
Theatre of the Oppressed 167
theology 32
Thomas, D.S. 139
Thomas, W.I. 139
three-dimensional model 58
Tirmare, P. 9, 12, 204–16, 219
TIUR project 137
Toennies, F. 3–4
Tohoku earthquake 179–80, 182
Tokelau 191, 196
tokenism 6–8, 25, 109, 114
Tolia-Kelly, D.P. 169
Tonga 191, 196
Tönnies, F. 176
Tormey, S. 224
tourism 160
Toynbee Hall 2
trade liberalization 220–2
transect walks 65
transparent classroom model 48
Treasury 218
Treatment Action Campaign (TAC) 3
triangulation 112
trust 122, 125, 131, 149–50, 152–3,
  177, 223

Tunick, S. 159
Tunisia 217, 224–5
Turkey 89, 167
Turunen, P. 10, 133
Tuvalu 196
Twelvetrees, A. 153, 234

Ubuntu 114
understanding 128, 130
unemployment 220–2
United Kingdom (UK) 63, 176, 189, 206–7, 210
United Nations Children's Fund (UNICEF) 120
United Nations Development Programmes (UNDP) 178
United Nations (UN) 25, 74, 160, 178; Convention on the Rights of the Child 107; Resolution on Gender Sensitive Disaster Responses 24
United States (US) 2, 5, 75, 120, 128; art projects 162; climate change 177–8; emancipatory frameworks 230; neo-liberalism 221–2, 224; Treasury 218
Universal Declaration of Human Rights (UDHR) 33, 160, 177
University of KwaZulu-Natal (UKZN) 76–7, 116, 232
University of the Western Cape (UWC) 59, 61, 65
Urban Imagination Network (UIN) 129
utilitarianism 27

vā 192, 195, 200
validation 116
values 26, 28, 30, 37–8, 88; climate change 175–7; contextual issues 124–5, 127–8, 130; emancipatory frameworks 233–4, 239–41; family violence 196, 198, 200; neighbourhood renewal 153; online

courses 99; social justice 234; welfare state 139
Van den Berg, A.M. 21, 25, 27
Venn diagrams 67
videos 116–17
Vike, H. 138
virtual books 89
virtual classrooms 88, 94
virtual communities of practice (VCoP) 11, 42, 45–50
virtues/virtuous practice 11, 20, 24–8
visas 136
visioning 60–1
Visser-Rotgans, R. 12, 159–72
visual mapping 61–4
Vrasti, W. 219
vulnerable people 133–44, 167, 178–82, 185, 204

Wacquant, L. 220
Waitangi, Treaty of 191, 198, 200
Wall Street 224
Wandersman, A. 181
war 177, 238, 241
Washington Consensus 218
water 9, 12, 23, 204–5, 213, 220, 242
weapons of mass destruction 4
Webb, J. 178
Weber, M. 31
websites 41, 45, 58, 62–4, 69; art projects 169–70; climate change 178; contextual issues 126; grassroots interventions 204; power 109, 116
Webster, M. 232
Weis, - 234
welfare state 37, 41, 133–44, 160, 220, 230, 243
Weltanschauung 30
Wenger, E. 42, 91, 155
West 2, 9, 20, 23, 33; art projects 160; climate change 177; emancipatory frameworks 232–3; family violence

189–90, 192, 194–5, 198; postmodernism 35–6; social action 208;
strengths 73–4
Western Sahara 225
Weyers, M.L. 21, 25, 27, 84
Wight, C. 224
Wittgenstein, L. 35
women 12, 24–5, 59, 63–4, 134; art
projects 167–8; climate change 180;
emancipatory frameworks 234, 239;
family violence 194–5;
neighbourhood renewal 148, 151,
153–5; neo-liberalism 219–20, 223;
social action 204, 206

workshops 64, 78–9, 112, 129;
contextual issues 130
World Bank 178, 206, 218
World Trade Organization (WTO)
206, 218

Young Leaders Development
Committee 110
Younghusband Report 232
YouTube 116
Yusuf-Khalil, Y. 58–9

Zaretsky, K. 165
Zuma, J. 222